THE MAGIC WORLD OF WINE

This book is dedicated to helping every wine drinker—from novice to connoisseur—get the most out of every bottle, and explore the wondrous varieties of pleasure that wine offers.

In clear, simple language, ENJOYING WINE shows you how to go about tasting wine, from assessing its color to judging its complexity and quality. It explains what to look for in every major variety, gives taste comparisons for specific groupings, suggests the best matchings between foods and wines, describes vital serving details, provides marvelous menus and recipes for wine cookery, and includes a complete wine dictionary.

Based on Paul Gillette's tremendously popular PBS television series, ENJOYING WINE takes its place as the one volume that every lover will want to place directly beside his favorite corkscrew.

SIGNET Books for Your Reference Shelf

ENJOYING WINE

Paul Gillette

A SIGNET BOOK

NEW AMERICAN LIBRARY

TIMES MIRROR

NAL BOOKS ARE ALSO AVAILABLE AT DISCOUNTS
IN BULK QUANTITY FOR INDUSTRIAL OR
SALES-PROMOTIONAL USE. FOR DETAILS, WRITE TO
PREMIUM MARKETING DIVISION, NEW AMERICAN LIBRARY, INC.,
1301 AVENUE OF THE AMERICAS, NEW YORK, NEW YORK 10019.

Copyright © 1976 by Paul Gillette

SIGNET, SIGNET CLASSICS, MENTOR, PLUME AND MERIDIAN BOOKS
are published by The New American Library, Inc.,
1301 Avenue of the Americas, New York, New York 10019

FIRST SIGNET PRINTING, NOVEMBER, 1976

1 2 3 4 5 6 7 8 9

PRINTED IN THE UNITED STATES OF AMERICA

To George and Cassie Carros

Contents

I wonder often what the vintners buy,
One half so precious as the stuff they sell.

—OMAR KHAYYAM

1

Enjoying Wine

When I told an Italian friend I was writing a book on wine, his brow furrowed. "You mean a textbook for oenology students? But, *caro Paolo,* you're not a chemist."

I explained that the book was for laymen.

"For laymen?" The furrows deepened. "But what interest would they have—? Ah, I understand. It is one of those arts and crafts books about how to make wine at home."

I explained that the book was not about making wine but simply about enjoying it.

For a moment he seemed genuinely bewildered. Then he laughed. "Ah, you Americans. You academize everything. For an Italian, it is enough to drink wine. We don't need a book to tell us how to enjoy it."

He's right and he's wrong.

Indisputably, Italy has the highest per capita wine consumption in the world: almost one gallon a week for every healthy adult. It's reasonable that Italians wouldn't drink so much of something they didn't enjoy.

On the other hand, while Italy produces some of the most sophisticated and highly respected wines in the world, most Italians have never heard of, much less tasted them. The typical Italian drinks only wines produced in his own *provincia.*

It's understandable that the average wage-earner in any country might not often have the opportunity to taste that Tuscan rarity, Brunello di Montalcino, probably the highest-priced wine in the world, with a single bottle of certain prime vintages commanding upwards of a thousand dollars. But Italy produces many other esteemed wines that are well within the average person's means. Most Italians never sample them. Nor do most Italians ever taste more than a few, if any, of the wines of Germany, France, Yugoslavia, Spain, and other countries that are Italy's regular trading partners in nonvinous commodities. Indeed, except in North America, England, Japan, and a few cities in South America, very few people have ever tasted wines produced in a country other than that in which they live.

Ultimately, I think, the question is not whether one *needs* to be told how to enjoy wine, but whether certain kinds of information can help one get *more* enjoyment from it. For myself, the answer is an emphatic yes.

As an Italo-American, both of whose parents were born in "the old country," I was exposed to wine virtually from the cradle. I don't remember ever not drinking it, and I don't remember ever not enjoying it. But I began enjoying it more as I learned more about it. Maybe some of the things I learned can enhance your enjoyment also—whatever your nationality.

What kinds of things? Well, take glasses. In fact, take two glasses. The first should be an ordinary juice glass or water tumbler, the second a large (at least eight ounces) stemmed wine glass the rim of which curves inward. Pour about three ounces of the same wine into each glass. Now hold the first glass beneath your nose. Inhale. Then repeat the procedure with the large-stemmed glass.

Chances are you perceived very little fragrance (or what wine professionals call "nose"*) in the first glass, whereas the second gave you a distinct and vivid impression. That's because the inward curve of the rim of the second glass helped capture the fragrance in the unfilled portion of the glass. With the juice glass or tumbler, most of the wine's olfactory properties dissipated. (And if you previously used the glass for beer, milk, or other beverages, chances are the aroma of one or more of these remained in the glass even after washing, thus cancelling what little of the wine's nose you might otherwise have perceived.)

All right, you say, what's the big deal about fragrance? Are we going to smell the wine or drink it? Hopefully we'll do both, because if we drink it without smelling it, we lose most of the wine's sensory value.

The fact is, there are only four taste sensations: sweet, salty, sour, and bitter. These may differ in intensity from

---

*I have tried wherever practical to define in the text all wine terms or special usages pertaining to wine. All wine terms used in the book—and quite a few not used in the book—are defined fully in the Wine Dictionary, beginning on page 173.)

one beverage or food to another, but the differences are relatively insignificant in terms of our overall perception of the beverage or food's character. Most of this perception comes via the nose.

This is why food often seems tasteless to a person with a head cold. Strictly speaking, the food *tastes* the same. What our sniffling diner misses are the olfactory subtleties that many of us erroneously regard as tastes.

These same subtleties are what separate a highly prized wine from one that's not so highly prized. If you serve a two-hundred-dollar bottle of Chambertin in juice glasses—or when you have a head cold—you won't get more than a hint of the qualities that distinguish it from a four-franc carafe of the house wine at your favorite Dijon *brasserie*. A glass with an inward curving rim, filled no more than halfway, "delivers" the wine's nose to yours at the same time that it delivers the wine itself to your mouth.

Here is another experiment. Pour a glass each of two very dissimilar wines—say, a German white and a Spanish red. Taste each in turn. Then have a friend blindfold you. Now eat a hot pepper. Let a moment pass after swallowing the last morsel. Then have your friend hand you one of the wines. Try to identify it. You almost certainly will have a difficult time doing so.

All right, you say, what's so important about being able to identify a wine while blindfolded? And how often do I eat a hot pepper?

Well, if two wines differ as much as those in this test, yet taste the same to you when you can't see them, isn't it rather pointless to buy the more expensive one? Why not limit your nonblindfolded consumption to the very cheapest pleasant-looking wine you can buy?

But wait, you say. The problem isn't the blindfold. The hot pepper destroyed your ability to perceive tastes and smells. Surely you'd be able to identify the wines under ordinary circumstances.

Maybe not. While the hot pepper was unusually dramatic evidence that certain stimuli can demolish the sensory capacities of the mouth, milder stimuli can also affect your perceptions to a point where dissimilar wines become indistinguishable, or to a somewhat less remote point where the character and balance of highly prized, expensively made wines (the qualities which separate them from run-of-the-mill, inexpensively made ones) are not fully perceived.

In a smoke-filled room, all wines taste pretty blah to nonsmokers—and to many smokers as well. This is why most wine *aficionados* get very annoyed with people who smoke at the dinner table, and why smoking is generally prohibited at wine tastings.

Distilled spirits—particularly highly aromatic ones, such as Byrrh, absinthe, gin, or brandy—dull or extinguish a taster's perceptions. A *pastis* or manhattan before dinner virtually guarantees that you will be wasting any sum over three dollars that you pay for the wine that accompanies the meal. I find that a martini has the same effect on my palate, although some wine professionals say it is not so with them.

With certain foods, a wine's most prized characteristics are overpowered or nullified. A spicy Mexican chili sauce or Pakistani curry will overpower the most assertive wine. You'll probably enjoy both dishes more with beer. Vinegar imparts its own taste to wine—the taste of acetic acid— which is one reason wine drinkers usually prefer their salad after the main course, as is traditional in Europe and South America, the prime wine-drinking continents.

Even the relatively mild spice level of a Neapolitan tomato sauce will dominate most wines. The effect is not as dramatic as with a curry or chili sauce, but the subtleties of most highly esteemed wines will be overcome by the strong acidity of the tomato sauce. Thus, the value-conscious wine-bibber will save his 1955 Borgogno Barolo for a meal that will com-plement it, serving only a relatively inexpensive wine with the pasta. (If you're not sure whether you can trust the advice of a wine seller, ask him to recommend a wine to serve with spaghetti and meatballs. Say that you really want to impress your dinner guests, that you've budgeted ten dollars for the wine, and that the spaghetti sauce will be very spicy. If the merchant is conscientious, he will tell you not to waste your money on a ten-dollar wine for that particular meal, and will recommend something in the two- to three-dollar range. If he recommends a wine costing more than five dollars, he's ripping you off.)

Similarly, an assertive wine can overpower a delicate food. Few dishes are more delectable than a gently steamed bass or filet of sole *à la meunière*. But serve either with a robust red wine, such as Egri Bikaver, and you'll scarcely taste the fish.

This is not to say that there are hard and fast rules about which wines to serve with which foods. If you *like* Egri Bikaver with your Dover sole, or egg in your beer, or maple syrup on your shish kebab, far be it from me to say you're wrong. There obviously are no rights or wrongs in matters of taste. But the traditional combinations of wines and foods did not evolve without reason. They have chemical validity as well as social currency. And even if you yourself favor maple syrup on your shish kebab, you almost certainly will please a greater percentage of your guests by sticking to more conventional pairings.

Here is another experiment in food/wine matchmaking. Tell a friend you are going to ask which of three glasses of wine he or she likes best. Blindfold your friend, then offer three glasses from the same bottle. After the first taste, ask him or her to clear the taste characteristic from the palate by eating a piece of apple. After the second, clear the palate with a piece of cheese. After the third, ask for a rating. If your friend wants to retaste, insist that again the palate be cleared—with bread before the first glass, apple before the second, and cheese before the third.

Your friend, unless he or she knows the trick, will probably prefer the third wine—which is, of course, identical to the "first" and "second." The reason for this preference is that the acid-sugar balance in apples tends to bring out the harshest qualities of a wine, while the taste and olfactory properties of cheese create a state of appetite in which (for most people, anyway) all wines taste better; bread is neutral. (There is a saying among French wine growers, "Buy over apples, sell over cheese." That is, you'll be at your most critical and your customer at his least critical.)

There is one last experiment, but it is so wasteful that you may prefer to take my word that it works. Buy two bottles of a highly prized chateau-bottled red wine from Bordeaux— say, Château Margaux in a vintage retailing at twenty dollars or more per bottle. Also buy two bottles of the least expensive red wine you can find from the same region, hopefully one selling for under two dollars a bottle, certainly none more expensive than five dollars. (The regional wine could be labeled "Margaux" [without the "Château"], "Medoc," "Haut Medoc," "Bordeaux," or by some trade name like "Grande Marque" or "Mouton-Cadet.") Refrigerate one bottle of each wine for at least three hours. Keep the remaining bottles at room temperature.

Now open the room temperature bottles and let them stand for half an hour. While standing, the wines will absorb oxygen. This process—aeration, or in the vernacular of wine people, "breathing"—intensifies taste and olfactory properties.

Next, have a friend pour a glass from each bottle. Use large-stemmed glasses, the rim of which curves inward, and fill them no more than one third. Without being told which wine is in which glass, smell and taste them.

You will probably immediately recognize the chateau-bottled wine by its powerful and complex nose and the subtle balance of its tastes. Compared to it, the regional wine will seem flat and uninteresting.

Now have your friend pour the refrigerated wines. Smell and taste each. Almost certainly you will not be able to tell which is which.

Somehow, refrigeration muffles or even extinguishes the nose of a red wine—but not of a white. This is one reason red wines are usually served at European room temperature (65 to 70 degrees Fahrenheit, as opposed to the 75 to 80 degrees often maintained in North America), and whites are usually chilled (40 to 60 degrees, depending on the type of wine).

In sum, the wine "rulebook," often scorned by people with limited tasting experience, is not merely a matter of formality or ritual. Many traditional practices make a great deal of sense—and can help you get much more enjoyment from wine.

This doesn't mean that the newcomer to wine must, as you might suspect from reading certain books, memorize long lists of do's and don't's or spend tedious hours studying tables of grape varieties, maps of wine-growing regions, and charts of vineyard classifications. Learning about wine should, in my view, be enjoyable at every step—and sip—along the way.

Suppose you could assemble a panel of congenial, extremely knowledgeable wine professionals. Suppose you could get each of them to tell you about his or her area of expertise, then give you pointers on how to get the most from each glass of wine. Suppose you could taste the specific wines these experts recommended and match your judgments against theirs.

Suppose you could tour some of the world's most celebrated vineyards, question the winemakers, sample the wines.

I have actually done all that for a series of television programs, "Enjoying Wine with Paul Gillette," seen in the United States on stations of the Public Broadcasting System. This book is a somewhat more leisurely trip over the same terrain, without the restrictions of a half-hour format.

The book doesn't aspire to be the last word in wine knowledge. It focuses on the basics and stresses the practical. My goal as a wine neophyte was simply to discover new wines that I liked. My next goal was to refine my selection techniques so that I got the most wine for my money. (It doesn't take a great deal of skill to buy palatable wines at fifty dollars a bottle. The skill comes, obviously enough, in buying wines you'll like as much—or almost as much—for a fraction of that price.)

In the chapters ahead, I'll share my discoveries with you. First, however, a caveat and a promise.

The caveat: There is no objectivity in the world of wine. There is only opinion. Sometimes it is informed opinion, sometimes it is less than informed, but even the best-informed opinion remains just that, one person's expression of personal preference.

So let no one say that one wine is great and another ordinary ("ordinary" being the wine snob's euphemism for awful). Let no one say that a wine is distinguished or unworthy, superior or inferior. It is all a matter of what one likes.

In this book, I've tried to label my own opinions as such whenever they appear. If my biases have led me to present some opinions as if they were facts, it has happened inadvertently.

The promise: I'll give you a straight count about my biases. They're all honestly derived, uninfluenced by personal economic interests.

I stress this fact because of my unhappy experience as a reader of wine books. Years ago, when I read my first book on wine, I unthinkingly accepted the author's assertion—presented as cold fact—that only France produces truly great wines, and that one region of France produces the greatest of the great. I subsequently learned that this writer was an exporter of wines from that region. But he didn't say so in his book.

As I went on to read other books and articles on wine, I perceived similar author biases. I learned that one author, who presently writes a syndicated newspaper column on wine, was a public relations man for the Bordeaux wine growers' association. Another was the head of an importing firm in New York, while a third was on the payroll of a California winery. Again, none of the books or articles identified the author's vested interest.

Offhand, I can think of only three people who write regularly about wine for national publications who are not present or former sellers of the product. I don't object to a seller writing about his or her product, but I do object to sellers not telling me where their economic loyalties lie.

To make the record crystal-clear on this point, let me state without equivocation: While I accept fees from restaurants for advising them about wine purchases and for drawing up wine lists, I am not now, nor have I ever been, an employee, agent, or stockholder of any company in the beverage industry, nor have I ever received payment from any such company under any circumstances whatsoever. When I write about wine, all I have to sell is books.

I hope this one adds to your enjoyment of wine.

2

A Beginner's Guide to Wine Tasting

To say that no wine is "better" than another is not to say that differences among wines are unimportant or purely a matter of chance. The ultimate character of a given glass of wine is the result of many decisions by the winemaker: whether to use grapes (as fully ninety-five percent of the world's producers do) or some other fruit or vegetable (wine can be made from elderberries, cherries, peaches, dandelions and even potatoes); which variety of the species to grow; when to harvest; how to ferment; whether to age and, if so, for how long and in what type of container. (Because so little nongrape wine is produced, all future references in this book will be to the grape-based variety, unless I specifically state otherwise.)

Geography also affects a wine's character. The same variety of grape planted in France, Germany, Australia, and the United States can—and usually will—produce four distinctly different wines, even if all other factors remain constant. Indeed, the same variety of grape planted on adjoining hillsides can produce distinctly different wines, even when they are made exactly the same way by the same winemaker.

Much of the joy of wine comes from perceiving these differences, which often are quite subtle. Many wine drinkers never perceive them fully because they have not developed the skill of wine tasting.

If it seems pretentious to describe wine tasting as a skill, recall the experiments described in the first chapter. Obviously, a great many factors can interfere with a person's ability to perceive the exact character of the wine he or she is tasting. The skill lies in minimizing these interferences and maximizing one's perceptions of the wine's unique properties.

Wine professionals have developed an approach that I think works extremely well. In fact, it works so well that I have never seen a wine professional anywhere in the world employ any other approach. Civilian wine lovers obviously do not have the same stake in tasting as the professional, who makes buy-and-sell decisions involving thousands of cases based on a single tasting. But the same approach is the best way I know for a civilian to develop tasting skills—and to get maximum enjoyment from each glass she or he tastes.

Let's try it, using a large (at least eight ounces) stemmed glass whose rim curves inward. Place it on a white tablecloth and pour about four ounces of a dry red wine. Actually, any wine may be used—white or red, sweet or dry—but the points I want to make will be illustrated best with a dry red. Ideally, the glass should never have been used for any beverage but wine or water. It should also have been rinsed thoroughly after its last washing—detergent that has not been rinsed away can affect the wine, even if the glass was washed days or weeks ago.

Now, holding the glass by the stem, look through the wine at the tablecloth. Note the wine's color and clarity.

Next, holding the base of the glass against the table, make several circular movements, causing the liquid to swirl around inside the bowl. Then lift the glass to your nose, inhale deeply, and note the fragrance of the wine.

Finally, take a sip. Hold the liquid for a moment at the front of your mouth, so that it is in contact with the tip of your tongue. Then slowly let it pass to the back of your mouth. Note the various taste sensations.

At this point, wine professionals tasting in the line of duty will generally spit out the wine. There are two reasons: first, the vapors of swallowed wine may remain on the breath, interfering with one's perception of wines yet to be tasted; and second, too much alcohol will dull one's perception in general. In any case, swallowing is not a necessary part of tasting: once the beverage has reached the back of the mouth, all visual, olfactory, and taste sensations have registered.

This having been said, let me add that I myself never spit out wine, and most professionals who are tasting recreationally don't either. Unless wines are extremely similar, the carryover effect from one to another should not be significant.

Now let's review the three steps described above and consider some of the factors professionals weigh in judging a wine. Not all these factors will be important to the civilian, but thinking about them from a professional's perspective can help sharpen perceptions.

When professionals evaluate a wine, they score it on sight, smell, and taste. The most common rating scale is a twenty-point evaluation such as the one on page 12, used by California State Fair wine judges. Some tasters prefer to rate more generally, assigning points to sight, smell, and taste, but not scoring specific attributes within these categories. One rating system allows 5 points each for sight, smell, and taste, and another 5 points for overall quality. Another system involves 2 points for sight, 3 each for smell and taste, and 2 for overall quality. Still other raters don't rate by category; they give the wine an overall numerical score, or they use verbal ratings such as "outstanding," "excellent," "very good," "good," and "unacceptable."

Whatever system they use, professionals assess the same basic qualities in a wine. Let's consider these qualities in the wine you have poured.

Visually, we are interested in clarity and color. Both have esthetic value, of course, but they also can reveal a great deal about the condition of a wine.

Cloudiness indicates that something has happened to the wine after it was bottled. If it is a young wine, air may have seeped in through the cork, causing a chemical reaction that converts wine to vinegar. Exposure to heat may have caused another sort of chemical reaction that mars a wine's original character. In either case, or in a host of other situations resulting in a cloudy young wine, the wine is considered defective.

Rating Scale Used by California State Fair Wine Judges*

Appearance:
  0-Cloudy
  1-Clear
  2-Brilliant
Color:
  0-Distinctly incorrect
  1-Slightly incorrect

*Note: I have paraphrased some terms on the scale that might be confusing to nonprofessionals.—P.G.

2-Correct

Olfactory character:
    0-None
    1-Indistinct
    2-Distinct but not varietal (i.e., characteristic of the dominant grape or grapes)
    3-Varietal
    (Substract 1 or 2 points for unpleasant odors.)

Acescence (i.e., presence of vinegar-like taste):
    0-Obvious
    1-Slight
    2-None

Total acidity:
    0-Distinctly low or high
    1-Slightly low or high
    2-Normal, well-balanced

Sweetness:
    0-Too little or too much
    1-Normal

Body:
    0-Too low or too high
    1-Normal

Flavor:
    0-Distinctly abnormal
    1-Slightly abnormal
    2-Normal

Bitterness:
    0-Distinctly high
    1-Slightly high
    2-Normal

Overall quality:
    0-Lacking
    1-Slight
    2-Impressive
    3-Extraordinary

RATINGS:

17-20 Outstanding

13-16 Excellent (i.e., a sound commercial wine but not considered particularly distinguished)

9-12 Commercial (i.e., saleable but with notable defect)

6-8 Seriously defective (i.e., not saleable by a person of good conscience)

0-6 Unsatisfactory (i.e., undrinkable)

This is not the same as saying you won't like it, although you probably won't. We have here a question not of preference but of essence. The wine has been transformed into something the winemaker did not intend. Conceivably there might be someone somewhere who actually likes a wine to taste this way, but it is not *good* wine. It is "bad" in the same sense that moldy bread, curdled milk, or a rotten apple is bad.

There are degrees of badness—and cloudiness. A wine that is less than crystal-clear need not be unpalatable. Wine professionals tend to be very fussy about clarity, because good-looking wines, like good-looking anything else, are more marketable. Don't reject the wine out-of-hand simply because it fails to throw off the sort of sparkle you get from diamonds. Complete the rest of your evaluation.

As for cloudy old wines, they need not be spoiled. The wine may simply have been suffused with sediment as a result of the bottle's having been moved. Letting the bottle stand should permit the sediment to settle again, clarifying the wine.

When evaluating color, the wine professional looks for indications of maturity, evidence of possible spoilage, and varietal authenticity—that is, whether the color is characteristic of the grape variety or combination of grape varieties making up the wine.

A brownish tinge at the circumference of the upmost surface of a red wine indicates that the wine is mature—that is, it has reached full development and is ready to drink. This state might be reached in only two or three years with wines produced under certain conditions, or it might take ten years or longer with other wines.

A brownish color throughout the wine, or through most of it, is generally an indication that peak development has passed, A purple color throughout suggests that the wine is not fully developed.

However, as with most precepts about wine, there are exceptions. Some red wines are intended by their producers to be drunk young. Though purple, they are fully developed. A fairly reliable general rule is, the less expensive a wine, the more quickly it matures.

Brownish color in a white wine usually indicates spoilage. In the wine industry, this particular variety of spoilage is called "maderization," after the Portuguese island of Madeira, which produces a wine with a distinct taste that some people characterize as woody, others as smoky, and still others as both woody and smoky. In the wines of Madeira, this taste is an intended characteristic. The somewhat similar taste of the maderized white wine is unintended and regarded as a defect.

If the wine is not defective, its color should be characteristic of the dominant grape variety or varieties. This may seem confusing to wine newcomers who have never noticed differences of hue more subtle than white-red-rosé. But there are substantial differences within each category. A wine made from the Chardonnay grape (grown chiefly in California and the Burgundy and Champagne regions of France) should have color characteristics significantly different from those of a wine made predominantly from Sauvignon Blanc (grown in California, the Bordeaux region of France, Argentina, and parts of northern Italy) or Riesling (prominent in Germany, Yugoslavia, Chile, Argentina, the Alsace region of France, California, and a few vineyards in New York and Canada), even though all three are white wines.

The wine professional, through years of experience, develops concepts of "correct" or typical varietal color. If a wine of a certain variety doesn't possess the expected characteristics, the pro suspects that something may have gone wrong in its development—or perhaps that the seller is misrepresenting the product.

Civilians usually won't be as concerned with varietal authenticity. Indeed, until you've tasted many bottles of a given type of wine, you'll have no basis of comparison. But you can start making deposits immediately in your visual memory bank, noting for future reference the color of each wine you taste. Meanwhile, if you're using a rating scale such as that of the California State Fair wine judges, award points for color in terms of your own likes and dislikes.

Does the wine look *good* to you? Then good enough! As importer Chuck Mueller points out, wines that look good and smell good to you usually taste good also. That applies whether you're a seasoned professional or a complete novice.

Several more brief points on the visual aspects of wine before we move along to the olfactory:

In testing for color, it's essential that you look through the wine at a white background. If a white tablecloth is not handy, use a napkin, a plate, or even a sheet of paper. A nonwhite surface will alter your perception of the wine's color.

It's also essential that your glass be colorless, and it's preferable that there be no engraving, design, indentations, facets, or other linear irregularities on the bowl. Irregularities of any sort can impede your ability to see the wine as it is.

The tasting room should be well lighted. Daylight is preferable, fluorescent light next best. Some people prefer to stage recreational tastings in dark, cavelike rooms with the atmosphere of a cellar. In this situation, a candle on the tasting table can be helpful.

In the test for clarity, if you cannot see through the wine to the tablecloth, hold the glass between you and the candle and look again. If you don't see the flame clearly, you may be sure the wine is cloudy.

If a red wine is particularly full-bodied, you may not be able to see through it clearly even in the most brightly lit room. In this case, test for clarity by holding your glass between you and the source of light. However, this technique is never effective in testing for color; the head-on brightness of the light impedes your vision.

Before moving on to the olfactory evaluation of the wine you're using in today's practice session, you may wish to repeat the visual tests. If you are keeping score on a rating scale, make your entries after each test rather than waiting to complete a section or the entire evaluation.

There is only one test for a wine's nose: smell it. But before you do, be sure to swirl the wine. Swirling exposes a larger surface of wine to the air. The interaction of wine and oxygen, or aeration, releases the fragrance.

The swirling technique I described earlier—holding the base of the glass against the table and making several circular movements—is probably the easiest and results in the least spilled wine. But if you're particularly dextrous, you can also swirl in midair, holding the glass at chest level.

As in visual tests, professionals learn a lot about a wine by considering its nose. Spoilage often is immediately apparent. A wine that has maderized will smell rather like charred wood that has been doused with water. Other wines, exposed to air because of an ill-fitting or dried cork, will have begun turning to vinegar and will smell like vinegar. Still other wines will, by their nose, reveal mustiness or other defects relating to aging, storage, and/or handling.

Again, this is not a question of preference but of essence. The wine has been transformed into something the wine-maker did not intend. It is "bad" the same way moldy bread, curdled milk, or a rotten apple is bad.

If a wine's nose indicates spoilage, the professional taster usually will reject it out-of-hand. If spoilage is not indicated, the taster will seek evidence of varietal character.

Olfactorily as well as visually, a wine usually will reveal the grape or grapes from which it was made. A variety like Cabernet Sauvignon (dominant in red wines from the French region of Bordeaux and prominent also in California, Chile, Italy, Australia, and Spain) will not smell exactly the same as Nebbiolo (the variety grown principally in the Italian region of Piemonte) or Sangiovese (grown principally in the Italian region of Tuscany) or Pinot Noir (dominant in most red wines from the French region of Burgundy and prominent also in California, Australia, and South Africa).

A wine's nose also will reveal a great deal about its aging and storage. A wine that was aged in fifty-gallon barrels of Limousin or Soane oak will have an olfactory character dif-ferent from that of a wine aged in hundred-thousand-gallon redwood tanks. A wine bottled thirty years ago should have a different olfactory character from one bottled last month.

Wine professionals make a distinction between the fra-grance of the grape variety(ies) and the other olfactory properties that develop in wine. They refer to the former as *aroma* and the latter as *bouquet,* terms often used synony-mously outside the wine industry. Among factors involved in bouquet are the reaction of the various grape varieties in a blended wine to each other (the "marriage" of the wines, professionals like to say) and the manner of aging and storing.

In the California rating scale, the highest rating for olfac-tory properties is 3 points, awarded to a wine whose nose is distinctly varietal. This would fall under the category of aroma and would be the most that could be expected from most inexpensively produced red wines and almost all whites. However, some versions of the California scale call for a bonus point if a wine possesses bouquet. Most twenty-point scales employed in Europe, South America, and Australia also award a fourth point for bouquet.

Much of this will be over the head of the newcomer to wine, but the newcomer can still appreciate the *smell* of what's in his glass (call it "nose," "fragrance," "aroma," "bouquet," or whatever) because, to restate importer Chuck Mueller's maxim, wines that taste good to you usually look good and smell good to you also, even if you're a complete novice.

A point about the olfactory condition of the tasting room: there should be no smells of any kind. The aromas of cooking, the fragrances of perfumes or flowers—indeed, any smell—can distort the perceptions of the tasters.

The effect of foreign smells on the judgment of even the most discriminating professionals was demonstrated dramatically a few years ago when a small California winery was destroyed by fire. Several huge vats were saved, and an insurance company offered the wines at auction. Dozens of professionals tasted them and concluded they were worthless, irreparably damaged by the smoke. The only bids received were for pennies a gallon from distillers who planned to convert the alcohol into brandy.

Then one man had the good sense to take a sample to his own office for tasting. He outbid the distillers and walked off with the wine for a fraction of its value. It hadn't been damaged by the smoke, but the odor of smoke that remained in the burned winery was so strong that everyone who tasted there concluded it was in the wine.

Let's turn now to the taste tests. Recall that we hold the wine for a moment in the front of the mouth, so that it is in contact with the tip of the tongue; then we slowly let it pass to the back of the mouth. For the wine's full taste to register, the liquid must be brought into contact with three sets of taste buds. Those at the tip of the tongue perceive sweet tastes and those that are the opposite of sweet, or "dry"; the buds at the sides record sour tastes, and those at the top of the tongue in back discern bitter tastes. Some people think of bitterness and sourness as synonymous, but they are not. Sourness is an acid taste, like that of citrus fruit or vinegar. Bitterness is acrid, like aspirin or strong tea.

To bring out taste characteristics more dramatically, wine professionals may whistle in or suck in a quantity of air with the wine. This exaggerates each of the taste characteristics. For further exaggeration, move the wine around inside your mouth a few seconds before swallowing.

Few civilian tasters will want to use these techniques in social situations, but whatever the setting, you can make it a point to leave the wine in your mouth for a moment or two before swallowing and make sure it comes into contact with the three appropriate sets of taste buds. If you just gulp the wine down, you'll be missing most of the taste pleasures.

When professionals evaluate the taste aspects of a wine, they are interested mainly in flaws—too much acescence; too much bitterness; or acidity or sweetness that is too high or too low. A wine that is not faulty gets the highest marks in each category. This is consistent with the facts about fragrance versus taste: the wine's *character* lies in its nose; undesired tastes can mar the taster's enjoyment of the wine's character, they can render the wine drinking experience unpleasant, but tastes do not *supply* character, they cannot of themselves carry the day.

Of course, taste judgments are, like so much else connected with wine, a matter of personal preference. If you and I rated the same wine on the California scale, our concepts of distinctly low or high sweetness or acidity might vary considerably. You might regard as substandard a wine that I prize, or vice versa. But this doesn't mean that taste ratings won't be useful to us individually. The whole point of systematic tasting is to develop a consistent and reliable technique for evaluating wines.

When professionals are doing the evaluating, their standards of judgment are a predetermination of what the character of a particular wine should be. A U.S. importer is in Verona, Italy, looking for a Soave to add to his line. He tastes samples from ten producers. He rates each on acidity, sweetness, flavor, et cetera, in terms of what he thinks a Soave should be like. He might find one too sweet *for a Soave*, whereas the same degree of sweetness in a California Chenin Blanc would be considered correct and in a Barsac (from Bordeaux) would be considered too low.

The taster's own general preference for sweet or dry wines will not—or at least should not—influence his judgment. He personally may prefer a sweeter wine; however, he is buying not for himself now but for (hopefully) hordes of Soave drinkers in the U.S., who expect their wine to taste a certain way. As their scout, he is seeking that elusive combination of visual, olfactory, and taste properties that will prove most appealing to them—and therefore most profitable for him.

The difference between personal preference and market judgment was illustrated once on my TV show by a panel of professionals conducting a "blind" tasting—that is, the wines had been poured into numbered glasses without the tasters knowing which was which. Indeed, the numbers were not the same from taster to taster—Taster A's Wine #1 might be Taster B's Wine #2. Only George Carros, host of the tasting table, knew who was drinking what.

(The purpose of a blind tasting is not to test the tasters but to test the wines without possible bias by the tasters. If I know that Wine #1 is, let us say, Paul Masson Rosé, about which I've written favorably on occasion, my awareness of what I'm drinking could make me judge the wine more harshly, because I fear I may have been too easy last time around, or too gently, because I don't want to contradict my previous judgment.)

Among the tasters on our rosé panel was importer Julius Wile. Pressed for an opinion on Wines #1 and #2, he said, "I'd rather sell #1, but I'd rather drink #2." Julius' commercial judgment was right on target: Wine #1 was Lancers Rosé, one of the world's best-selling brands. But everyone on this panel—George Carros, writer Madeline Greenberg, importer Knight M. Fee, and Alan Olsen, director of the German Wine Information Bureau—had a personal preference for Wine #2, Chateau d'Acqueria Tavel Rosé. None of them, I might add, sells it.

The success of a brand such as Lancers often spawns imitations. Some years ago, Italian Swiss Colony, a California producer (which happens, interestingly, to be owned by Heublein, Inc., the corporate parent of Lancers U.S. importers), decided to follow Lancers example. Italian Swiss winemakers worked at duplicating Lancers character, then offered samples of both wines to visitors at the Italian Swiss public tasting room in Asti, California. I have it on good authority that Italian Swiss kept changing its blend until the visitors, tasting blind, said they could not distinguish between the two. The latter, by the way, sells at about three times the price of the former. If you like Lancers, you might find it both interesting and profitable to taste it blind against Italian Swiss.

In any case, the systematic approach to taste properties

can be useful to the civilian as well as the professional. If you don't choose to make judgments about individual properties like acescence and acidity, you can nonetheless make a judgment about the wine's taste in general.

Two additional factors which wine professionals frequently take into account when evaluating taste, though these factors do not appear on the California State Fair wine judge's rating scale, are aftertaste and "memory," the latter defined as the length of time the aftertaste remains on the palate.

The aftertaste should, of course, be consistent—that is, the same as the taste of the wine. Sometimes, especially with inexpensively made wines, it will verge closer to the taste of water. With wines that have been mishandled in storage, there may be an aftertaste of burned wood (maderization) or various chemicals. With still other wines, generally in the lower price categories (though I've also found it to be true of some medium-priced varieties from Inglenook), there will be virtually no aftertaste.

As a general rule, the longer the aftertaste stays on the palate, the better *aficionados* like the wine. Indeed, many professional tasters count the seconds that it remains on the palate and speak of a four-second wine versus a ten-second wine. "Memory," suggests importer Chuck Mueller, "is certainly one of the most distinguishing marks of a fine wine, and from my experience it is perhaps the easiest for the amateur to appreciate."

Finally, having evaluated the wine on sight, smell, and taste, you are ready to pronounce your judgment of general quality. Adding this rating to the others, you have the wine's overall rating—highly subjective, to be sure, but that's the way it should be, because the ultimate test of the wine is the response it evokes from *you*.

If you follow this approach in tasting, I think you'll find within a very short time that wines seem much more varied to you than they ever did before. Awareness of their variety leads automatically to greater enjoyment of the ones that appeal to your particular sight-smell-taste preferences—at least, it has for everyone with whom I've ever discussed wine.

The process is similar, I think, to that involved in appreciating anything that has any degree of complexity, whether it's architecture, music, or football. If you don't know the game, the activity that you perceive has little value to you.

Once you learn what's going on—who's trying to accomplish what, and how others have accomplished it in other situations —everything suddenly becomes much more meaningful . . . and enjoyable.

3

Developing A Wine Taster's Palate

Once you know *how* to taste wine, the next step is to refine your tasting abilities so that you can perceive the subtle qualities inherent in the most sophisticated examples of the winemaker's art.

But wait, you say. What happened to all the discussion about everything being subjective? If it's all subjective, what's this sophistication stuff? Who's to say A is more sophisticated than B?

You are, dear reader. And that's what the game is all about. Returning to the football analogy, you'll almost certainly enjoy the sport more once you develop an eye for the moves of the players. This doesn't mean that you and I must agree on the individual merits of players. But at least we have some basis for discussion.

Discussion, by the way, can be a big part of enjoying wine—any discussion over wine glasses, of course, but also discussion *of* wine. As wine consultant David Milligan, former president of Dennis & Huppert Importers of Miami, points out, the pleasures of wine are rather like the pleasures of a good book: you enjoy reading it, but you also enjoy having discovered it and having helped your friends discover it, and you enjoy talking with them about it.

Some wines don't lend themselves to much discussion. Oh, they may be drinkable, especially if nothing else is available. But they don't hold your interest after your thirst is slaked. They lack that certain something that makes you want to share them with someone else.

If you don't know quite what I mean, it's probably because you haven't yet come to appreciate the infinite varieties in wine. The most effective way I know to develop that appreciation is to taste wines comparatively, under controlled conditions.

What follows is a six-lesson palate development course, designed to demonstrate some of the differences among similar wines. Follow the lessons in sequence. It's more fun if you do it with a friend, or a number of friends, and it's also more helpful, because comparing each other's reactions forces you to think more precisely about your own.

Don't forget the points made in Chapter Two. The tastings should take place in a quiet, well-lighted, odor-free room. No smoking! The tasting table should be covered with a white cloth. Use a large (at least eight ounces) stemmed glass whose rim curves inward. Use a different glass for each wine. If you don't have that many glasses, be sure to rinse thoroughly between wines, lest the properties of the first distort your perceptions of the second.

For every wine you taste, perform the following operations in sequence:

(1) Look through the wine at the white tablecloth. Note the wine's color and clarity.

(2) Swirl the wine inside the glass. Then lift the glass to your nose, inhale deeply, and note the fragrance of the wine.

(3) Take a sip. Hold the liquid for a moment at the front of your mouth, so that it is in contact with the tip of your tongue. Then slowly let it pass to the back of your mouth. (Swallow or spit, as you prefer.)

Now let's begin.

LESSON #1: Buy any two wines labeled "Chablis" that sell for under three dollars a fifth. (An example would be Christian Brothers' Chablis and Beringer Chablis, each selling for around two dollars.) Refrigerate the bottles for one to three hours. Ideal serving temperature is 45 to 50 degrees Fahrenheit.

The tasting must be blind. This means that the tasters don't know which wine they are tasting. One way to achieve this is to place numbered paper bags over the bottles or numbered paper sleeves around them. Another way is to pour the wines into numbered carafes.

The best way, in my experience—but also the most complicated—is to enlist the help of someone who is not part of the tasting. That person numbers the individual glasses (a grease pencil works perfectly for this) and keeps track of which wine is in which glass, but the tasters do not have the same wine in the glass of the same number. It is not until the end of the session that everyone knows which wine was eliciting which reaction. This eliminates the possibility that the tasters fall prey to each other's power of suggestion.

Whatever method you use, taste Wine #1 and make notes about it. Be sure to go through all three operations—visual, olfactory, and gustatory—with this first wine before proceeding to the second. Rate it on the California State Fair twenty-point scale, if you like, or use some other numerical or verbal system. For beginners, the easiest approach probably is to allow 3 points overall for visual character, 5 points for nose, 5 for taste, and 7 for overall quality.

Whatever scale you use, do rate both wines. Then expose the bottle and talk with your fellow tasters about how you reacted to each one.

Remember, the point of this exercise is not to reach a unanimous judgment about which is the "better" wine; it is to think systematically about the visual, olfactory, and gustatory properties of each. It doesn't even matter whether you *like* the wines (at least for the purposes of the exercise), so long as you think in terms of the individual characteristics.

If you and your fellow tasters want to compare total scores and declare one wine a winner, by all means do. But the exercise's greatest benefit should come from thinking and talking about the individual properties of the wines. Is #1 too sweet, not sweet enough, or just right? Is #2 cloudy, clear, or brilliant?

If you're so inclined, and if there's any wine left after this first tasting, repeat it, start-to-finish. Yes, mask the bottles again, then discuss and evaluate the wines as if you hadn't tasted them before. And when you complete your ratings the second time, compare them to those from the first time around.

Don't be disappointed if there is a considerable difference between both sets. As a newcomer to tasting, you haven't developed a reliable wine memory. You don't know what you consider sweet or dry—at least, you don't know with the kind of second-nature certainty that most professionals possess. These exercises are the way you develop that kind of certainty.

Actually, most professionals are not unfailingly reliable in their judgments. Many factors affect people's perceptions:

their state of health, what they ate that day, what olfactory stimuli they've been subjected to, even their levels of anxiety or tension. It's not unheard of for even the most consistent professional to make an inconsistent judgment on occasion.

Maynard Amerine, retired professor of oenology and viticulture at the University of California at Davis, widely recognized as one of the world's leading wine scholars, tells this story on himself. After tasting the same two wines comparatively each day for a year—one from California, the other from France—he was asked by the hostess at a dinner party if he thought he could identify them in a blind tasting. He replied that he wasn't certain he could but would be happy to try.

The hostess vanished into the kitchen and returned with two glasses of wine. Dr. Amerine tasted them and reported that, yes, without question, he knew which wine was which. He then very confidently identified the California wine as French.

The fact is, day-to-day changes in many variables can nullify a taster's best efforts. But over the long run, the skilled taster will be reliable in a vast majority of situations. And in any case, to repeat a precept you'll encounter again and again in this book, the blind tasting is not a test of the taster, it's a test of the wine.

So . . . you have completed your first tasting. You may be impatient to go on to Lesson #2. I urge that you don't. Instead, repeat Lesson #1 for four or five more nights, comparing your ratings from night to night. Try not to think about the previous night's ratings until you've completed those for the present night. Your goal should not be to show how consistent you can be but rather to elicit from yourself a candid judgment of the wine every time you taste it.

You'll almost certainly find that your ratings vary substantially from night to night. But you're learning. And the variations are not only a result of your inexperience. They reflect changes in your palate and possibly changes in the wine. If you used a fresh bottle each night and both came from the same case, it's unlikely that there would be any change in the wine; but if you used the same bottle on two nights—as, for example, with a gallon jug—the wine could change significantly from day to day. Wine is a living thing, and it is particularly responsive to air. Change the air-wine ratio in the bottle, and you change the wine.

LESSON #2: Find a producer whose line includes at least three varietally-named white wines. If that seems terribly complex, you may want to enlist your wine merchant's help. In any case, a varietally named wine is one named after the dominant grape variety: Chardonnay, Johannisberg Riesling, Sauvignon Blanc, Pinot Gris, Chenin Blanc, Moore's Diamond, etc.

You want a bottle each of three such wines, all made by the same producer. This is important, because the purpose of this lesson is to explore the differences among white grape varieties. Those differences should be most pronounced when all other factors—geography, vinification techniques, et cetera —remain constant.

Ideally, the three wines to be tasted will contain only grapes of the variety after which the wine is named. If the wine comes from France, that's a fairly safe bet; the law there (which is not always obeyed—but then, where is the law always obeyed?) requires that one hundred percent of the grapes in a varietally labeled wine be of that variety. In California, the requirement is only fifty-one percent; however, most wineries use a higher percentage, and many use one hundred percent.

It is not, mind you, disastrous if the grapes are less than one hundred percent of the named variety. Once in a blind tasting I used three varietals from Gallo, California's largest producer: Sauvignon Blanc, Chenin Blanc, and French Colombard. Members of the tasting panel included importer Chuck Mueller, of Kobrand Corporation, and French wineman Gerard Yvernault, of Château Margaux. Both promptly recognized all three grapes—whatever percentage Gallo happened to be using.

So you have three white varietals from the same producer, and you can taste them against each other. Compare your reaction. Make notes. You are not interested now so much in which wine you *like* best as in what are the essential characteristics of each. You are learning the wines, not judging them.

Repeat the lesson four or five times with the same wines before going on.

LESSON #3: Use the same varietally named white wine from three different producers, one of which was the same wine from Lesson #2. In other words, if your wines for

Lesson #2 were a Gewürzraminer, Green Hungarian, and Chardonnay from Sebastiani of California, take one of these —say, the Chardonnay—to match against the same varietal of two other producers—say, Sterling and Beringer.

Ideally, the producers of wines for Lesson #3 will be from the same country. This insures relative (though by no means absolute) uniformity of grape-growing conditions and legal regulations, creating the presumption that the differences you perceive among the wines will be fundamentally the result of vinification techniques.

Now we proceed to taste the wines comparatively. Do it for four or five evenings, rating the wines numerically and/or verbally. This time, by the way, you *are* interested in which wine you like best. Since the wines are essentially the same, grape-wise, you are judging the producers against each other.

A significant factor in your judgment should be the price of the wine. If you are tasting three Chardonnays, priced at four, seven, and nine dollars, do you like the nine-dollar wine best? If not, why buy it?

Let's say that you do like the nine-dollar Chardonnay best. Do you like it twice as much as the one that sells for four dollars? In exercises of this sort, the technique of tasting blind is especially valuable.

You might, if you're inclined, repeat Lesson #3 on successive weeks with different white varietals—say, a Chardonnay first, a Johannisberg Riesling second, a Sauvignon Blanc third. If the investigation interests you, don't feel pressured to move on.

LESSON #4: Now we move from whites to reds. This time, while using the same varietal, we'll select producers from different countries. The emphasis now is not only on vinification techniques but also on geographic differences.

In performing this exercise for my TV show, I selected as the grape variety Cabernet Sauvignon, by far the most widely grown internationally among red wine grapes. The wines were: Concha y Toros Cabernet Sauvignon, Chile; Ginestet Cabernet Sauvignon, France; Louis Martini Cabernet Sauvignon, United States; Kettmaier Cabernet Sauvignon, Italy; Adriatica Cabernet Sauvignon, Yugoslavia.

Taste the wines comparatively. Do it for four or five evenings, employing numerical and/or verbal ratings. Remember, you're still tasting blind!

LESSON #5: This is a test not of the wines but of your palate. Your goal is to taste one wine, then remember it accurately enough to pick it out from a group of other wines.

Use the same wines you used for Lesson #3 or #4. The only difference should be the arrangement of the glasses.

A friend will have to set things up for you. He or she should arrange a row that includes one glass of each wine in the test. Just before that row, there should be another glass that contains one of the wines in the row.

In other words, there are two glasses on the table containing the same wine. Your job is to taste the sample glass, then locate its mate.

If you find the experiment too easy done this way (ha!), try it the really hard way: place five glasses in a circle and use four wines. Two glasses contain the same wine, but you don't have a sample glass as a starting point, so you don't know which one you're looking for. If you can match the identical wines consistently, you've got an extraordinarily well-developed palate.

Repeat the lesson four or five times. If you find it interesting, repeat it additional times with other varietals from different producers and/or different countries.

LESSON #6: This is a test of differences among vintages of the same wine.

By definition, a vintage is the year in which were harvested the majority of the grapes that went into the wine. In some countries, it is illegal to use a vintage designation unless ninety percent of the wine was made from grapes grown in that year. In most countries, the figure is seventy-five percent.

In any case, because weather changes from year to year—especially in countries with fragile growing seasons, such as France, Germany, and Chile, but also in places with more consistently sunny climes, such as Italy, California and Argentina—the character of a given wine may (and usually will) also change. Thus we have "good" and "very good" and "great" and "outstanding" years. (The industry is, not surprisingly, less than eager officially to term a year "poor.")

In Lesson #6, we taste wines by the same producer in three different years: one, a so-called "off year," meaning one in which the wine was regarded as less than superior but by no means undrinkable; two, a prime vintage that has not reached full maturity; three, a prime vintage that has reached full maturity.

On my TV show we tasted three wines from Château Pedesclaux, a classified growth from the Bordeaux township of Pauillac, home of those oenological superstars, Château Lafite-Rothschild, Château Latour, and Château Mouton-Rothschild. (Pedesclaux, whose vines are within a few hundred meters of these celebrated vineyards, sells at about one-tenth their inflated prices.)

Our off-year was 1968, regarded by many as one of the worst vintages in recent times. (Indeed, a few days before our tasting, *New York Times* wine writer Frank J. Prial wrote a piece warning consumers away from the 1968 Bordeaux.) Our premature year was 1970, regarded as potentially a great year. Our prime year at peak development was 1966, considered Pedesclaux' best since 1961, which in turn has been hailed as the vintage of the century.

Looking at the three wines was almost as instructive as nosing and tasting them. The '68 was brick red, brown at the edges—obviously quite ready for drinking, despite its relative youth. The '70 was closer to purple—holding great promise, but not a wine for immediate consumption. The '66 was close to the '68, but with more intensity to the red; its edges also were brown, so it was fully mature.

We nosed. The '68 had the distinctive Bordeaux nose, described by some as "nutty" or "smokey." (I try to avoid describing nose or taste, because I've found that no two people get the same message from the same adjective. I'm not very enthusiastic about describing a wine's visual character, either. But, of course, it's impossible to discuss wines in the present context without *some* description.) The '70 had a strong and pungent aroma (defined, you will recall, as the smell of the grapes) but no significant bouquet (reflecting the development of the wine itself as it aged, first in barrels, then in the bottle). The '66 had rich bouquet.

The most instructive nose comparison was between the '66 and the '68. The latter, while far from undistinguished, lacked the sophistication and complexity of the former. Even newcomers to wine, including some people whose prior exposure to wines was limited to the Boone's Farm and Annie Green Springs genre, were able to differentiate the two Pedesclaux; in blind "nosings," they consistently identified the '66.

The taste test supported our visual and olfactory impressions. The '70 was much too young; drinking it amounted to oenological infanticide. The '66 was the essence of a Pauillac whose time has come. The '68 was not nearly as sophisticated, but it was very drinkable.

In some ways, the '68 was the most instructive wine of the tasting—particularly in view of the *New York Times* writer's warning. Granted, the wine would not inspire the enthusiasms *aficionados* accord the '66 or other celebrated vintages. But it certainly was not a wine to be shunned.

In fact, selling at $2.75 a bottle in New York City at the time of our tasting, Pedesclaux '68 was—in my view and that of most of our tasters, professional and amateur—a much better buy than such highly advertised wines as Grande Marque (selling at $3.79) or the regional wines of leading shippers like B&G ($8.49 a bottle for a regional Margaux, $4.89 for a regional Médoc), Cruse ($9.65 for a St. Julien, $4.99 for a Médoc), and deLuze ($3.99 for a Médoc). The moral is, be very skeptical about what you read about wine, even in the *New York Times*. Perhaps I should say *especially* in the *New York Times*.

Enlist the aid of your favorite wine merchant in setting up a similar tasting. Don't use the three Pedesclaux vintages we've discussed here, because by the time you stage your tasting their character will have changed considerably. A knowledgeable wine merchant will be able to help you select another wine with three currently available vintages that are not outrageously priced and that demonstrate the points the tasting seeks to make.

Be sure to taste the wines in the same order we did: first the off-year, then the immature prime year, then the mature prime year. Placing the immature prime year between the other two accents the differences among the three wines.

It also is instructive to taste the off-year immediately before the mature prime year. Try this in a later tasting. Or try it in the same tasting, after clearing your palate with bread or a cracker.

4

Wine Tasting for Fun and Enlightenment

If you'd like to pursue palate development beyond the six lessons in the last chapter, there is a much more extensive course—eighteen lessons—in *Playboy's Book of Wine*. If you wish to go further still, the University of California at Davis offers a program for aspiring wine judges. The ultimate act of aspiring connoisseurship is to become a student in oenology and viticulture at either the University of California, the French wine academies at Montpelier or Bordeaux, the German academy at Mains, or other schools for aspiring wine professionals.

However, as a civilian with no aspirations to turn pro, bear in mind that you will be developing your palate *whenever* you taste wines and especially when you taste them comparatively. Many wine lovers hold tastings rather than cocktail parties. Sometimes groups of wine enthusiasts share expenses in order to taste high-priced vintages (such as those Bordeaux and Burgundy superstars selling at fifty dollars a bottle) which members individually might not ordinarily get the opportunity to taste.

I suggest setting a goal for each tasting rather than selecting wines randomly. For example, it's more instructive to taste the same varietally named wine (say Cabernet Sauvignon) of three producers than to taste three totally unrelated wines (for instance, a New York State white, a Hungarian red, and a Russian sparkling rosé). Decide in advance what you want your tasting to demonstrate: for example, differences among California Cabernets Sauvignons, differences among Cabernets Sauvignons produced in various parts of the world, differences among varietally named white wines from the same region of production, differences among various regional bottlings of the same varietal.

Here are thirteen testing ideas to get you started:

1. Five Dramatically Different Approaches to Rosé
NEW YORK: Taylor Rosé
CALIFORNIA: Paul Masson Rosé
PORTUGAL: Mateus Rosé
YUGOSLAVIA: Adriatica Opolo Rosé
GREECE: Roditis Rosé

In this and other suggested tastings, when no vintage is recommended, any current vintage will do. In rosé wines, vinification techniques and blending are such that there is extremely little difference in the same producer's product from year to year. However, there are considerable differences in the approaches of individual producers and considerable differences in the styles of wine produced in different countries.

(Though New York and California are both in the same country, differences in climate and terrain are so great that the wines produced in these states are quite unlike each other; thus, we treat both separately here. More than two dozen other of the United States produce wine, but in such small amounts that virtually the entire production is consumed locally. The wines of these states are generally much more similar in style to those of New York than to those of California.)

Rosé is a good starting point for wine neophytes. It has a softness and freshness that most newcomers find quite palatable. These same newcomers often dislike the more complex wines which long-time *aficionados* generally favor.

There are wide differences in regional approaches to rosé, ranging from Taylor's, which many drinkers will find cloyingly sweet, to the Yugoslav Opolo, which has a unique tartness that some people will incorrectly characterize as "sour" or "bitter."

2. Four Rosé Wines from France
ANJOU: Moc-Baril Cabernet d'Anjou Rosé
TAVEL: Château d'Aqueria Tavel Rosé
PROVENCE: Château de Selle
PROVENCE: Château Ste. Roseline

The differences among these wines are not nearly as dramatic as in the first group, but they are nonetheless significant. This tasting not only demonstrates regional differences (Anjou *vs.* Tavel *vs.* Provence) but also the differences in the approaches of two vintners from the same region, Provence.

3. Five Generic Chablis

CALIFORNIA: Beringer Chablis

CALIFORNIA: Sonoma Vineyards Chablis

CALIFORNIA: Almaden Chablis

CALIFORNIA: Pedrizzetti Chablis

NEW YORK: Great Western Moore's Diamond Chablis

A "generic" wine is one named after a place other than that in which it was produced. Why would anyone name a wine that way? The producers say they do so because the wine is made in the same style as that of the region whose name is being used; thus, the generic name helps consumers who know regional types discover new wines they will like.

Nonsense, reply the producers of the region whose name is being used. These generic wines have next to nothing in common with the style of our wines. The generic producers don't use the same grapes that we do, they don't use the same aging techniques, and the wines don't taste at all like ours. The whole thing is a ripoff; they are trying to capitalize on our good name.

I tend to favor the regional producers' point of view. I find about as much similarity between Almaden Chablis and Pic Chablis Grand Cru "Bougrots," produced in the region of France named Chablis, as I find between Pepsi-Cola and Vichy: the latter two are both liquid and both effervescent, but that's as close as they get.

This is not to say that the generically named Chablis are not palatable. I consider several of them delightful—but in ways quite different from the wines of the region of Chablis. Some also are very good buys. I regard Beringer Chablis, at $1.90 a fifth, one of the better white wine bargains presently available in the United States.

4. A Generic Chablis vs. Two Regional Chablis

CALIFORNIA: Christian Brothers Chablis

FRANCE: Pic Chablis

FRANCE: Pic Chablis Grand Cru "Bougrots" 1970

With this tasting, you can compare and see what I mean. I don't think you'll confuse the Beringer—or any other generic—with the regional.

Both regionals, you'll note, are from the same producer. The *grand cru* is the premium product, made from specially selected grapes in a prime year. "Bougrots" is the name of the vineyard where they are grown. The other Chablis was made from grapes grown in vineyards throughout the region of Chablis.

French law, by the way, requires that all wine labeled Chablis be made exclusively from the Chardonnay grape. Beringer and many other California producers make a wine predominantly, if not exclusively, from the same grape, but they do not call it Chablis; they call it Chardonnay or Pinot Chardonnay and sell it for quite a bit more than (sometimes double or even triple) their generically named Chablis.

Not surprisingly, Chardonnay is an expensive, low-yield grape that calls for small-barrel aging and other expensive vinification techniques. The generic Chablis, which sell for quite a bit less than the regionals or the varietally named Chardonnays and Pinot Chardonnays, usually are made from blends of Chenin Blanc, French Colombard, Thompson Seedless, and other relatively inexpensive grapes. However, some California producers use some Chardonnay in the blend.

5. Generic Chablis vs. Chardonnay vs. Chablis
CALIFORNIA: Christian Brothers Chablis
CALIFORNIA: Christian Brothers Pinot Chardonnay
CALIFORNIA: Wente Bros. Pinot Chardonnay
FRANCE: Sichel Pinot Chardonnay
FRANCE: Jouvet Pinot Chardonnay Mâcon
FRANCE: Pic Chablis
FRANCE: Pic Chablis Grand Cru "Bougrots" 1970

This tasting reveals more subtle shades of difference between the original (regional) Chablis, other wines made predominantly of the same grape, and the generic Chablis.

There are, really, several tastings within the main tasting; that is, several comparisons involving two or three wines, each of these comparisons being revealing of itself in addition to being revealing as part of the overall seven-wine tasting.

Tasting the Christian Brothers Chablis versus that producer's Pinot Chardonnay (or the generic Chablis of any producer against the same producer's Chardonnay or Pinot Chardonnay) reveals much about the respective character of generic versus varietal wines. The latter almost inevitably are more complex, more sophisticated. They are Beethoven compared to Vivaldi, Giotto compared to Cimabue. None of this is to say that the former are not interesting in their own right (there are times I'm much more in the mood for Vivaldi), but simply that they are different experiences.

Tasting the Christian Brothers Pinot Chardonnay against that of Wente Bros. demonstrates the differing approaches to the same wine by two respected California winemakers, the former in the Napa Valley, the latter in the Livermore Valley. Until recently, individual regions of production were not often designated in California, and many people (including quite a few prominent wine writers) assumed that wines from these different regions did not vary significantly. Taste comparisons put that myth to rest, and future years almost certainly will see regional designations within California take on great importance. (Future years also will see, I think, the abandonment of generic labeling by most California wineries.)

Tasting the California Pinot Chardonnay against those of Sichel and Jouvet reveals dramatic differences in style. In France, a varietally labeled wine must contain only grapes of the named variety; in California, a varietal name may be used if fifty-one percent of the wine comes from grapes of that variety. But the differences between the French and California wines here are as much a matter of grape-growing conditions (soil, drainage, climate) and vinification techniques as of grape variety.

None of this should be taken as a qualitative statement about any of the wines. My own ranking order of preference would be (1) Wente Bros., (2) Christian Bros., (3) Sichel, and (4) Jouvet. Your order might very well be different, and neither one of us is "right."

Pinot Chardonnay, by the way, is what people used to call the grape before viticulturists decided it is not a member of the Pinot family (along with Pinot Blanc, Pinot Gris, and several others) as originally believed. The grape is now usually called simply Chardonnay, although most producers continue to label the wines Pinot Chardonnay, probably because they don't want consumers who have grown accustomed to buying it under that name to think the wine has been changed.

"Pinot Chardonnay Mâcon" is a regional as well as a varietal designation. The term tells us that the wine was made from Chardonnay grapes grown exclusively in the region of Mâcon, a short distance south of Chablis. Both are within the region of Burgundy. (Strictly speaking, Burgundy is a "region" and Chablis and Mâcon are "districts" within the region.) The Sichel Pinot Chardonnay does not carry a regional designation, the absence of which suggests that grapes came from more than one district—although that need not necessarily be the case.

Comparing the Sichel and Jouvet with the two Pics reveals not only geographic differences (Mâcon *vs.* Chablis *vs.* Burgundy-at-large) but also differences in vinification styles among three well-known French producers.

In sum, it's a revealing tasting at many levels. It should prove especially revealing to newcomers who thought all wines labeled "Chablis" were the same, or who felt that there were no significant differences among white wines, period.

6. White Wines of Burgundy

Pic Chablis 1973
Pic Chablis Grand Cru "Bougrots" 1970
Mâcon Blanc Villages Jadot 1973
Jadot Hospices de Beaune Meursault "Jean Humblot" 1972
L'Heritier-Guyot Clos Blanc de Vougeot 1972
Jadot Puligny Montrachet 1972
Montrachet Jadot 1971

Here is an array of white wines from Burgundy, most produced by the same firm, Louis Jadot. Using wines of the same producer at a tasting is especially instructive, because the vinification approach is basically the same, as is the underlying oenological philosophy, and the differences that result are chiefly the result of geography and grape variety.

Jadot, unfortunately, does not produce a Chablis; however, those by Pic are imported into the United States by

Kobrand Corporation, which also imports Jadot. Staying with wines of the same importer is useful, particularly if the importer is a small firm like Kobrand, because all wines generally have been chosen by the same buyer or committee of buyers and thus reflect to only a slightly lesser extent the consistency of the wines of a single producer.

Incidentally, buying by the producer or importer's name when you don't know the individual wines can be helpful. Chances are, if you like those of his wines that you do know, you share the palate biases of his winemaker or buyer, and you'll also like those of his wines that you don't know. This is less apt to be true with the larger importing firms, where more people participate in buy decisions and where an attempt often is made to offer something for everyone. However, even at large firms there is a certain consistency of approach.

Schieffelin & Co., for example, represents an extremely broad spectrum of wines, and while not all of them are in line with my palate biases, I've never had reason to fault any of them qualitatively. I'd be more comfortable buying an unknown wine imported by Schieffelin than one imported by a firm about whose wines I had not formed an overall impression or a firm that had imported one or two wines I found very disappointing.

Some smaller firms, in addition to Kobrand, whose buyers generally share my palate biases are Frederick Wildman & Sons, House of Banfi, Julius Wile & Sons, Crosse & Blackwell, and Charles Morganstern. I've never been disappointed by a wine imported by any of these companies.

In this tasting of white Burgundies, there are many interesting stylistic contrasts. The regional Chablis, the Mâcon Blanc Villages, and the Puligny Montrachet are relatively inexpensive; they are young and fresh. The other wines are mature and well-rounded; they possess a complexity and sophistication no young wine could match.

Montrachet is one of the most celebrated white wines in the world. Its price reflects its celebrity: over twenty-five dollars a bottle New York retail at this writing. The Puligny Montrachet is similar in basic style and sells at a fifth the price. Puligny Montrachet is the name of the community where the wine was produced—one of two communities which the vineyard, Montrachet, straddles. Over the years, communities in Burgundy took to attaching to their original name the name of their most celebrated vineyard. Thus, what once was the community of Vosne has become Vosne Romanée; it is home of the vineyard, Romanée-Conti. Aloxe, home of the vineyard, Corton, has become Aloxe-Corton.

Clos de Vougeot and Meursault are two no less famous names of Burgundy. Tasting these wines alongside Montrachet reveals the subtle but very significant differences among three of the most highly prized white wines in the world.

7. Beaujolais

> Jouvet Beaujolais
> Louis Latour Beaujolais Supérieur
> Louis Latour Beaujolais Villages 1973
> Louis Jadot Beaujolais Villages 1973
> Louis Jadot Moulin-a-Vent 1973

Beaujolais has long been the favorite carafe wine in Paris and has become quite popular over the past two decades in the United States. Many people think there is only one wine produced under that name, or that differences among wines carrying the names are insignificant. Actually, Beaujolais covers an extremely broad spectrum of wine qualities within the same basic style.

The Beaujolais region produces four legally defined categories of wine: Beaujolais, Beaujolais Supérieur, Beaujolais Villages, and special *crus*, or "growths," named after nine communities where production is authorized. Governmental restrictions concerning conditions of production are, not surprisingly, increasingly limiting as we proceed up the scale. Prices rise correspondingly.

The wines in this tasting cover the full spectrum and invite paired comparisons as we proceed up the scale: a simple Beaujolais next to a Supérieur, the Supérieur next to the same producer's Beaujolais Villages, that Beaujolais Villages next to one from another producer, and this second Beaujolais Villages next to the same producer's Moulin-a-Vent, probably the most celebrated of the nine *crus* (the others are Fleurie, Juliénas, Chénas, Morgon, Brouilly, Côte de Brouilly, Saint-Amour, and Chiroubles).

A type of Beaujolais not mentioned here is Beaujolais Nouveau. This is not a legally defined category; it refers to any Beaujolais intended for quick consumption. These wines, which almost inevitably come from the simple Beaujolais classification, are put to market as soon as forty-five days following the harvest.

A nineteenth-century tradition had producers literally racing to Paris with Beaujolais Nouveaux on horse-drawn carts. Their arrival in the City of Light triggered a sort of mini-New Year's Eve celebration, with Parisians greeting the new wine year by guzzling the first specimens from the *vendange*. The tradition continues today, with trucks replacing horsecarts—although they no longer literally race.

Generally a wine that is drinkable young is not drinkable old, and these Beaujolais Nouveaux are no exception. They lose their character rapidly; most are considered undrinkable after May of the following year.

Some importers have in recent years introduced Beaujolais Nouveaux to the United States, but many French wine growers privately advise against drinking them. Gerard Yvernault, a representative of Château Margaux in Bordeaux, is not so private about his advice. He told television viewers that he wouldn't drink a Beaujolais Nouveau in the United States. They don't travel well unless pasteurized, and pasteurization destroys their character.

8. Red Wines of Burgundy

Domaine A. Ropiteau-Mignon Pommard Chanlains (Premiere Cuvée) 1969
Jadot Beaune Boucherottes 1969
Jadot Le Musigny 1971
Domaine Jacques Prieur Chambertin 1969

Pommard is one of the best known red wines of Burgundy. It is interesting to taste this superb example of the species (imported to the United States by Frederick Wildman & Sons) against the Boucherottes, an estate-bottled Côte de Beaune, the vineyard of which is immediately adjacent to the Pommard district. (The Côte de Beaune is one of two *côtes*, or "coasts," that make up the Côte d'Or, or "Gold Coast," the central area of Burgundy and home of its most celebrated vineyards. The other, just north of the Côte de Beaune, is the Côte de Nuits.)

The Jadot Le Musigny is a non-estate bottled Côte de Nuits, and the Chambertin is probably that district's most prized wine, reportedly Napoleon's favorite.

9. Red Wines of Bordeaux
    Ginestet Fort Médoc 1971
    Ginestet Margaux 1971
    Château Margaux 1971

This tasting reveals significant differences between regional and chateau wines by the same producer.

Château Margaux, owned by Bernard Ginestet (who happens also to be the mayor of the town of Margaux), is one of the four top-ranked growths of Bordeaux in the official classification of 1855. (The other three are Château Lafite, now Château Lafite-Rothschild, of Pauillac; Château Latour, of Pauillac; and Château Haut Brion, of Pessac, Graves.)

In Bordeaux, a chateau-bottled wine is one in which all the grapes come from the same vineyard. The Ginestet Margaux was made by the same producer, but from grapes drawn from throughout the township of Margaux. The Ginestet Fort Médoc was made from grapes grown in the district of Médoc, of which Margaux is a part. Generally, the smaller the geographic area from which the grapes are drawn, the more distinctive the character of the wine.

These three wines clearly show differences in color, style, intensity of bouquet, and overall quality. The tasting could be expanded to include another chateau-bottled wine from the same township, perhaps Château Rausan-Ségla, rated a "second growth" in the official classification of 1855.

10. An Introduction to German Wines
    Madrigal Liebfraumilch 1973
    Madrigal Johannisberg Riesling 1973
    Madrigal Wehlener Sonnenuhr Riesling Kabinett 1971
    Piesporter Goldtropfchen Auslese, Erzeuger-Abfullung
       Lehnert Matheus, Estate Bottled 1971

Germany produces an almost incredible range of wines, ranging from such popular favorites as Liebfraumilch to such rarities as *Trockenbeerenauslese,* made from individually selected raisin-like grape berries that have developed *Edelfaule,* or "noble rot," a benign fungus that reduces water content, thereby sweetening the grape's remaining juice. Until recently a relatively small number of German wines was known in the United States and Canada. Fortunately, that situation rapidly is being remedied.

This tasting starts with Liebfraumilch, probably the best known of German wines among North Americans, and continues with more sophisticated examples of the same basic style. The Johannisberg Riesling is varietally named, meaning under German wine laws that all the grapes are of that variety. The Liebfraumilch also contains Riesling grapes, but blended with others to produce a softer, fresher wine.

German wine laws establish three categories of wine: *Tafelwein*, or "table wine," given very little aging and meant to be drunk quite young; *Qualitaetswein*, or "quality wine," produced under more restrictive conditions; and *Qualitaetswein mit Praedikat*, or "quality wine with special attributes." These attributes are: *Kabinett*, literally "cabinet" in the sense of a body of ministers, a governmental cabinet; wines so designated are made under conditions even more restrictive than *Qualitaetswein* and receive special aging; *Auslese*, designating wines made from individually selected bunches of grapes; *Spaetlese*, made from grapes infected with *Edelfaule*, the noble fungus; *Beerenauslese*, made from individually selected *Edelfaule* berries; and *Trockenbeerenauslese*, made, as has been noted, from individually selected raisin-like (literally, "dry") *Edelfaule* berries.

In our tasting, both the Liebfraumilch and Madrigal Johannisberg Riesling are of the *Qualitaetswein* category; the remaining two are classified as *Qualitaetswein mit Praedikat*, the respective *Praedikaten* being *Kabinett* and *Auslese*. The first three, as will be noted from the trade name, are made by the same producr; all four come from the same exporter, Weinexport Hattenheim.

11. Chianti
Ruffino Chianti
Oliveri Chianti Classico 1971
Straccali Chianti Classico 1971
Melini Chianti Classico 1971
Melini Chianti Classico Riserva 1968
Nozzole Chianti Classico Riserva 1968
Nozzole Chianti Classico Riserva 1964

Chianti is probably the Italian wine best known in the United States and Canada. It comes from a region in Tuscany, extending from Florence to Siena. The region is named "Chianti" for oenological purposes only; the name derives from the Latin word, *clangor,* a horn used for fox hunting.

Chianti is one of the few wines in the world made from a blend of red and white grapes. It is, for this reason, quite light. It is produced in great volume: more gallonage annually than any single type of Italian wine. But the differences among wines named Chianti are considerable, as this tasting will show.

There are three legally defined categories: simple Chianti, which may be made from grapes grown anywhere in the region; Chianti Classico, made from grapes grown at higher elevations in a subdivision of the region; and Chianti Classico Riserva, produced under more restrictive conditions and given special aging.

This tasting contains several instructive pairings: a simple Chianti (from Ruffino, the region's largest producer) against a *classico,* this *classico* against two others of the same year, the Melini *classico* against the same producer's *riserva,* this *riserva* against another of the same year by Nozzole, and the Nozzole '68 against a Nozzole '64.

12. Four from Verona
Ruffino Bardolino
Mirafiore Bardolino
Mirafiore Valpolicella
Amarone Classico Recioto della Valpolicella 1968

Next to Chianti, the best known Italian reds in the United States and Canada probably are those Veronese twins, Bardolino and Valpolicella. They really are twins: in blind tastings, few nonprofessionals can tell them apart—and sometimes even professionals are fooled.

But though the two wines, which are named after communities in Verona, are quite alike stylistically, there are significant differences from producer to producer. In this tasting, we compare two very popular Bardolini, then comparatively taste a popular Valpolicella against a more prestigious one. The *classico* designation in Valpolicella, as in Chianti, designates a regional subdivision at higher altitude.

After you've tasted the four against each other, you might find it interesting to repeat Lesson #5 from the palate development course in Chapter Three, using any of the four

Veronese wines as the constant to be identified in a blind tasting of the entire four.

If you can manage that, try tasting the two Mirafiore and the Ruffino blind and—no fair peeking—identify the Valpolicella.

13. Three Royal Italians
Grumello Enologica Valtellinese 1971
Gattinara Antoniolo 1964
Barolo Giri 1966
Barolo Borgogno 1955

Italian wine growers often speak of Nebbiolo as the nation's most noble grape. It produces very full-bodied wines of extraordinary character, closer to those of Burgundy than to any other Italian wine that comes immediately to mind. In a tasting presided over by Lucio M. Sorre of Frederick Wildman & Sons, I tasted the three best known of the Nebbiolo wines, all from the region of Piemonte.

Extending the nobility metaphor, wine professionals sometimes speak of these three as the king, the queen, and the prince. The king is Barolo, the queen Gattinara, the prince Grumello. I won't try to verbalize the visual, olfactory, and taste differences that inspire these characterizations. Suffice it to say that all three wines represent a unique tasting experience, and if after tasting them you think the royalty roles should be interchanged—or scrapped—characterize them as you like.

Note, by the way, that Barolo, Gattinara, and Grumello are wine *types*, not sole examples of the species. As with Chianti, Bardolino, and Valpolicella—or Liebfraumilch, Beaujolais, and Chablis—different producers make distinctly different wines.

In this tasting, we stress differences among the basic wine types. Though the producers differ, all four wines are imported to the U.S. by House of Banfi, reflecting a consistency of the buyer's palate.

Later tastings might explore one type from three producers or different vintages from the same producer. The comparison of the Borgogno and Giri is somewhat unfair to the Giri, since the Borgogno has an eleven-year age advantage. However, the tasting demonstrates differences between a prized Barolo of relatively recent vintage and a genuine classic. It would be interesting also to taste a Borgogno and Giri of the same year against each other.

The '55 Barolo, by the way, is regarded by many wine professionals, including Banfi's representative, Ferdinando D. Garbani, as that wine's vintage of the century. Other cognoscenti favor the '47. I'll settle for either.

These Nebbiolo-based wines are among the longest lived that Italy produces, with some vintages not reaching their peak for thirty years.

5

How to Serve Wine

If you're having guests for dinner, should you use a decanter to serve wine? Or is it better to serve from the bottle?

If you're serving white wine, should you chill it first? Should you chill red wine? What shape glass should you use for Champagne?

Is one corkscrew better than another? How do you avoid pushing the cork into the bottle? If the mouth of the bottle is dirty when you remove the cork, should you wipe it off with a napkin or just pretend you don't see it?

These questions are not exactly earth-shaking and certainly don't deserve the kind of deliberation that would go into solving the balance-of-payments deficit or deciding where your children should go to school. But certain approaches to wine service can, I think, make for a more comfortable and enjoyable experience for your guests and yourself. These approaches can also enhance both your own and your guests' appreciation of the wines that you serve.

Try them and see if you don't agree.

Glasses

Importer Julius Wile says he has only one requirement of a wine glass: it shouldn't leak. I share his view that wine can be enjoyed in any glass, and I'm sure he shares mine that it's more enjoyable in some glasses than others. Let's pursue the point by repeating the first experiment we performed, this time with a few added touches.

Take three glasses: first, an ordinary juice glass or water tumbler; second, one of those small (six ounces or less) stemmed glasses that department stores often advertise as wine glasses; third, a large (at least twelve ounces), colorless, unengraved, stemmed glass whose rim curves inward.

Place the glasses side-by-side on a white tablecloth and pour about three ounces of the same red wine into each. Taste the wines, starting with the juice glass or tumbler, then using the small stemmed glass, then the large stemmed glass. Be sure to perform all three tasting operations discussed in Chapter Two. In case you've forgotten:

(1) Look through the wine at the tablecloth. Note color and clarity.

(2) Swirl and nose the wine.

(3) Sip and let the liquid come into contact with the three appropriate sets of taste buds.

Now compare what you perceived with each glass.

When you used the juice glass or tumbler and looked through the wine, chances are you didn't notice much. Your hand probably blocked your view of most of the wine, and your hand's shadow probably created a prism effect that made it impossible for you actually to see through the wine; you couldn't be sure whether it was slightly cloudy, clear, or brilliant. Your fingertips on the glass probably made your visual task even more difficult. If there was a drawing or design on the glass, you probably saw even less. And if the glass was colored, you couldn't accurately perceive the color of the wine.

With the stemmed glasses, none of these problems arose. Holding the glass by the stem permitted you to see the entire bowl of wine. There were no obstructions or shadows, and you didn't fingerprint the bowl. Assuming the small glass was neither colored nor engraved, there were no interferences with your perception of color or clarity.

But the large stemmed glass had one advantage over the small: you were able to tip the bowl without spilling wine; this allowed you to experiment with the best angle of vision. That could be important with a wine about whose maturity you were unsure; the transition from brownish circumference to brick-red center is better observable when the glass is tipped to create the largest possible circumference.

And there is an esthetic fillip: the wine—any wine—looks richer and more elegant in the larger glass, now doesn't it?

On to the test for nose. Performing this experiment in Chapter One, you found that the juice glass or tumbler didn't really give you a vivid impression. This time, experimenting with three glasses, you almost certainly found that you didn't get a very vivid impression from the small stemmed glass, either.

The fact is, wines tend to be rather shy about their fragrance. They don't fill the room with it. If you want it, you've got to pursue it. Italian reds are particularly bashful; the nose must be coaxed out. Hungarian, Yugoslav, and Greek reds are only slightly less shy. Those from Spain, France, and California tend to be assertive—particularly the mature Burgundies and Bordeaux—but even they do not reveal themselves fully without some persuasion. The most persuasive conditions are (a) a large glass that (b) curves inward at the rim and (c) is only partially filled.

Why? The large glass exposes a correspondingly large surface of wine to the air. It is aeration that releases the fragrance of wine—or any other liquid. By only partially filling the glass, we provide an enclosed area for the fragrance to accumulate. The ideal serving is three to four ounces at a time in a glass at least double and preferably triple or quadruple that size. Whatever its size, the glass should never be more than half full—and if you use a four-ounce glass, the one to two ounces you pour simply do not expose enough surface to the air.

The inward curving rim helps capture the nose in the unfilled portion of the glass. Swirling the wine increases aeration and thus magnifies nose. In a three- or four-ounce glass, swirling is virtually impossible.

Some classic wine glasses do not have an inward curve to the rim. The traditional claret glass is basically U-shaped, as is the flute. Perhaps these shapes came into being because the wines served in the glasses (Bordeaux reds in the claret, sparkling wines in the flute) are among the olfactorily more assertive and don't need the help of the inward curve. But the curve will be found on most other classic shapes: the tulip, the Moselle glass, the pear-shaped tastevin (not to be confused with the sommelier's shallow silver tasting cup, also called a "tastevin"), and of course the Burgundy bowl.

I personally prefer the inward curve, so I usually serve Bordeaux reds and other Cabernet Sauvignon types in the tastevin and sparkling wines in the tulip. I bear in mind that tradition is not always the best guide: witness that abomination, the *coupe*, or saucer-shaped Champagne glass, whose rim is so broad as to dispel nose completely and hasten the departure of bubbles, making the wine quickly go flat. Happily, most people no longer use the *coupe* for serving anything more important than ice cream.

If protocol is important to you, the following shapes probably would be deemed "correct" by most people:

For sparkling wines: tulip, flute.

For younger whites: Moselle, tulip, tastevin.

For mature whites: tastevin or, in rare cases, if wine is a real superstar, Burgundy bowl.

For younger reds, including Beaujolais, Zinfandel, Chianti, and other light-bodied wines: claret, tastevin.

For Cabernet Sauvignon and other light-bodied mature reds: claret, tastevin.

For Pinot Noir and other full-bodied mature reds, including Barolo and Egri Bikaver: Burgundy bowl.

For fortified wines, including Sherry, Port, Madeira, and Malvasia Bianca, a variety of special glasses is available; among general glasses, the most suitable probably is the tulip.

The best all-purpose glass probably is the tastevin, though some professionals recommend the claret. In my view, this is because they are afraid a funny-shaped glass like the tastevin will scare away some squeamish potential buyers of wine.

Continuing on to the taste test, we find that there are no significant differences in the three glasses being used in our experiment. This, of course, is because once the wine has been delivered to the mouth, the glass has done its job. But you'll recall that nose is far more important than taste in perceiving the subtleties that make wine drinking something more than a mere thirst-quenching enterprise. Without a glass that meets the criteria listed above, you—and your guests—will not get the most out of the wines you serve.

For emphasis, let's recap these criteria:

1. Large glass (at least eight ounces, ideally twelve to twenty-six).
2. Stemmed.
3. Colorless.
4. No engraving on bowl.
5. Curves inward at rim.

6. Pour three or four ounces at a time, never more than half a glass.

Temperature

Shortly after beginning work on this book, I had lunch with the U.S. importer of some of Europe's most highly reputed wines. When I mentioned that I intended to write about Chinese rice-based wines along with the more popular Western grape-based varieties, he quite visibly winced. "I frankly don't know how they manage to drink them," he said.

Not long afterward we lunched again, this time at the home of writer-editor-filmmaker Brian Richard Boylan, who, his ethnic origins notwithstanding, happens to be a bang-up *chef de cuisine Chinoise.* The importer and I got chatting about the difficulty of matching Western wines to Chinese food in general, and to the very spicy Szechuan cooking in particular. The conventional wisdom is that only one French wine can hold up against these dishes, Hermitage, but even that has a struggle, so ultimately you're better off serving tea. Enter Brian Richard Boylan carrying three handleless ceramic containers of about three-ounce capacity.

We sip. The liquid is warm—indeed, about body temperature. It rather reminds one of a tepid but particularly pungent tea that has been spiked with—well?—well, something. "Good," says the importer, nodding approvingly. "What is it?"

It is Shao Hsing, Chinese rice-based wine, served at body temperature, as the Chinese are wont to serve it. The reason my importer friend previously found it so unpalatable was that on the very few occasions when he sampled it, it had been served at the much cooler temperatures traditional for white wines.

I don't say that a difference in serving temperature will have the same dramatic effect on everyone's reaction to every wine, but there is no question that temperature is an important consideration. Recall the experiment in Chapter One in which refrigeration frosted the nose of a celebrated Bordeaux. Conversely, refrigeration helps a white wine assert its most prized characteristics; serve the same white warm, and it's like drinking room-temperature Coke.

There are no hard and fast rules about serving temperatures, and of course *de gustibus non est disputandum,* so if you like room-temperature Coke, far be it from me to tell you you shouldn't. Still, wine professionals, whose only vested interest in this instance is helping you get the most pleasure from the wines they sell, recommend certain temperatures as most likely to provide that pleasure. These are the ranges they generally regard as ideal:

Sweet white wines, including Sauternes, Barsac, *Spaetlese, Auslese, Beerenauslese, Trockenbeerenauslese,* South African "late-picked" vintages, California and New York "late harvested" wines, Champagnes labeled "extra dry," "dry," "semi-dry," "sweet," "sec," "demi-sec" or "doux," Asti Spumante, Sekt, all other sparkling wines not specifically labeled "brut," "natur" or "natural"—1 to 5 degrees Centigrade (34 to 41 degrees Fahrenheit).

Red sparkling wines, including sparkling Burgundy and *Kalte Ente* ("Cold Duck")—1 to 5 degrees Centigrade (34 to 41 degrees Fahrenheit).

Aromatized wines, sweet or dry, including Vermouth, Marsala, Dubonnet, and such flavored wines as Sparkling Life, Annie Green Springs, Boone's Farm, etc.—1 to 5 degrees Centigrade (34 to 41 degrees Fahrenheit) or over ice.

Dry sparking wines, including all Champagnes and other sparkling wines labeled "brut," "natur" or "natural," and *Spumante Secco* (sometimes also labeled "brut," but *not* Asti Spumante, which is sweet)—5 to 7 degrees Centigrade (41 to 45 degrees Fahrenheit).

Young dry whites, including all generics, German wines below the rank of *Qualitaetswein mit Praedikat,* and varietals intended to be consumed under three years, generally including Chenin Blanc, Sauvignon Blanc, Pinot Gris, Green Hungarian and Gewürztraminer (but not Chardonnay and usually not Riesling) 7 to 12 degrees Centigrade (45 to 53 degrees Fahrenheit).

Young reds, sweet or dry, including Beaujolais, Zinfandel, all generics, all Canadian reds, and all non-California reds produced in the U.S., but *not* fortified wines, like Port—11 to 15 degrees Centigrade (52 to 59 degrees Fahrenheit).

Aged dry whites (over three years)—11 to 16 degrees Centigrade (52 to 61 degrees Fahrenheit).

Aged dry full-bodied reds, including Barolo, Gattinara, Barbaresco, Grumello, and others made predominantly from the Nebbiolo grape; Brunello di Montalcino; wines made predominantly from Pinot Noir, including Burgundy (that

produced in France, *not* generics); wines of the Côte du
Rhone, including Hermitage and Châteauneuf-du-Pape; South
African and Australian full-bodied blends, including Pinotage;
the Moroccan Vieux Papes—15 to 17 degrees Centigrade
(59 to 63 degrees Fahrenheit).

Dry fortified wines, principally Sherry, sometimes called
"Fino," "Dry Sherry," or "Cocktail Sherry," and Madeira
Secco ("Dry Madeira")—12 to 18 degrees Centigrade (54
to 64 degrees Fahrenheit). Some people like these wines over
ice. I myself wouldn't drink them that way; I find that the
dilution kills their character completely. This can be a relatively small loss with many inexpensive (under two dollars a
bottle) brands now on the market, but a great loss with such
classics as Dos Cortados, Don Zoilo, Pando, La Iña, and Tio
Pepe. If one of my guests *asked* for a dry fortified wine on
the rocks, I suppose I'd manage to serve it that way without
wincing. But I wouldn't volunteer it, and I really don't think
rocks drinkers get more than a fraction of what the wine has
to offer.

Aged dry light-bodied reds, including Chianti and wines
made predominantly from Cabernet Sauvignon (including the
reds of Bordeaux)—17 to 20 degrees Centigrade (63 to 68 degrees Fahrenheit).

Medium-sweetness fortified wines, including Sherry (sometimes simply named "Sherry," more often qualified as "Medium Sherry" or "Amontillado") and tawny (i.e., brownish
rather than red) Port—18 to 25 degrees Centigrade (65 to 77
degrees Fahrenheit). Again, some people like these over ice,
and a leading imported brand, Dry Sack, advertises itself on
TV and in magazines as an on-the-rocks drink. But I think
this is an awful waste of good Sherry.

Sweet fortified wines, including Cream Sherry, Port (sometimes called "Ruby Port"), Malvasia Bianca, Mammertino,
Santol and other Philippine wines made from plums and
relatives of the plum—22 to 27 degrees Centigrade (72 to 78
degrees Fahrenheit).

Shao-Hsing and other rice-based Chinese wines—36 to 38
degrees Centigrade (97 to 100 degrees Fahrenheit).

Sake and other Japanese rice-based wines—1 to 5 degrees
Centigrade (34 to 41 degrees Fahrenheit) or 41 to 45 degrees
Centigrade (105 to 115 degrees Fahrenheit). Most Japanese
whom I know prefer the warmer temperature; the wine is

hcated in a carafe which is lowered into hot water. Some people also serve Sake over ice.

This may seem overly complicated, and I grant that it would be quite a chore to memorize the entire table. But I don't think it terribly burdensome to consult the table once you've decided which wines you are going to serve. If you want an easier way out, a rough rule of thumb is to serve reds and medium or sweet fortified wines at room temperature and everything else chilled.

Service

Some people who have no fear of differential calculus or laser physics nonetheless are intimidated by a bottle with a cork in it. No one need be. Wine service can be simplicity itself.

If you use a suitable glass, you've taken care of the most important part. Now all that remains is to open the bottle and pour the wine.

There are many corkscrews on the market, and most of them will do the job with a minimum of difficulty. However, some are more reliable than others. The most important factors are that the screw itself be both long (at least two inches) and hollow—long so that it can penetrate the cork deeply enough, hollow so that it can get a good grip.

If the word "hollow" seems confusing, examine a corkscrew. The screw will have one of two forms: either there will be a solid central core to which the grooves of the screw are attached, as in a plumber's steel worm; or there will be no grooves as such, rather a continuous strand of metal that works its way in a spiral from top to bottom. In the latter case, you can insert a matchstick or drinking straw through the center.

The spiral configuration permits the metal to imbed itself more firmly in the cork, whereas the device with a solid central core pushes a gaping hole into the cork, making it difficult for the grooves to grip, particularly if the cork is less than fully moist.

A point on moistness: all corks should possess it. If a cork is dry, not only will it be likely to disintegrate when you try to remove it, but also, long before you open the bottle, air may begin seeping in through tiny openings in the cork. This will oxidize the wine and ultimately spoil it, generally by turning it to vinegar.

A cork is kept moist by wine from inside the bottle. If the bottle is upright, wine does not reach the cork. This is why wine professionals advise against upright storage. But despite this advice, many wine merchants store their bottles that way. If you see a bottle stored upright, don't buy it.

The preferred position for storage is with the bottle on its side and the neck very slightly elevated. This not only keeps the cork moist but also permits sediment to accumulate in the lowermost portion of the bottle. By keeping the bottle in this position when you move it from its storage place to the place where you're going to serve it, you prevent the sediment from entering the wine, clouding it, and imparting a harshly acetic taste.

Sediment is not a problem with any wine except an aged (five years or older) red. Younger reds, whites, sparkling wines, fortified wines, aromatized wines, and flavored wines do not produce sediment. Fortified wines may develop some crystallization, but this does not mix with the wine and is easily separated when you pour.

I'll go into more detail about sediment and crystallization later. First, however, let's get back to storage.

Though wines other than aged reds usually don't develop sediment, most can be damaged by air. The exception is fortified wines, which are protected by their higher alcohol level. So store fortified wines any way you find convenient— upright, on their sides, or neck down—and store all other corked bottles in a position that keeps the cork moist. If you're using a refrigerator or wine rack for storage, you'll generally keep the bottles on their sides. You can do this also if you store them in the case in which you bought them. If for some reason—like irregular shape of the bottles—you can't store them on their sides, store them neck down. However, if a wine stored this way is an aged red, it will have to be kept upright or on its side for at least two days before serving so that sediment which has accumulated in the neck can settle in the bottom of the bottle before you pour.

If all this sounds complicated, let me reduce it to a simple rule: store fortified wines any way you like; store all others on their sides.

(Wines in gallon jugs or other screw-top containers are meant for quick consumption and will begin losing character if stored for longer than a few months after they leave the winery. During their short shelf span, there is minimal oxidation through the screw cap. Store them upright; they may leak in other positions.)

Now back to the corkscrew. There are four basic types: (a) the sommelier; (b) the double screw; (c) the levered screw; (d) the plain screw.

Sommelier (pronounced somm-ell-YAY) is the French term for the wine steward in a restaurant. Traditionally, he is the oenological equivalent of the chef: he buys the wines, stores them, determines when they are ready to be served, prepares a list of those that are available, and serves them.

The sommelier-type corkscrew is named after this fellow, and it is the type most sommeliers use. It is shaped somewhat like a jackknife. There is a metal piece that fits against the rim of the bottle. Then the screw pulls out at a right angle to the main body of the instrument. You twist in the screw, fit the metal piece against the rim, lift the opposite end, and leverage extracts the cork. Often there is a folding blade in the lifting end; this is used to cut away the foil or plastic hood on the neck of the bottle.

The double screw is generally made of wood and consists of a hood which fits over the mouth of the bottle, a metal screw attached to a larger wooden screw, and two turning handles atop the wooden screw. You position the hood, then turn the upper handle, which drives the metal screw into the cork. When you can turn the upper handle no further, you turn the lower one. This lifts the wooden screw into which the metal screw is imbedded, thus extracting the cork. (It's more complicated to describe than to do.)

The levered screw consists of a metal hood with a metal screw inside and two levers, resembling rabbit ears, connected to the screw by gears. You position the hood and twist the screw into the cork. This causes the levers to raise. Lower them, and the cork is extracted.

The plain screw is just that, attached to some sort of crosspiece. You twist into the cork and lift the crosspiece. Out comes the cork by sheer muscle action rather than leverage.

Most wine professionals I know favor the sommelier because it's efficient and compact. Those who don't favor the sommelier generally like the double screw. I don't because the hood makes it difficult for me to position the screw precisely in the center of the cork. The levered screw, though not preferred, is generally acceptable; its chief problem is that the levers require both hands, which creates problems with a bottle that is not upright. The plain screw is unwieldy, and even when handled by an expert can result in spills and splashes—to say nothing of jarring the sediment in aged red wines.

Several nonscrew bottle opening devices have appeared in recent years. One involves a long needle which goes through the cork and injects air into the bottle. The air theoretically expels the cork. I say "theoretically," because I've often seen it tried but I've never seen it work consistently.

Another is a tweezer-like affair whose blades slide down alongside the cork and, theoretically, lift it out. I say "theoretically" for the same reason as above.

I don't doubt that someone someday will invent a better corkscrew—or better nonscrew cork remover. But it's not high on my list of things I'd like to see happen. I'm quite happy with the sommelier.

Whatever corkscrew you use, the procedure for opening the bottle is basically the same. To keep things simple, let's assume for this illustration that your bottle contains a young white wine.

Okay, there is no sediment. The position of the bottle therefore does not matter. Place it upright on the table. Remove the foil or plastic hood over the neck. Some people like to remove the entire hood; others prefer to cut away only that portion covering the mouth of the bottle. It's a matter of esthetics; take your choice.

The mouth of the bottle having been exposed, use a napkin to clean away any dust or other matter that may have accumulated around the mouth or cork. With a young white wine, there shouldn't be much of anything to clean. With an older wine, there is apt to be a substantial accumulation. In either case, on both esthetic and hygienic grounds, remove what is there.

Next, place a screw dead center on the cork, twist it in, and extract the cork. You may expose additional dust or other matter. If so, clean it away.

Now pour a dollop—no more than an ounce—in your own glass. That's right—do this before serving your guests. The custom dates back to the days when people used to have guests over to the castle and poison them. The host would taste the wine to demonstrate his good faith.

Actually, the procedure is a courtesy as well as a tradition. If there are cork particles or other matter in the neck of the bottle, they will go into your glass rather than those of your guests.

Don't sip the wine immediately. First look at it and nose it, as in our standard tasting format. This, too, is a courtesy to your guests. You are testing the wine to make sure it is satisfactory before serving them.

If for some reason it is unsatisfactory, get another bottle and start again. If, as is far more likely, the wine is satisfactory, pour. Start with the senior lady present and work your way back by any convenient route to yourself. And that's all there is to it.

With an aged red wine, the procedure is fundamentally the same, but there is an extra step: decanting. This is done to separate the wine from the sediment. If the wine is a red wine that should be aged but hasn't been—at least not sufficiently —decanting can serve the second function of increasing aeration, thereby taking off some of the rougher edges and giving the wine a character more closely resembling maturity (although, to be sure, decanting is no substitute for aging; you still won't achieve the same mature character you would if you permitted the wine to develop fully).

Let's approach decanting obliquely, starting in the cellar— or wherever else you may happen to have stored the bottle. Remember, it was on its side to permit sediment to collect in the bottom. Or, in rare instances, it may have been stored neck down, which means the sediment has accumulated in the neck.

Now, you have decided which wine you are going to serve. If you're a real plan-ahead type, you may have decided several days in advance. In this case, you can bring the wine to the room where it will be served. Stand it upright. Leave it in place for two days. Any sediment shaken loose on the trip from storage will settle during this time. You are now ready to open the bottle and decant. (If you had the bottle neck down, you will have to plan at least two days ahead to give the sediment time to settle.)

If, like most people, you make your decision about what to serve only a short time before you serve it, the stored wine must be on its side. Lift it gingerly from its resting place. Holding the bottle at the same angle, carry it to where you are going to serve it. There are baskets for this purpose, or you can carry it in your hands. In either case, the thing to remember is not to shake it. If the sediment is stirred up, you'll have undone the effects of aging. The wine should be fine again once the sediment has resettled, but that may take a day or two.

Still holding the bottle on its side, take it into the room where it will be served. If it is lying in a basket, open it right there—without changing the angle of the bottle. If you are holding it in your hands, very slowly and gingerly set it upright on a table, always holding downmost the surface that was downmost in storage, thus minimizing the risk of stirring up the sediment. If time permits, leave the bottle upright for an hour or so before opening; this will permit resettlement of small particles of sediment that may have shaken free. In any case, open as in the previously discussed example involving a young white wine.

Now that the bottle is open, fetch a decanter—any kind will do, even a carafe or water pitcher, although more elegant vessels may be more pleasing to your esthetic sense. Light a candle. Hold the neck of the decanter near the flame of the candle as you lift the bottle over the candle and pour into the decanter.

The angle as you pour must permit you to look through the neck of the bottle at the flame. As you do, you can watch the wine. If you've done everything correctly so far, you should see very clear wine coursing over the flame. Let it course until you see the first traces of sediment, which should happen when you've got an ounce or two left in the bottle. As soon as sediment appears, stop pouring.

The remaining sediment-infused wine can be discarded. Or you can save it for cooking. Or you can drink it, if you're so inclined. It's not unhygienic. It will be somewhat harsh, but it will retain the essential character of the mature wine. I sometimes invite guests to taste it before tasting the mature wine as an interesting comparison. In any case, don't remix it with the mature wine, or you defeat the whole purpose of separating it.

Back to the decanter. Once the wine is inside, you are ready to pour, just as if from a bottle. Sample it first. If it is too young, you may wish to increase aeration by pouring it from one decanter to another two or three times before pouring for your guests. Or you may choose to let it sit in the decanter for fifteen minutes to half an hour before serving. In this connection, the larger the mouth of the decanter, the greater the aeration, so you can use a small-mouthed decanter for an old wine that you know to be fully mature and a large-mouthed one for a relatively young wine that needs a little help.

I shudder as I give this advice, because I'm very fussy about not serving wines that are less than fully mature. I'd rather let them lie in my cellar and age gracefully, in the meanwhile serving wines intended to be drunk young. But if you insist on serving a wine before it is mature, large-mouthed decanting is the way to do it.

I should add that it isn't absolutely necessary to decant. If the wine is younger than ten to fifteen years, it may have thrown off a relatively small amount of sediment. In this instance, it can be poured directly from the bottle. But it's a good idea to let the bottle stand on the table for an hour or so before pouring. In any case, note the side of the bottle which was lowermost during storage (and which therefore held the sediment). Pour with this side downward to minimize chances that any sediment that may have adhered to it will break free and enter the wine.

In this connection, even if you don't decant, some professionals say it's a good idea to open a bottle of red wine and let it stand for at least fifteen minutes to half an hour before serving. This aerates the wine, bringing out its nose. Winemen refer to the practice as "letting the wine breathe." There is controversy on the practice, however. Some professionals say "breathing" does not help the wine and in some cases diminishes the wine's character. They advise opening the bottle immediately before serving. (I myself line up with the breathers.)

Among fortified wines, vintage Port throws off a great deal of sediment and should be treated even more gingerly than other aged reds. With other fortified wines, service is not much more complicated than with whiskey. Most bottles have a cap-top cork. Simply twist off the cap and pour. If a fortified wine is fairly old—say, five to ten years—some crystals may have formed in the bottle. If you pour carefully, they'll stay inside till the wine has been emptied. If they enter a glass, they may simply be lifted out with a spoon.

It's less important to taste a fortified wine before serving guests than to taste an ordinary white or red, because there are fewer things that can go wrong with it. But it's traditional to taste. On the practical side, you can ascertain that the wine is the right temperature and that it hasn't fallen prey to one of the freak accidents that might render it undrinkable.

With sparkling wines, the uncorking procedure is quite different. These wines are bottled under pressure. The cork is held in place by a wire cage and by its own expansion immediately beneath the mouth of the bottle.

Begin by carrying the bottle gingerly from the refrigerator where it has been stored to the room where it will be served. As noted in the previous section on temperature, it should be quite cold. This not only enhances its nose and taste, it also keeps the wine from popping its cork.

Now you are ready to serve. Peel away the foil hood. Next, hold a napkin around the neck of the bottle, covering the top of the cork with it and holding it in place with your index finger. When it is positioned this way, the loop that fastens the wire cage should be exposed. The finger action is to keep the cork from shooting out prematurely.

Now untwist the wire, freeing the cage. Lift off the cage. With the next step, there is some disagreement among professionals. One school holds that you should cover the cork with a napkin with one hand while with the other you twist the bottle away from the cork. I'm of this school. The other school contends that a napkin is not necessary and that you have more control if you grip the bare neck of the bottle while holding your thumb on the closure, then, with your free hand, twist the bottle away from the cork. Experiment and take your pick. In any case, you definitely twist the bottle, not the cork.

That's right, the bottle not the cork. For reasons I've never been able to deduce—though my physicist friends tell me it has something to do with leverage—twisting the cork instead of the bottle causes the cork to pop, which, movies like *Gigi* notwithstanding, is a very gauche thing to do. As you twist the bottle while holding the cork firm, the cork should come out with a soft, satisfying *thump!,* leaving you holding a bottle from whose neck emits a lovely white puff of vapor.

Sample and serve. Applause.

6

How to Wine Friends and Affluent People

The question of which wine to serve when and with what perplexes many people—and with good reason. True, *de gustibus non est disputandum,* there's no disputing tastes, so if you like to drink a certain wine under circumstances where others would find it unpalatable, so much the worse for them—after all, it's your palate. But suppose you are serving guests who may not share your tastes. Or suppose you'd like to explore possibilities and combinations that might make wine even more enjoyable for you than it is now. Is there some formula you can follow, hopefully without having to memorize a lot of complicated rules?

I know of no formula, as such. But there are a few precepts that are easy to learn and will set you straight on the basics. After that, it's all a matter of using common sense, your tasting experience, and your imagination.

I'll enumerate here what I consider the three most important general rules. I'll ask you to take them on faith, because I think I can use to better advantage the space that would otherwise be devoted to explaining why they work. Suffice it to say that they've evolved over many centuries of wine drinking and reflect what apparently are fundamental gastro-chemical truths.

1. Match the color of the food with the color of the wine.

This is a drastic oversimplification, but it's the best general rule-of-thumb I can construct. It certainly beats trying to memorize things like "white wine with fish and poultry, red wine with roasts and game . . ."

Color of food, color of wine. Okay. Fish, poultry,

veal, and pork are white—more or less. Serve white wine. Beef and game are red, tomato sauce is red—more or less. Serve red wine. Ham is pink. Serve rosé.

You can comfortably serve a dry sparkling wine—for example, a brut Champagne—with just about anything (though I'd be less than comfortable about serving—or drinking—it with steak). Some people say you can serve rosé with anything; I'm comfortable matching it with a light sandwich on a hot day, with ham, and that's about it.

So you start with the basic rule, experiment with various food-wine combinations, and decide what works best for your palate. Assess the reaction of your guests, read a few good menu-type cookbooks that suggest wines to accompany various courses, talk to friends about combinations they like, and eventually you come up with a workable set of precepts that cover just about any occasion.

If your attempts to achieve the perfect match sometimes prove discouraging, chin up! Even the supposed experts have trouble deciding on the perfect match. For example, *Le Point*, the French newsmagazine, recently polled that nation's food writers on what wines they would match with *foie gras* and fresh oysters, served in successive courses. Four of the six writers picked a sweet white for the *foie gras*, a fifth opted for a dry white sparkling wine, and the sixth chose Port—which the rulebook generally banishes to dessert and after-dinner drinking. To accompany the fresh oysters, three writers selected a dry white, another selected a light-bodied dry red, another a full-bodied dry red, and the sixth chose water (which the French are mistakenly believed never to drink). Frankly, I'd be happy with any of the above choices except the water.

2. Dry to stimulate, sweet to dampen.

This is easy enough to remember. Just pair the d's and s's. Now what does it mean?

Dry things stimulate the appetite, sweet things dampen it. That's why we generally serve grapefruit before the meal and ice cream after it, not vice versa. Of course, there are exceptions, such as melon as an appetizer and *caffè espresso* after dinner. But the rule is generally sound.

It works with wine as with food. If you're not sure about which wine to serve in which circumstances, ask yourself what you're trying to accomplish. If you want to stimulate your guests' appetites—before dinner, during dinner—serve a dry wine. If you want to dampen the appetite or simply provide a compatible taste sensation for someone whose appetite has been satisfied, serve something on the sweet side.

Particularly good bets before a meal are a dry fortified wine, such as Sherry, and a dry sparkling wine, such as brut Champagne. Particularly good with dessert or after dinner are sweet sparkling wines (Asti Spumante, Doux Champagne) and sweet fortified wines (Cream Sherry, Port, Malvasia Bianca).

3. Light on top, heavy on bottom.

Here's another that's easy to remember. Just think about how much easier it is for a light person to stand on a heavy person's shoulders than vice versa.

Light and heavy wines interact the same way. If you want to prove it in an experiment, pour two glasses: a light dry white and a full-bodied dry red. Taste the white, then the red. No problem. The full character of each comes through. Now taste the red again. Take a good healthy swallow. Then taste the white. It's almost like drinking water, isn't it?

In tastings, wine professionals almost invariably proceed from light to full-bodied, white to red. In multi-course dinners, the same pattern usually obtains—though there are occasional exceptions. The rule even seems to hold with regard to time of day: light wines go swimmingly with lunch, full-bodied wines are better suited for dinner.

Those are the three general rules. Now you can mix and match on your own, using common sense, your tasting experience and your imagination.

Meanwhile, let me share with you the mix-and-match choices of four of my favorite professional hosts: Leo Bossolini, proprietor and chef of Leo in Santa Croce, Florence, Italy; Julie Fine, creater and host of Julie's Mansion, Toronto,

Ontario; Marjorie Lumm, director of the home advisory service of the Wine Institute, San Francisco, and editorial director of the California Wine Advisory Board Cookbooks; and finally, George Carros, host of the tasting table on "Enjoying Wine with Paul Gillette" and creator and host of the Monaco Room, Scranton, Pennsylvania.

I asked each to select a traditional regional or ethnic meal and match each course with a wine. I didn't specify that each wine should be of the same national origin as the food, but it often worked out that way, supporting one of my private precepts, which is not shared by a majority of wine professionals. (My reasoning is that each nation's wines and cuisine evolved together and influenced each other's development; wines of another nation may be compatible, but they rarely if ever achieve the same harmonic blend.)

Here are the professional hosts' menus, including recipes:

ITALIAN//LEO BOSSOLINI//LEO IN SANTA CROCE, FLORENCE

Menu

Frascati/FONTANA CANDIDA FRASCATI SUPERIORE 1976
    Prosciutto con Melone

Firenze/VILLA ANTINORI BIANCO 1975
    Crostino Caldo al Re Guido d'Andrea

Firenze/VILLA ANTINORI CHIANTI CLASSICO RISERVA 1968
    Perciatelli alla Carrettiera

Pontassieve/RUFFINO CHIANTI CLASSICO RISERVA DUCALE 1964
    Filetto alla Wizard of Sherwood
    Insalata Verde con Cetriolo

Greve/NOZZOLE CHIANTI CLASSICO RISERVA 1964
    Formaggi Assortiti

Asti/CINZANO ASTI SPUMANTE
Pesca Duracina

Recipes

Prosciutto con Melone
Drape a thin slice of prosciutto (variety of Italian smoked ham) over a piece of canteloupe; serve cold.

Crostino Caldo al Re Guido d'Andrea

Slice of toast (per person)	Tomatoes
Mozzarella cheese	Parmigiano cheese
Capers	Prosciutto
Anchovies	Small mushrooms
Parsley	Truffles
Basil	Pepper
Gruyère cheese	Olive oil

Arrange on a piece of toast, from the bottom up: sliced mozzarella, capers, anchovies, sliced small mushrooms, truffles, chopped fresh parsley and basil, Gruyère cheese, tomatoes, Parmigiano cheese, and a slice of prosciutto. Coat lightly with oil, sprinkle with pepper, bake at 400° for about 10 minutes, or until cheeses have melted slightly. Serve immediately.

Perciatelli alla Carrettiera

Parsley	Oil
Small hot peppers	Perciatelli (style of pasta)
Black olives	Salt
Capers	Pepper
Basil	Garlic
Tomatoes	

Boil oil. Add garlic, basil, parsley and small peppers. very slowly fold in sliced olives, capers and tomatoes. Sprinkle with pepper. Cook for two minutes.

Independently, boil salted water, add perciatelli, cook to very firm (*molto al dente*) texture (about 10 minutes). Fold into the sauce, and salt and pepper while mixing. Serve immediately.

Filetto alla Wizard of Sherwood

One filet mignon or heart of T-bone per person	Mushrooms
	Prosciutto
Butter	Cream
Cognac	Worcestershire sauce
Pâté de foie gras	Pepper
Truffles	Salt

Place meat in frying pan with butter, cook very slowly, basting each piece with 2 ounces of cognac as it cooks. Next, smear cooking meat with paté de foie gras, then cover it with truffles and chopped mushrooms, and top with a slice of prosciutto. To pan add cream, Worcestershire sauce, pepper and salt. Let everything cook slowly together for 15 minutes, then serve meat bathed in its own sauce.

Insalata Verde con Cetrioli

When diners have been served meat—but not until—begin making salad. Break pieces of lettuce into dishes, peel cucumbers (do not peel them beforehand; they must be virginly fresh) and add to lettuce, season with —in this order—salt, just a drop or two of vinegar, much olive oil, pepper.

Pesca Duracina (Clingstone Peach)

Do not peel until diners have begun eating cheeses. Then peel, quarter, and place into a bowl containing about 5 ounces of Asti Spumante. Serve additional Asti Spumante in glasses to accompany course.

CANADIAN//JULIE FINE//JULIE'S MANSION, TORONTO*

Menu
Niagara Falls/CHÂTEAU-GAI BRUT CHAMPAGNE

Islington/CHÂTEAU CARTIER RIESLING
Cold Garnish Salmon Pie Frontenac

---

*Julie points out that this dinner is made up entirely of foods grown within the Dominion, accompanied by Canadian wines. To those North Americans—whether from the U.S. or Canada—who have not discovered the unique and exquisite flavors of native Canadian cuisine, here's what you've been missing.

Niagara Falls/BRIGHT'S MANOR ST. DAVIDS
    SAUTERNE
    Cape Breton Chowder

Niagara Falls/CHÂTEAU-GAI CANADIAN CLARET
    Boneless Breast of Brome Lake Duckling with Wild
        Rice and Mountain Cranberries
    Fiddlehead Salad

Niagara Falls/CHÂTEAU-GAI HAUT SAUTERNES
    Apple Fritters with Maple Syrup

Recipes
Cold Garnish Salmon Pie Frontenac

Pastry:
½ lb. flour
9 oz. shortening
½ cup warm water
Pinch salt
1 egg
Filling:
2 lbs. fresh salmon
    sliced thinly as fillets

1 tablespoon pistachio nuts
    chopped finely
2 hard boiled eggs, chopped
8 medium-sized mush-
    rooms, sliced
¼ teaspoon salt
¼ teaspoon pepper
2 oz. granulated gelatine
    softened in warm water

Place all pastry ingredients into bowl and make standard crust to cover a 9″ pie shell.

Place layers of filling on the pastry starting with salmon, pistachio nuts, eggs, mushrooms, repeating until all filling is used up. Cover with thin layer of pastry.

Leave a hole in the center of the pastry for steam to escape. Bake in hot oven (450°) for 10 minutes and then turn down heat to 400° for 20 minutes.

Remove pie from oven and let stand until cold. Through the hole in the top of the pie shell, pour in the gelatine, which should be cool and slightly set. Refrigerate for 2 hours. Slice pie and serve with mayonnaise sauce.

Cape Breton Chowder

1 green pepper, diced
1 large potato, diced

Pinch thyme
Pinch salt and pepper

1 medium onion, diced
1 stalk of leeks, diced
¼ stalk of celery, diced
2 slices bacon
½ cup navy beans
(soaked overnight in
cold water)
2 peeled tomatoes,
chopped
2 bay leaves
Pinch thyme

Pinch salt and pepper
Pinch nutmeg
14 oz. tin fresh whole clams
with natural juice (Cher-
rystone or Steamers)
Few drops of Worcestershire
sauce
Chopped parsley
1 cup water or fish stock
½ cup grated soda crackers

Sauté onion and bacon in large, deep skillet. Add rest of ingredients and moisten with 1 cup of water or fish stock. Simmer (do not boil) uncovered until vegetables are cooked. When vegetables are cooked, thicken with grated soda crackers.

Boneless Breast of Brome Lake Duckling with Wild Rice and Mountain Cranberries

2 large whole duckling
breasts boned
2 cups Château-Gai
Canadian claret
2 bay leaves

Pinch oregano
4 tablespoons olive oil
Pinch salt and pepper
Flour
½ cup clarified butter

Marinate breasts the day before in wine, bay leaves, oregano, olive oil, salt, pepper. Place the breasts in a dish large enough to allow them to lie flat and be totally immersed in the marinade. Cover and refrigerate overnight.

Dry with paper towels and dip breasts into flour. In a skillet, brown both sides using clarified butter. Place breasts in roasting pan. Bake uncovered in a hot oven (450°) for 15 minutes.

Remove breasts from oven, drain off extra fat from pan. Place breasts in a circle on serving dish surrounded with wild rice. Place mountain cranberries in center.

Sauce:
Strain ½ of remaining marinade and swill roasting pan. Heat to boiling point. The flour already in the pan will cause sauce to thicken.

Serve with duckling breasts on side.

Fiddlehead Salad

16 oz. frozen fiddlehead greens cooked as directed on package in salted boiling water	¾ cup olive oil
	¼ cup red wine vinegar
	¼ onion, finely chopped
⅛ teaspoon dry mustard	Salt and pepper to taste
1 teaspoon lemon juice	Touch of garlic, or to taste

Be sure not to overcook fiddleheads. Once they have come to rolling boil take off heat and place under cold water tap until greens are cold to touch. Strain. Set aside.

Mix rest of ingredients together and pour over fiddleheads. Let stand for an hour to marinate.

Serve on pieces of fresh lettuce and garnish with sliced tomatoes and wedges of hard-boiled eggs. Sprinkle chopped parsley or chives on top.

Apple Fritters with Maple Syrup

2 large apples, peeled and cored	1 teaspoon vegetable oil
	1 egg
1 teaspoon ground cinnamon	8 oz. Château-Gai Johannisberger Riesling*
4 teaspoons sugar	Pinch salt
½ teaspoon ground cloves	4 egg whites whipped to firm froth
½ fresh lemon	2 teaspoons sifted icing sugar
8 oz. flour, sifted	

Slice apples into ¼″ slices. Place enough slices to cover surface of standard-size dinner plate and sprinkle with cinnamon, sugar, cloves and few drops fresh lemon juice. Add another layer of sliced apples and repeat

---

*A long-standing precept has it that foods should be cooked with the same wine that is served to accompany them. That may have been okay for Louis XIV, but I don't know too many people today who would cook with a fifty-dollar bottle of Romanée-Conti or Château Latour. Fortunately, Château-Gai Canadian Claret, used here for cooking the Brome Lake Duckling, is at $1.35 a bottle one of the least expensive wines presently available in North America; accordingly, there is no problem both serving it and cooking with it. The Château-Gai Johannisberg Riesling used in the apple fritters is not much more expensive: $2.10 a bottle. However, a different wine, which happens to sell at the same price, is served with the fritters as a matter of taste.

cinnamon, sugar, cloves and lemon juice. Continue until all apple slices are used. Refrigerate for 1 hour.

Mix flour, salt, oil, egg and wine. Stir until batter has a thick consistency. Fold in egg whites.

Pour enough vegetable oil in a skillet to fill one inch. Heat oil until hot, but not smoking. Dip apple slices in batter, then fry in oil until each side is golden brown. Place slices on paper towels to absorb oil.

Sprinkle with icing sugar and serve with maple syrup.

UNITED STATES//PAUL WALLACH//FOUNDER, EPICUREAN SOCIETY OF NORTH AMERICA; AUTHOR; RADIO-TV PERSONALITY

Menu

Paicines/ALMADEN FINO DRY SHERRY (not vintage dated)
 Mushrooms Magnifique

San José/Mirasou GAMAY BEAUJOLAIS 1975
 Wine Country Onion Soup
 Spinach Salad and Dressing

St. Helena/LOUIS MARTINI PINOT NOIR 1970
 Beef Ragout

Napa/BERINGER LATE HARVEST JOHANNISBERG RIESLING 1974
 Chilled Pears
 Gourmandise Cheese

Recipes

Mushrooms Magnifique

1 4-oz. can buttered mushrooms, or 30 freshly cooked button mushrooms	⅓ cup dry Sherry (use the same wine that will be served with this course)
¼ cup butter or margarine	Finely chopped fresh parsley or chives

Drain mushrooms; heat in butter in shallow pan. Add Sherry; simmer gently until liquid is almost completely evaporated. Sprinkle with chopped parsley or chives. Serve hot with cocktail picks.

Wine Country Onion Soup

¼ cup butter or margarine	1 cup dry or medium-dry white wine
6 medium-size onions, thinly sliced	Salt and pepper
4 cups bouillon (canned or bouillon-cube broth may be used)	6 slices French bread, toasted and buttered
	½ cup grated Parmesan cheese

Melt butter in large saucepan; sauté onions until clear. Add bouillon; cover and cook slowly until onions are very tender. Add wine, salt and pepper; bring to boiling. Pour into 6 individual casseroles or 1 large one. Float buttered pieces of toasted French bread on top; sprinkle with grated Parmesan cheese. Bake on upper rack of hot oven (450°) until cheese browns lightly (about 10 minutes).

Spinach Salad and Dressing

⅔ cup salad oil	½ teaspoon salt
¼ cup wine vinegar	½ teaspoon garlic salt
2 tablespoons dry white wine	1 teaspoon freshly ground pepper
2 teaspoons soy sauce	2 bunches (about 4 qts.) young spinach
1 teaspoon sugar	1 pound bacon
1 teaspoon dry mustard	2 hard-cooked eggs, coarsely grated
¼ to 1 teaspoon curry powder	

Combine oil, wine vinegar, wine, soy sauce, sugar and seasonings in a covered jar. Shake well; chill; meanwhile, thoroughly wash the spinach; tear into pieces, removing stems. Dice bacon, fry until crisp. Mix the bacon and eggs with spinach. Shake dressing again; pour over spinach.

Beef Ragout

3 pounds boneless beef chuck, cut into 1-inch cubes
Flour
1 10½-oz. can condensed consommé
½ cup dry Sherry
2 small onions, thinly sliced
½ teaspoon curry powder
¼ teaspoon dried basil leaves
1 whole clove
1 bay leaf
Dash of garlic salt
Dash freshly ground black pepper
½ strip bacon
1 coarse celery stalk
12 to 15 whole baby carrots, scraped and sliced
1 mint leaf or pinch of dried mint
4 small tomatoes, peeled and cubed
½ pound sliced fresh mushrooms or
1 6-oz. can sliced mushrooms, drained
2 tablespoons flour
1 8-oz. can tomato puree
½ cup finely chopped celery
½ cup finely chopped parsley

Roll beef pieces in flour to coat evenly. Place meat, consommé, Sherry, onions, curry powder, basil leaves, clove, bay leaf, garlic salt and pepper in an ovenproof Dutch oven. Place over moderate heat (about 250°) and heat until mixture begins to boil. Add bacon and celery stalk. Cover Dutch oven and place in a preheated 350° oven. Bake about 2 hours, or until meat is fork-tender. While meat is cooking, place carrots and mint leaf in a saucepan. Add about 1 cup water. Place over moderately low heat and cook 10 to 15 minutes or until tender. Drain. When meat is fork-tender, take Dutch oven out of oven and remove bacon and celery stalk. Place Dutch oven over moderate heat. Add tomatoes and mushrooms; sprinkle the 2 tablespoons flour over mixture and stir to blend. Simmer, covered, 10 to 15 minutes. Add cooked carrots, tomato puree, the chopped celery and parsley and stir to blend. Season to taste with salt and pepper. (6 to 8 servings.)

GREEK//GEORGE CARROS//THE MONACO ROOM, SCRANTON, PENNSYLVANIA

Menu

Patras/ACHAIA ST. HELENA
>   Dolmadakia (Small Stuffed Grapevine Leaves)
>   Spanakopetes (Spinach-Cheese Triangles)
>   Taramasalata (Fish Roe Spread)
>   Kalamata Olives (Marinated Dark Olives)
>   Anchovies
>   Feta Cheese (Goat's Milk Cheese)
>   Soupa Avgolemono (Chicken Soup with Egg-Lemon
>   Sauce)

**Patras/ACHAIA CLAUSS DEMESTICA ASPRO
(WHITE)**
>   Psari Mayoneza (Fish with Mayonnaise Sauce)

Patras/CASTEL DANIELS (RED)
>   Arni Psito Me Anginares (Roast Lamb with Arti-
>   chokes)
>   Pastichio (Baked Macaroni with Cream Sauce)
>   Salata Horyiatiki (Greek Country Salad)

Patras/ACHAIA CLAUSS MAVRODAPHNE
Social period between final course and dessert*
>   Galatabourikos (Custard Strudel)
>   Fraoules (Strawberries)
>   Greek Coffee/Metaxa Brandy

Recipes

Dolmadakia

50 vine leaves	1 lemon
2 cups rice	1 cup chopped parsley
3 medium onions,	Salt
chopped	Pepper
1½ cups olive oil	

Fry chopped onions in oil until golden brown. Add
washed rice and other ingredients and 1 cup water. Cover
and let simmer for 3 minutes. Let mixture cool. Wash
vine leaves thoroughly to remove all brine. Separate

---

*The social period between the final course and dessert is a tradition in
Mediterranean countries. In many, dessert and coffee are not available
at the restaurant; instead, after a salad, cheese or fruit course, the
diners adjourn to a bar for dessert, coffee, and brandy.

leaves carefully, removing thick stem portions. Fill each leaf, using one large or two small ones for each dolma. Be sure the shiny side of each leaf is on the outside.

A teaspoon of filling is enough per leaf. Do not roll too tightly; allow room for rice to expand. Place a few coarse leaves on bottom of pot and arrange dolmathes side by side and layer upon layer until all leaves and filling are used. Add 3 cups water, salt and pepper to taste, and juice of 1 lemon. Cover with a heavy plate and let simmer until rice is cooked (40-45 minutes). Serve cold.

Spanakopetes

1 medium onion, finely chopped	½ pound feta cheese
¼ cup olive oil	6 ounces pot cheese or cottage cheese
1 pound fresh spinach, well-washed, well-drained and finely chopped	3 eggs, beaten
	½ pound phyllo pastry sheets
	¼ pound butter, melted

Sauté onion in olive oil for 5 minutes. Add spinach. Simmer over low flame, stirring occasionally, until most of moisture has evaporated.

Crumble feta cheese into small pieces. Add pot cheese and blend well. Add beaten eggs and mix well. Add spinach-onion mixture, stir until well blended. Melt butter.

Cut phyllo pastry into 3 equal parts. Refrigerate ⅔ until needed later. Place remaining sheet on flat surface and butter well. Then fold in the long sides toward the middle, making a strip about 2 inches wide. Butter again. Then place 1 tablespoon spinach-cheese mixture 1 inch from narrow edge of sheet. Fold the inch margin over mixture. Fold long edges in toward middle. Butter again and roll compactly to end. Repeat with remaining shells.

Bake the spanakopetes at 425° for 20 minutes or until golden-brown, turning once. Allow to cool about 5 minutes before serving. Serve warm. (Yield: 40-50 pieces.)

Taramasalata

⅓ of 8-ounce jar fish roe
1 small onion, finely grated

2 cups olive oil
5 slices white bread, trimmed
Juice of 3 lemons

Mash fish roe and add grated onion. Add some olive
oil and beat thoroughly to a smooth paste. Moisten bread
and squeeze out excess water. Continue beating mixture,
alternately adding small bits of olive oil, moistened bread
and lemon juice. When all ingredients have been added,
beat until cream-colored, then serve cold.

Soupa Avgolemono

1 4- to 5-lb. stewing hen, ready to cook	1 stalk celery
1 small carrot	1 cup rice
1 onion	Salt to taste

Place hen in heavy kettle. Cover with boiling water
and add carrot, onion and celery stalk. Cover and simmer over low heat until hen is tender (2-4 hours), adding
salt to taste after 1 hour.
Strain broth. Remove extra fat. Add rice and continue
to cook until rice is tender. Remove broth from heat
and wait for boiling to stop. Add avgolemono sauce below, according to directions.

Avgolemono Sauce

4 eggs
Juice of 2 lemons

Beat eggs until light and fluffy. Gradually beat in lemon
juice. Add broth slowly to egg sauce, return soup to low
heat, and stir until thickened.

Psari Mayoneza

1 5-lb. bass, cleaned
2 carrots, sliced
2 celery stalks, sliced
4 scallions, chopped
Salt

Wash and scale fish. Salt well. Tie in cheesecloth and
place on rack in fish kettle with carrots, celery and

scallions. Add water and bring to a simmer. Cover kettle and simmer fish for 35 minutes. Cool in broth. Remove fish and place on platter. Remove cheesecloth.

Mayoneza Sauce

5 egg yolks
2 tablespoons pre-
    pared mustard
1 cup olive oil
½ cup lemon juice

Beat egg yolks and mustard in an electric mixer at medium speed until thick. Very slowly pour in olive oil and lemon juice. Continue to beat until sauce is smooth and thick.

Pour over fish. Garnish with lemon slices.

Arni Psito Me Anginares

6 artichokes	1 tablespoon oregano
Cold water, salted	2 cups water
Juice of 6 lemons	Parsley sprigs
2 tablespoons flour	Salt
4-pound lamb roast	Pepper

Remove outer leaves of artichokes and cut off stems. Cut ½ to 1 inch from tips of remaining leaves. Rub cut stems with lemon and cut in half, lengthwise. Rub cut surfaces with lemon.

Cut and scrape fuzz from artichoke hearts, then place hearts in a bowl of cold salted water into which the juice of 2 lemons and the flour have been stirred; water should cover artichoke hearts. Soak for ½ hour to 1 hour.

Preheat oven to 450°. Rub lamb with salt, pepper, oregano, and juice of 1 lemon. Roast 20 minutes, then reduce heat to 350°. Add 1 cup water to roasting pan, cook another 15 minutes. Add remaining water to pan and continue cooking for 30 minutes or until lamb is done to taste. Baste occasionally with pan drippings. If needed, add more water. There should be 2 cups of liquid drippings in pan when meat is done.

Transfer lamb to a warm platter. Add artichokes to roasting pan. Bake them, cut side down, 1 hour or until tender—do not overcook. Baste occasionally while cooking. Arrange artichokes around the lamb, and garnish with parsley. (6 servings.)

Pastichio

Thin cream sauce: 2 cups hot milk
  4 tablespoons butter   2 egg yolks
⅓ cup flour

Melt butter in saucepan. Stir in flour and cook until mixture turns golden. Gradually stir in hot milk and cook, stirring, until sauce is smooth and hot. Beat egg yolks with a little of the hot milk and stir into sauce. Remove from heat without cooking the eggs.

Thick cream sauce: ½ cup flour
2 cups milk   2 cups cold milk
4 eggs

Heat 2 cups milk to simmering. Beat eggs with flour. Stir in cold milk. Gradually stir in hot milk and cook, stirring constantly, until mixture is quite thick. But do not let boil after eggs are added.

Additional preparation: 1¼ pounds macaroni
Ingredients: Grated cheese
  3 onions, chopped   Garlic powder
1½ pounds chopped   Salt
    beef   Pepper
  4 tablespoons butter
  2 cups tomato sauce

Brown chopped onions and meat in butter. Add tomato sauce, spices and seasonings. Cover and simmer for 1 hour. Cook macaroni and drain.

Into buttered 11x16x2-inch baking pan put layer of macaroni, then layer of meat with sauce, then half the thin cream sauce. Sprinkle with grated cheese. Add another layer of macaroni and sprinkle with cheese. Cover with remaining thin cream sauce. Spread the thick cream sauce over top and sprinkle with cheese. Bake in 350° oven for 1 hour. Cool and slice into squares. When ready to serve, reheat in hot oven.

Galatabourikos

1 lb. pastry sheets	2 qts. milk
10 eggs	¾ cup farina
1 cup sugar	

Scald milk, remove from stove to cool. Separate eggs and beat 10 yolks with only 5 whites. When eggs are fluffy and light, add sugar and beat until creamy. Stir in farina. Slowly spoon in milk, beating constantly.

Cook mixture over low heat until slightly thickened, then remove from heat and allow to cool. Grease 10x15″ baking pan with melted butter and line bottom with 8 pastry sheets. Brush with butter.

Pour slightly cooled mixture over pastry sheets and cover with 8 more pastry sheets. Fold in pastry edges to contain mixture. Bake at 375° for 15 minutes, then reduce heat to 275° and bake for 30 more minutes.

7

Stocking Your Own Wine Cellar

In certain parts of China, when a child is born his parents put away a quantity of the best wine they can buy. Years later, when the child marries, the long-cellared birthday wines of the bride and groom are opened and drunk at the wedding feast.

In France, Italy, Spain, and many other European nations, it is customary to lay away wines in a cellar for special occasions. The French don't call a home wine cellar *cave, cellier,* or *chai,* as they do those of the commercial variety. They call it *bibliothèque,* which translates into English as "library." A Lyonnaise proverb has it that a person who does not have two libraries in his home is deficient either in mind or in spirit.

The custom of cellaring wines has a great deal to recommend it. If you cellar wisely, you not only have handy a suitable wine for every occasion but you also preserve your wines in optimum condition—and you can save a great deal of money. For instance, my parents cellared a case of Marquès de Riscal, a Spanish red wine, for me in 1938, the year I was born. At the time, it cost eight cents a bottle. Today the same vintage is selling at auctions for over fifty dollars a bottle.

Of course, not every wine will benefit from cellaring. Some, as I've noted in earlier chapters, are made to be drunk young. They pass their peak within a year after they leave the winery, and within a few years they become well-nigh undrinkable. The wine to lay away is one made with lots of tannin, a product of grape skins and seeds. If drunk young, it will be very harsh—so harsh that within the first year or two after the harvest, it is hard to get down. But as it ages, first in barrels, then in the bottle, the wine mellows. Soon it takes on a distinct character, unlike that of any younger wine. Some wines continue to change character—to mellow, to mature—for fifty years or longer.

Unfortunately, tannin alone is not sufficient to give a wine this kind of elegant longevity. If it were, producers all over the world would be creating their own versions of Brunello di Montalcino from such inexpensive high-yield grapes as Concord and Thompson Seedless. To make a long-lasting wine—one, that is, that's worth waiting to drink—you need a lot of things, all of them hard to come by; the right combination of sunshine, rain, and temperature; the right soil; the right aging techniques; the right winemaker.

So how does a newcomer to wine determine whether one is worth laying away? I asked that question of wine consultant David Milligan, who provided what I consider the most useful rule-of-thumb: the more expensive a wine is when it initially goes on the market, the more likely it will be to age well.

That business about "going on the market" can be slightly confusing. The fact is, wines intended to be consumed young generally appear in retail establishments the same year as the harvest. Wines that require aging—and almost without exception these are dry reds—usually are held at the winery for a number of years, being aged first in barrels, then in their own bottles. Thus, a long-lived 1966 (the year is always the one in which the grapes were picked) might not leave the winery until 1971 or 1972. If the year is regarded by professionals as really superior, the wine may remain in sellers' warehouses for another five years as they wait for the wine to mature—and the demand to build, along with the price.

As with any rule, there are exceptions to David Milligan's. But you've got to start somewhere, and I think this is as good a place as any. Of course, if you've developed a relationship with a wine merchant who has won your confidence, he can be an excellent source of more precise advice on wines worth cellaring. But beware! Even the most sincere wine merchants are not always as knowledgeable as they think. There is a fellow in New York who is widely regarded by wine snobs as one of the most knowledgeable wine sellers around. Not long ago in a blind tasting on a TV show (not mine), he mistook Manischewitz White Concord for a *Beerenauslese*.

Speaking of white wines, the standard intelligence is that, with few exceptions, they are not to be laid away. It's a good general rule, as anyone knows who let too much time pass before drinking the last bottle in his one-dollar-a-bottle case of Gomez-Crusado. But like all general rules, it was made to be broken.

On "Enjoying Wine with Paul Gillette," German wine authority Herbert Weiss, of Schieffelin & Co., produced from his own cellar a bottle of 1921 Blue Nun. As a light-bodied Liebfraumilch, intended for immediate consumption, this was the last wine in the world you would expect to survive fifty-five years. But it did—magnificently!

In general, however, cellar only red wines and only those made predominantly from grape varieties such as Nebbiolo, Brunello, Cabernet Sauvignon, and Pinot Noir, which traditionally produce long-lasting wines. I lay away a few whites— a Sauternes (the original Sauternes, that is, not a generic!), a Barsac, a Meursault, a Montrachet—but not nearly as many of these as reds.

A few pages hence, I'll present sample cellars in various price ranges recommended by six wine professionals. But first a few words about your own cellar.

First of all, don't let the term "cellar" fool you. It need not be subterranean. While an underground vault with walls six feet thick and a constant temperature of 11 to 13 degrees Centigrade (52 to 55 degrees Fahrenheit) is ideal, you can safely store wine in just about any place that meets four criteria:

(1) Temperature should be fairly constant. Wide swings are particularly undesirable. Your wines will mature more gracefully at a steady 13 degrees Centigrade (55 degrees Fahrenheit) than at 21 degrees Centigrade (70 degrees Fahrenheit), but they will be better off at a steady 21 degrees Centigrade than in a room where there are daily fluctuations between 13 and 21 degrees Centigrade. Probably the maximum safe temperature is 21 to 25 degrees Centigrade (70 to 77 degrees Fahrenheit), but this is really pushing the limits of safety; I would not be at all comfortable about a wine I had left in a room constantly warmer than 21 degrees Centigrade. As for minimum temperature, wine generally crystallizes and is damaged around −2 degrees Centigrade (28 to 29 degrees Fahrenheit), but I'd be uncomfortable about leaving any wine I like in a room where the temperature was apt to

fall below 3 to 4 degrees Centigrade (37 to 40 degrees Fahrenheit).

(2) Vibrations—there should be none. A shaken wine ages much too rapidly. So don't store wine near an air conditioner, an oil burner, or any other kind of motor.

(3) Darkness—the darker the better. There is no harm in turning on a light when you go into the cellar, or even in leaving one on for a few hours. But constant light and particularly bright sunlight are damaging to wine. Be skeptical of any wine merchant who displays bottles in sunlight. Chances are the wine has been damaged.

(4) Odors should not be present. They can enter the bottle through the cork, pervade the wine, and destroy its prime asset—its nose.

Working within these criteria, you doubtless can find many places in your house or apartment that are suitable for wine storage: a closet, a corner of a garage, a spare room or a section of one, even a refrigerator. A basement is ideal, but —I stress—not necessary.

Now how to stock your cellar? If you don't have particular wines that you've learned from experience (your own or a friend's) to be good for laying away, and if you don't know a wine merchant you can trust, one way of getting help making your selection is to phone any winery or wine importer whose products you have enjoyed in the past. Ask to speak to someone in the sales department. Tell her or him that you want a recommendation on wines to lay away. A prospective long-time customer will receive good service.

I recently asked six wine professionals a more complicated version of that same question. I asked them to recommend cellars valued at (if purchases were made today at typical U.S. retail prices) $500, $1,000, $5,000, $10,000, and $100,000. I told them I would not mind if they made up their selections entirely from products which they themselves sell, nor would I care if they introduced wines sold by competitors. Their choices follow. When a vintage date follows the wine's name, the recommendation applies only to that vintage.

If no date is given, the most recent available vintage is recommended. (These wines generally are a blend of grape varieties or of the same variety grown in a number of vineyards. The blend retains the same basic character from year to year, and the wine usually is intended to be consumed within a year after it is put on sale.) Some producers do not use a vintage date. These wines, which often are blends of more than one vintage, also are intended to be consumed within a year. They are identified by the letters "N.V." in the lists that follow.

HARRY G. SERLIS, ROBERT MONDAVI WINERY,
OAKVILLE, CALIFORNIA

$500 Wine Cellar

California Napa Valley White Wines by Robert Mondavi	Price per unit (case)
Chardonnay '73 or '74	$ 51.00
Chenin Blanc '74 or '75	35.00
Fumé Blanc '74	51.00
Johannisberg Riesling '75	51.00
Traminer '74	33.00
White Table N.V.	24.00

California Napa Valley Red Wines by Robert Mondavi	
Cabernet Sauvignon '72	65.00
Gamay '73 or '74	36.00
Gamay Rosé '74	30.00
Petite Sirah '72 or '73	51.00
Pinot Noir '73	57.00
Red Table N.V.	24.00

$1,000 Wine Cellar

California Champagne	Price per unit (case)
Hanns Kornell Brut Champagne (2 cases)	63.00

White California	
Almaden Gewürztraminer N.V.	$ 32.00
Robert Mondavi Chardonnay '73 or '74	51.00
Robert Mondavi Chenin Blanc '74 or '75	35.00

	Price per unit (case)
Robert Mondavi Fumé Blanc '74	51.00
Robert Mondavi Johannisberg Riesling '75	51.00
Robert Mondavi Traminer '74	33.00
Robert Mondavi White Table Wine N.V.	24.00
Wente Sauvignon Blanc '73	30.00

Red California

Christian Brothers Pinot St. George N.V.	44.00
Fino Eleven Cellars Napa Claret	22.00
Fino Eleven Cellars Napa Zinfandel	30.00
Gallo Hearty Burgundy N.V.	16.00
Louis Martini Merlot '73	38.00
Louis Martini Mountain Zinfandel '72	35.00
Robert Mondavi Cabernet Sauvignon '72 (2 cases)	65.00
Robert Mondavi Gamay '73 or '74	36.00
Robert Mondavi Gamay Rosé '74	35.00
Robert Mondavi Petite Sirah '72 or '73	51.00
Robert Mondavi Pinot Noir '73	57.00
Robert Mondavi Red Table Wine N.V.	24.00
Robert Mondavi Zinfandel '73	51.00
Winemasters Guild Zinfandel N.V.	21.00
Winemasters Guild Zinfandel	21.00

$5,000 Wine Cellar

	Price per unit (case)
California Champagne	
Almaden Blanc de Blanc '73 (2 cases)	$ 71.00
Hanns Kornell Brut (2 cases)	63.00
Hanns Kornell Sehr Trocken (2 cases)	80.00
White California	
Almaden Gewürztraminer N.V. (2 cases)	32.00
Beaulieu Vineyard Beaufort Chardonnay '73 (2 cases)	51.00
Christian Brothers Chardonnay N.V. (2 cases)	44.00

Price per
unit (case)

Charles Krug Pinot Chardonnay '73
(2 cases)   51.00
Mirassou Harvest Selection
Gewürztraminer '74 (2 cases)   51.00
Mirassou Harvest Selection Pinot
Chardonnay '73 (2 cases)   62.00
Robert Mondavi Chardonnay
'73 or '74 (2 cases)   51.00
Robert Mondavi Chenin Blanc
'74 or '75 (2 cases)   35.00
Robert Mondavi Fumé Blanc '74
(2 cases)   51.00
Robert Mondavi Fumé Blanc Reserve
'73 (2 cases)   65.00
Robert Mondavi Johannisberg Riesling
'75 (2 cases)   51.00
Robert Mondavi Traminer '74
(2 cases)   33.00
Robert Mondavi White Table Wine
N.V. (2 cases)   24.00
Simi Gewürztraminer '74 (2 cases)   44.00
Wente Le Blanc de Blancs (2 cases)   27.00
Wente Sauvignon Blanc '73 (2 cases)   30.00

Red California

Beaulieu Vineyard Private Reserve
Cabernet Sauvignon '71 (2 cases)   90.00
Beringer Zinfandel (2 cases)   27.00
Christian Brothers Cabernet Sauvignon
N.V. (2 cases)   38.00
Christian Brothers Pinot St. George
N.V. (2 cases)   44.00
Christian Brothers Zinfandel
N.V. (2 cases)   36.00
Concannon Petite Sirah '71
(Limited bottling) (2 cases)   55.00
Cresta Blanca Grignolino (2 cases)   27.00
Cresta Blanca Zinfandel (2 cases)   30.00
Fino Eleven Cellars Napa Claret
(2 cases)   22.00

	Price per unit (case)
Fino Eleven Cellars Napa Zinfandel (2 cases)	30.00
Gallo Hearty Burgundy N.V. (2 cases)	16.00
Inglenook Charbono '71 (Limited bottling) (2 cases)	51.00
Charles Krug Cabernet Sauvignon '71 (2 cases)	51.00
Charles Krug Vintage Select Cabernet Sauvignon '70 (2 cases)	72.00
Louis Martini Barbera '68 (2 cases)	30.00
Louis Martini Merlot '73 (2 cases)	38.00
Louis Martini Mountain Zinfandel '72 (2 cases)	35.00
Robert Mondavi Cabernet Sauvignon '71 (2 cases)	65.00
Robert Mondavi Cabernet Sauvignon Reserve '71 (2 cases)	130.00
Robert Mondavi Gamay '73 or '74 (2 cases)	36.00
Robert Mondavi Gamay Rosé '74 (2 cases)	35.00
Robert Mondavi Petite Sirah '72 or '73 (2 cases)	51.00
Robert Mondavi Pinot Noir '73 (2 cases)	57.00
Robert Mondavi Pinot Noir Reserve '71 (2 cases)	95.00
Robert Mondavi Red Table Wine N.V. (2 cases)	24.00
Robert Mondavi Zinfandel '73 (2 cases)	51.00
Sebastiani Special Vintage Select Barbara '69 (2 cases)	51.00
Sebastiani Special Vintage Select Cabernet Sauvignon '68 (2 cases)	70.00
Sebastiani Special Vintage Select Pinot Noir '68 (2 cases)	58.00
Simi Rosé of Cabernet '74 (2 cases)	38.00
Winemasters Guild Zinfandel (4 cases)	21.00

	Price per unit (case)
Red Bordeaux	
Château Mouton Baron Philippe '71	85.00
Château Mouton Baron Philippe '69	64.00
Château Margaux '71	225.00
Château Cheval Blanc '71	170.00
Château Mouton Rothschild '71	200.00
Château Beychevelle '70	135.00

White Bordeaux

Château d'Yquem Sauternes '67	215.00

Red Burgundy

Gevrey Chambertin Louis Jadot '72	120.00
Gevrey Chambertin P. Bouchard '71	75.00
Domaine de la Romanée Conti La Tache '70	280.00
Domaine de la Romanée Conti Grand Echezeaux	200.00
Volnay Clos de Rhenes P. Bouchard '71	82.00
Clos Vougeot '70, Domaine M. Jean Grivot	220.00

White Burgundy

Puligny Montrachet '74 Armand Roux	95.00
Meursault Clos du Cromin, Domaine Poil '74	120.00

Alsatian

F. E. Hugel el Fils Gewürztraminer Reserve Exceptionelle '70	70.00

Moselle

Wehlener Sonnenuhr Qualitaetswein mit Praedikat H. Thanish '72	90.00

$10,000 Wine Cellar

	Price per unit (case)
California Champagne	
Almaden Blanc de Blanc '73 (2 cases)	$ 71.00

	Price per unit (case)
Korbel Brut	65.00
Korbel Natural	75.00
Hanns Kornell Brut	63.00
Hanns Kornell Muscat Alexandria	80.00
Hanns Kornell Sehr Trocken (2 cases)	80.00

White California

Almaden Special Selection Pinot Chardonnay '72	48.00
Almaden Gewürztraminer N.V.	32.00
Beaulieu Vineyards Beaufort Chardonnay '73 (2 cases)	51.00
Chappellet Chardonnay '73	85.00
Christian Brothers Chardonnay N.V. (2 cases)	44.00
Christian Brothers Brother Timothy Special Selection Pinot de La Loire N.V.	45.00
Fino Eleven Cellars Napa Sauvignon Blanc	30.00
Charles Krug Moscato di Canelli '73	55.00
Charles Krug Pinot Chardonnay '73 (2 cases)	51.00
Mirassou Harvest Selection Gewürztraminer '74 (2 cases)	51.00
Mirassou Harvest Selection Pinot Chardonnay '73 (2 cases)	62.00
Robert Mondavi Chardonnay '73 or '74 (2 cases)	51.00
Robert Mondavi Chardonnay Reserve '73	71.00
Robert Mondavi Chenin Blanc '74 or '75	35.00
Robert Mondavi Fumé Blanc '74 (2 cases)	51.00
Robert Mondavi Johannisberg Riesling '75	51.00
Robert Mondavi Traminer '74	33.00
Robert Mondavi White Table Wine, N.V.	24.00
Simi Gewürztraminer '74 (2 cases)	44.00

	Price per unit (case)
Wente Le Blanc de Blancs (2 cases)	27.00
Wente Sauvignon Blanc '73	30.00

Red California

Almaden Special Selection Gamay Beaujolais '72	48.00
Beaulieu Vineyards Private Reserve Cabernet Sauvignon '71 (2 cases)	90.00
Beringer Cabernet Sauvignon '69	80.00
Beringer Grignolino '73	30.00
Beringer Zinfandel (2 cases)	27.00
Chappellet Cabernet Sauvignon '72	85.00
Christian Brothers Cabernet Sauvignon N.V. (2 cases)	38.00
Christian Brothers Bro. Timothy Special Selection Gamay Noir N.V.	50.00
Christian Brothers Pinot St. George N.V.	44.00
Christian Brothers Zinfandel N.V. (2 cases)	36.00
Concannon Petite Sirah '71 (Limited bottling) (2 cases)	55.00
Cresta Blanca Grignolino (2 cases)	27.00
Cresta Blanca Zinfandel (2 cases)	30.00
Fino Eleven Cellars Napa Claret	22.00
Fino Eleven Cellars Napa Zinfandel	30.00
Foppiano Zinfandel '71	30.00
Gallo Barbera	22.00
Gallo Hearty Burgundy N.V.	16.00
Inglenook Charbono '59	300.00
Inglenook Charbono '71 (Limited bottling) (2 cases)	51.00
Charles Krug Cabernet Sauvignon '71 (2 cases)	51.00
Charles Krug Vintage Selection Cabernet Sauvignon '70 (2 cases)	72.00
Louis Martini Barbera '68 (2 cases)	30.00
Louis Martini Merlot '73	38.00
Louis Martini Mountain Zinfandel '72	35.00

	Price per *unit (case)*
Robert Mondavi Cabernet Sauvignon '72 (2 cases)	65.00
Robert Mondavi Cabernet Sauvignon Reserve '71 (2 cases)	130.00
Robert Mondavi Gamay '73 or '74	36.00
Robert Mondavi Gamay Rosé '74	35.00
Robert Mondavi Petite Sirah '72 or '73	51.00
Robert Mondavi Pinot Noir '73 (2 cases)	57.00
Robert Mondavi Red Table Wine N.V.	24.00
Robert Mondavi Zinfandel '73	51.00
Sebastiani Special Vintage Selection Barbera '69 (2 cases)	51.00
Sebastiani Special Vintage Selection Cabernet Sauvignon '68 (2 cases)	70.00
Sebastiani Special Vintage Selection Pinot Noir '68 (2 cases)	58.00
Simi Rosé of Cabernet '74 (2 cases)	38.00
Souverain of Rutherford Cabernet Sauvignon '70	70.00
Souverain of Rutherford Zinfandel '72	45.00
Winemasters Guild Zinfandel (2 cases)	21.00

Red Burgundy

Gevrey Chambertin Louis Jadot '72	120.00
Gevrey Chambertin P. Bouchard '71	75.00
Domaine de la Romanée Conti La Tache '70	280.00
Domaine de la Romanée Grand Echezeaux	200.00
Volnay Cos de Rhenes P. Bouchard '71	82.00
Clos Vougeot '70, Domaine M. Jean Grivot	220.00

White Burgundy

Puligny Montrachet '74 Armand Roux	95.00

Price per
unit (case)

Meursault Clos du Cromin, Domaine
Poil '74   120.00

Alsatian
F. E. Hugel et Fils Gewürztraminer
Reserve Exceptionelle 1970   70.00

Moselle
Wehlener Sonnenuhr Kabinett H.
Thanish '72   90.00

Rhine Valley
Schloss Johannisberger Rotlack
Kabinett Fuerst Von Metternich '73   85.00
Schloss Vollrads Spaetlese '71,
Rosa-Kapsel   200.00

Italian
Pio Cesare Barbaresco Riserva '64   120.00

Moselle
Bernkasteler Doktor und Graben
Kabinet H. Thanisch '73   190.00

Red Bordeaux
Château Mouton Rothschild '61
(Pauillac)   1,000.00
Château Mouton Baron Philippe '71
(Pauillac)   85.00
Château Mouton Baron Philippe '69
(Pauillac)   64.00
Château Margaux '71 (Margaux)   225.00
Château Cheval Blanc '71
(St. Emilion)   170.00
Château Mouton Rothschild '71
(Pauillac)   200.00
Château Beychevelle '70 (St. Julien)   135.00

White Bordeaux
Château d'Yquem (Sauternes) '67   215.00
Château Bouscat (Graves) '72
(2 cases)   80.00

White Burgundy
Bienvenues Batard Montrachet '73   210.00

	Price per unit (case)
Louis Jadot Meursault Genevrieres '72	150.00

Loire Valley
Remy Pannier Sancerre '73	60.00

Champagne
Moët & Chandon Brut Imperial	130.00
Taittinger Brut Reserve	190.00

$100,000 Wine Cellar

California Champagne
	Price per unit (case)
Almaden Blanc de Blanc '73 (2 cases)	$ 71.00
Korbel Brut (2 cases)	65.00
Korbel Natural (2 cases)	75.00
Hanns Kornell Brut (2 cases)	63.00
Hanns Kornell Muscat Alexandria (2 cases)	80.00
Hanns Kornell Sehr Trocken (2 cases)	80.00

White California
Almaden Special Selection Pinot Chardonnay '72 (2 cases)	48.00
Almaden Gewürztraminer N.V. (2 cases)	32.00
Beaulieu Vineyards Beaufort Chardonnay '73 (2 cases)	51.00
Chappellet Chardonnay '73 (2 cases)	85.00
Christian Brothers Chardonnay N.V. (2 cases)	44.00
Christian Brothers Brother Timothy Special Selection Pinot de La Loire N.V. (2 cases)	45.00
Fino Eleven Cellars Napa Sauvignon Blanc (2 cases)	30.00
Charles Krug Moscato di Canelli '73 (2 cases)	51.00
Charles Krug Pinot Chardonnay '73 (2 cases)	51.00
Mirassou Harvest Selection	

	Price per unit (case)
Gewürztraminer '74 (2 cases)	51.00
Mirassou Harvest Selection Pinot Chardonnay '73 (2 cases)	62.00
Robert Mondavi Chardonnay '73 or '74 (2 cases)	51.00
Robert Mondavi Chardonnay Reserve '73 (2 cases)	71.00
Robert Mondavi Chenin Blanc '74 or '75 (2 cases)	35.00
Robert Mondavi Fumé Blanc '74 (2 cases)	51.00
Robert Mondavi Johannisberg Riesling '75 (2 cases)	51.00
Robert Mondavi Traminer '74 (2 cases)	33.00
Robert Mondavi White Table Wine, N.V. (2 cases)	24.00
Simi Gewürztraminer '74 (2 cases)	44.00
Wente Johannisberg Riesling Spatlese '74 (2 cases)	70.00
Wente Le Blanc de Blancs (2 cases)	27.00
Wente Sauvignon Blanc '73 (2 cases)	30.00

Red California

Almaden Special Selection Gamay Beaujolais '72 (2 cases)	48.00
Beaulieu Vineyards Private Res. Cabernet Sauvignon '71 (2 cases)	90.00
Beringer Cabernet Sauvignon '69 (2 cases)	80.00
Beringer Grignolino '73 (2 cases)	30.00
Beringer Zinfandel (2 cases)	27.00
Chappellet Cabernet Sauvignon '72 (2 cases)	85.00
Christian Brothers Cabernet Sauvignon N.V. (2 cases)	38.00
Christian Brothers Brother Timothy Special Selection Gamay Noir N.V. (2 cases)	50.00
Christian Brothers Pinot St. George N.V. (2 cases)	44.00

	Price per unit (case)
Christian Brothers Zinfandel N.V. (2 cases)	36.00
Concannon Petite Sirah '71 (Limited bottling) (2 cases)	55.00
Cresta Blanca Grignolino (2 cases)	27.00
Cresta Blanca Zinfandel (2 cases)	30.00
Fino Eleven Cellars Napa Claret (2 cases)	22.00
Fino Eleven Cellars Napa Zinfandel (2 cases)	30.00
Foppiano Zinfandel '71 (2 cases)	30.00
Gallo Barbera (2 cases)	22.00
Gallo Hearty Burgundy N.V. (2 cases)	16.00
Hanzell Pinot Noir '71 (2 cases)	100.00
Inglenook Charbono '59 (2 cases)	150.00
Inglenook Charbono '71 (Limited bottling) (2 cases)	51.00
Charles Krug Cabernet Sauvignon (2 cases)	51.00
Charles Krug Vintage Selection Cabernet Sauvignon '70 (2 cases)	72.00
Louis Martini Barbera '68 (2 cases)	30.00
Louis Martini Cabernet Sauvignon '62 (2 cases)	250.00
Louis Martini Merlot '73 (2 cases)	38.00
Louis Martini Mountain Zinfandel '72 (2 cases)	35.00
Robert Mondavi Cabernet Sauvignon '72 (2 cases)	65.00
Robert Mondavi Cabernet Sauvignon Reserve '71 (2 cases)	130.00
Robert Mondavi Gamay '73 or '74 (2 cases)	36.00
Robert Mondavi Gamay Rosé '74 (2 cases)	35.00
Robert Mondavi Petite Sirah '72 or '73 (2 cases)	51.00
Robert Mondavi Pinot Noir '73 (2 cases)	57.00
Robert Mondavi Red Table Wine N.V. (2 cases)	24.00

	Price per unit (case)
Robert Mondavi Zinfandel '73 (2 cases)	51.00
Sebastiani Special Vintage Selection Barbera '69 (2 cases)	51.00
Sebastiani Special Vintage Selection Cabernet Sauvignon '68 (2 cases)	70.00
Sebastiani Special Vintage Selection Pinot Noir '68 (2 cases)	58.00
Simi Rosé of Cabernet '74 (2 cases)	38.00
Souverain of Rutherford Cabernet Sauvignon (2 cases)	70.00
Souverain of Rutherford Zinfandel '72 (2 cases)	45.00
Winemasters Guild Zinfandel (2 cases)	21.00

Alsatian

F. E. Hugel et Fils Gewürztraminer Reserve Exceptionelle '71 (2 cases)	85.00

Spanish

Jean Leon Cabernet Sauvignon '70 (2 cases)	75.00

Rhine

Dienhard Bernkasteler Doktor Kabinett '71 (2 cases)	220.00
Gersenheimer Mauerchen Rulander Auslese '71 Lehr und Forschung (2 cases)	125.00
Winkeler Dachsberg Scheurebe Auslese Von Hessen '71 (2 cases)	175.00
Erbacher Markobrunn Beernauslese, Staatsweingut '71 (2 cases)	500.00
Erbacher Markobrunn Trockenbeerenauslese '71 (2 cases)	950.00
Hocheimer Domdechaney Trockenbeerenauslese '71 Werner (2 cases)	850.00
Rauenthaler Gehrn Beerenauslese '71 Schloss Eltzl (2 cases)	500.00
Schloss Vollrade Beerenauslese '71 Graf Matuscka-Grieffendau (2 cases)	660.00

Wachenheimer Mandelgarten Scheurebe

*Price per
unit (case)*

Trockenbeerenauslese Dr. Bruklin-
Wolfe '71 (2 cases) 800.00
Serriger Vogelsange Beerenauslese
Staatliche Weinbaudomane '71
(2 cases) 700.00
Dienhard Bernkasteler Doktor
Kabinett '72 (2 cases) 215.00
Niersteiner Floss Traminer Beeren-
auslese '70 (2 cases) 300.00
Niersteiner Auflangen Riesling,
Auslese Eiswein '70 (2 cases) 350.00
Oppenheimer Sacktrager
Trockenbeerenauslese '71 (2 cases) 595.00

Italian
Antinori Riserva '64 (2 cases) 90.00
Monsecco Gattinara, Ravizza '64
(2 cases) 140.00
Monsecco Gattinara, Ravizza '57
(2 cases) 180.00
Brunello di Montalcino Tenuta
d'Orcia '69 (2 cases) 185.00
Brunello di Montalcino Tenuta
d'Orcia '70 (2 cases) 125.00
Ruffino Riserva Ducale Gold Chianti
(2 cases) 95.00
Recioto Amarone Della Valpolicella
'66 (2 cases) 70.00
Barolo Franco-Fiorina '67 (2 cases) .. 100.00

Red Rhone
Rochette-Châteauneuf-du-Pape '72
(2 cases) 100.00
Fleurie-Sichel (2 cases) 70.00
Margon-Sichel (2 cases) 60.00
M. Chapoutier-Châteauneuf-du-Pape
La Marcelle '70 (2 cases) 100.00
M. Chapoutier-Hermitage (2 cases) .. 85.00

White Bordeaux
Domaine de Chevalier '71 (2 cases) .. 140.00
Château Smith Haut Lafite '72
(2 cases) 60.00

	Price per unit (case)
Rothschild Barsac '72 (2 cases)	65.00
Château d'Yquem Sauternes (2 cases)	550.00
Entre Deux Mers-Sichel (2 cases)	60.00
Sauternes "Grand Terrasse" (2 cases)	65.00

Red Bordeaux

Château Haut Brion (Graves) '61 (2 cases)	850.00
Château Haut Brion (Graves) '55 (2 cases)	650.00
Château Haut Brion (Graves) '64 (2 cases)	300.00
Château Haut Brion (Graves) '66 (2 cases)	300.00
Château Lafite Rothschild (Pauillac) '61 (3 cases)	1,350.00
Château Lafite Rothschild (Pauillac) '64 (2 cases)	450.00
Château Lafite Rothschild (Pauillac) '66 (2 cases)	450.00
Château Lafite Rothschild (Pauillac) '70 (2 cases)	400.00
Château Latour (Pauillac) '61 (3 cases)	1,050.00
Château Latour (Pauillac) '64 (2 cases)	400.00
Château Mouton Rothschild (Pauillac) '55 (2 cases)	650.00
Château Mouton Rothschild (Pauillac) '64 (2 cases)	450.00
Château Mouton Rothschild (Pauillac) '67 (2 cases)	400.00
Château Mouton Rothschild (Pauillac) '70 (2 cases)	400.00
Château Mouton Rothschild (Pauillac) '71 (2 cases)	400.00
Château Petrus (Pomerol) '64 (2 cases)	500.00
Château Petrus (Pomerol) '71 (2 cases)	450.00

	Price per unit (case)
Château Petrus (Pomerol) '61 (3 cases)	1,100.00
Château l'Angelus (St. Emilion) '66 (2 cases)	130.00
Château Figeac (St. Emilion) '66 (2 cases)	210.00
Château Beychevelle (St. Julien) '61 (2 cases)	300.00
Château Beychevelle (St. Julien) '64 (2 cases)	200.00
Château Rausan Gassies (Margaux) '61 (2 cases)	300.00
Château Cos Labory (St. Estèphe) '71 (2 cases)	150.00
Château D'Angludet (Cantenac-Margaux) '70 (2 cases)	170.00
Château Bouscat (Graves) '53 magnum (3)	300.00
Château Margaux (Margaux) '59 magnum (3)	1,000.00
Château Cheval Blanc (St. Emilion) '61 magnum (3)	850.00
Château Mouton Rothschild (Pauillac) '64 magnum (3)	550.00
Château Mouton Rothschild (Pauillac) '66 magnum (3)	550.00
Château Rausan Segla (Margaux) '62 (2 cases)	135.00
Château Rausan Segla (Margaux) '64 (2 cases)	135.00
Château Rausan Segla (Margaux) '67 (2 cases)	125.00

Champagne

Bollinger Brut '70 (3 cases)	185.00
Dom Perignon '69 (2 cases)	325.00
Dom Perignon '69 magnum (2 cases)	325.00
Taittinger Brut Reserve (2 cases)	210.00
Taittinger Brut Reserve magnum (3 cases)	210.00
Taittinger Blanc de Blanc (3 cases)	350.00

	Price per unit (case)
Laurent Perrier Blanc de Blanc Grand Siecle '70 (3 cases)	290.00

White Burgundy

Batard-Montrachet, EB Ramonet Prudhom '73 (2 cases)	180.00
Sichel Pouilly Fuissé '71 (2 cases)	65.00
Sichel Puligny Montrachet '71 (2 cases)	120.00
Chablis, A. Bichot '70 (2 cases)	75.00
Meursault, A. Bichot '69 (2 cases)	85.00
Corton Charlemagne '70 (2 cases)	85.00
Pouilly Fuissé, Bouchard '72 (2 cases)	65.00
Montrachet La Guiche, Drouhin '71 (2 cases)	325.00
Chevalier Montrachet, Drouhin '71 (2 cases)	185.00

Red Burgundy

Grand Echezeaux, Romanée Conti '61 (3 cases)	450.00
La Tâche, Romanée Conti '59 (3 cases)	600.00
Richebourg, Romanée Conti '61 (3 cases)	750.00
La Tâche, Romanée Conti '62 (2 cases)	450.00
Gevrey Chambertin "Combottes" Remoissenet '66 (2 cases)	230.00
Musigny, P. Ponnelle '69 (2 cases)	200.00
Clos-de-Vougeot, Mongeard Mugneret '71 (2 cases)	160.00
Richebourg, Jean Gros '71 (2 cases)	75.00
Romanée Conti '70, Domaine Gros (3 cases)	900.00
Romanée Conti '67, Domaine Gros (2 cases)	675.00
Gevrey Chambertin, Faiveley '71 (2 cases)	125.00
Gevrey Chambertin, Drouhin '71 (2 cases)	125.00

	Price per unit (case)
La Romanée Monopole '70 (2 cases)	300.00
Corton Grancey Louis Latour '69 (2 cases)	335.00
Corton Charlemagne Louis Latour '73 (2 cases)	300.00
Pommard Louis Jadot '72 (2 cases)	155.00
Pommard Armand Roux '70 (2 cases)	110.00
Chambolle-Musigny '70 Domaine Comte George de Vogue (2 cases)	100.00
Musigny '71 Domaine Comte George de Vogue (2 cases)	200.00
Domaine de Clos Frantin Vosne Romanée Les Malconsorts '66 (2 cases)	150.00
Domaine de Clos Frantin Clos de Vougeot '66 (2 cases)	215.00
Domaine de La Romanée, La Romanée Monopole '67 (2 cases)	315.00
Domaine de La Romanée, La Romanée Monopole '71 (2 cases)	520.00
Bouchard-Pommard '72 (2 cases)	150.00
Bouchard, Nuits St. George '72 (2 cases)	120.00

DON DIANDRA, DORO'S RESTAURANT, SAN FRANCISCO, AND
NATIONAL RESTAURANT ASSOCIATION

$500 Wine Cellar

Red California

	Price per unit (case)
Foppiano Vineyards Cabernet Sauvignon '71 Russian River-Sonoma	37.80
Robert Mondavi Pinot Noir '73 Napa Valley	56.70

White California

| Mirassou Chardonnay '74 Monterey | 54.00 |
| Robert Mondavi Fumé Blanc '74 (Unfiltered) Napa Valley | 48.60 |

	Price per unit (case)
Red Bordeaux	
Château Ferrande '73 Graves	43.10
Red Burgundy	
Beaujolais Villages '73 Domaine Comte de Chabanne	43.10
White Burgundy	
Pouilly Fuissé '74 Domaine Desrayaund	62.55
Loire Valley	
Muscadet '73 Les Montry	42.65
Red Italian—Verona	
Fratelli Poggi Bardolino '71	35.10
White Italian—Umbria	
Barberani Orvieto Classico	35.10
White German	
Piesporter Goldtropfchen Kabinett '73 Wilhelm Wasum	40.95

$1,000 Wine Cellar

Red California

	Price per unit (case)
Foppiano Vineyards, Cabernet Sauvignon '71 Russian River-Sonoma	37.80
Robert Mondavi, Pinot Noir '73 Napa Valley	56.70
Robert Mondavi, Cabernet Sauvignon '73 Napa Valley	64.80
White California	
Mirassou Chardonnay '74 Monterey	54.00
Robert Mondavi, Fumé Blanc '74 (Unfiltered) Napa Valley	48.60
Robert Mondavi, Johannisberg Riesling '75 Napa Valley	48.60
Red Bordeaux	
Château Ferrande '72 Graves	50.65
White Bordeaux	
Château Ferrande '74 Graves	40.50

	Price per unit (case)
Château Romer du Hayot '73 Barsac	64.75

Red Burgundy

Beaujolais Villages '73 Domaine Comte de Chabanne	43.10
Beaune les Cent Vignes '69 Domaine Coron	129.05

White Burgundy

Pouilly Fuissé '74 Domaine Desrayaund	62.55
Chablis Grand Cru Valmur '73 Domaine J. Moreau & Fils	99.25

Red Italian—Verona

Fratelli Poggi Bardolino '71	35.10

Red Italian—Tuscany

Contessa Albani Masetti Chianti Classico Uzzano '71	53.90

White Italian—Umbria

Barberani Orvieto Classico '73	35.10
Roberto Bianchi Verdicchio dei Castelli di Jesi Classico	35.10

White German

Wilhelm Wasum Piesporter Goldtropfchen Kabinett '73	40.95

$5,000 Wine Cellar

	Price per unit (case)

Red California

Foppiano Vineyards Petite Sirah Russian River-Sonoma	27.00
Foppiano Vineyards Zinfandel '72 Russian River-Sonoma	27.00
Mirassou Pinot Noir '72 Monterey	54.00
Mirassou Cabernet Sauvignon '72 Monterey	54.00
Foppiano Vineyards Pinot Noir '71 Russian River-Sonoma	37.80

	Price per unit (case)
Foppiano Vineyards Cabernet Sauvignon '71 Russian River-Sonoma	37.80
Robert Mondavi Petite Sirah '73 Napa Valley	48.60
Robert Mondavi Pinot Noir '73 Napa Valley	56.70
Robert Mondavi Cabernet Sauvignon '73 Napa Valley	64.80

White California

Mirassou Pinot Chardonnay '74 Monterey	54.00
Foppiano Vineyards Chablis '74 Russian River-Sonoma	24.30
Robert Mondavi Chenin Blanc '75 Napa Valley	37.80
Robert Mondavi Fumé Blanc '74 (Unfiltered) Napa Valley	48.60
Robert Mondavi Johannisberg Riesling '75 Napa Valley	46.80
Robert Mondavi Chardonnay '74 Napa Valley	70.20

Red Bordeaux

Château Ferrande '73 (Graves)	43.10
Château Ferrande '71 (Graves)	50.65
Château Pape Clement '73 (Graves)	114.80
Château la Clusière '70 (St. Emilion)	75.00
Château Pavie Decesse '73 (St. Emilion)	75.00
Château Cheval Blanc '70 (St. Emilion)	309.00
Château du Tertre '70 (Margaux)	120.00
Château Brane-Cantenac '73 (Margaux)	114.80
Château Grand St. Julien '70 (St. Julien)	54.00
Château Beauregard '70 (St. Julien)	75.00
Château Beauregard '71 (St. Julien)	75.00
Château Léoville las Cases '73 (St. Julien)	108.00
Château Belle Rosé '73 (Pauillac)	54.00

	Price per unit (case)
Château Batailley '70 (Pauillac)	134.25
Château Batailley '73 (Pauillac)	80.90
Château Pichon Lalande '63 (Pauillac)	108.00
Château Capbern Gasqueton '70 (St. Estèphe)	94.50
Château Beau-Site (St. Estèphe)	54.00
Château Calon Segur '70 (St. Estèphe)	134.50

White Bordeaux

Château Ferrande '73 Graves	40.50
Château Romer du Hayot '73 Sauternes	64.25

Red Burgundy

Beajolais Villages '74 Domaine Comte de Chabanne	43.10
Beaune les Cent Vignes '64 Domaine Coron	126.00
Beaune les Cent Vignes '69 Domaine Coron	129.00
Côte de Beaune Villages '69 Domaine Doreau	77.25
Pommard '72 Domaine Carré	130.50
Nuits-Saint-Georges '70 Clos de l'Arlot, Domaine Jules Belin	119.00
Clos Vougeot '70 Domaine Dufouleur	201.50

White Burgundy

Chassagne Montrachet '73 Domaine Delagrange	121.50
Meursault '71 Clos du Cromin, Domaine Poil	121.50
Pouilly Fuissé '74 Domaine Desrayaund	62.55
Chablis Grand Cru Valmur '70 Domaine J. Moreau et Fils	99.25
Puligny Montrachet '73 Perrières, Domaine Bellicard	121.50
Corton Charlemagne '73 Domaine Gordot	180.90

Red Italian—Tuscany

Contessa Albani Masetti Chianti Classico Uzzano '71	53.00

Price per
unit (case)

Red Italian—Verona
Estate Bottled, Fratelli Poggi Bardolino
'71   35.10
Produttori Associati Soave Valpolicella
'71   35.10

White Italian—Verona
Produttori Associati Soave Classico '74   35.10

Red Italian—Lombardy
Inferno '69 Valtellina, Produced by
Enologica   48.60
Sasella '64 Valtellina, Produced by
Enologica   48.60

Red Italian—Piedmont
Alfredo Prunotto Grignolino '71   42.65
Pio Cesare Barbera '70 Alba   42.65
Pio Cesare Nebbiolo d'Alba '67   62.10
Pio Cesare Barbaresco '64 Riserva   121.50
Pio Cesare Barolo '67   107.45

White Italian—Latium
Frascati '73 Vigneti di Colle Portella:
A. De Sanctis   35.10

White Italian—Umbria
Barberani Orvieto Classico   35.10
Roberto Bianchi Verdicchio dei Castelli
di Jesi Classico   35.10

White German
Piesporter Goldtropfchen Kabinett '73
Wilhelm Wasum   40.95

$10,000 Wine Cellar

Price per
unit (case)

Red California
Foppiano Vineyards Petite Sirah '71
Russian River-Sonoma   27.00
Foppiano Vineyards Zinfandel '72
Russian River-Sonoma   27.00
Mirassou Vineyards Pinot Noir '72
Monterey   54.00

Price per
unit (case)

Mirassou Vineyards Cabernet Sauvignon
  '72 Monterey   54.00

Foppiano Vineyards Pinot Noir '71
  Russian River-Sonoma   37.80

Foppiano Vineyards Cabernet
  Sauvignon '71 Russian River-Sonoma   37.80

Robert Mondavi Petite Sirah '73
  Napa Valley   48.60

Robert Mondavi Pinot Noir '73
  Napa Valley   56.70

Robert Mondavi Cabernet Sauvignon
  '73 Napa Valley   64.80

Robert Mondavi Cabernet Sauvignon
  Reserve '71 Napa Valley   129.60

White California

Mirassou Vineyards Pinot Chardonnay
  '74 Monterey   54.00

Foppiano Vineyards Chablis '74
  Russian River-Sonoma   24.30

Robert Mondavi Chenin Blanc '75
  Napa Valley   37.80

Robert Mondavi Fumé Blanc '74
  Napa Valley   48.60

Robert Mondavi Johannisberg Riesling
  '75 Napa Valley   48.60

Robert Mondavi Chardonnay '74
  Napa Valley   70.20

Red Bordeaux

Château Ferrande '73 (Graves)   43.10
Château Ferrande '71 (Graves)   50.65
Château Haut Brion '73 (Graves)   226.80
Château Pape Clement '73 (Graves)   114.80
Château la Clusière '70 (St. Emilion)   75.00
Château Pavie Decesse '73
  (St. Emilion)   75.00
Château Cheval Blanc '70
  (St. Emilion)   309.00
Château l'Evangile '70 (Pomerol)   183.00
Château Petrus '67 (Pomerol)   400.00
Château du Tertre '67 (Margaux)   120.00

	Price per unit (case)
Château Prieure Lichine '70 (Margaux)	134.50
Château Brane Cantenac '73 (Margaux)	114.80
Château Margaux '70 (Margaux)	282.00
Château Beauregard '70, '71 (St. Julien)	75.00
Château Grand St. Julien '73 (St. Julien)	54.00
Château Léoville las Cases '73 (St. Julien)	108.00
Château Belle Rosé '73 (Pauillac)	54.00
Château Pichon Lalande '73 (Pauillac)	108.00
Château Batailley '70 (Pauillac)	134.25
Château Batailley '73 (Pauillac)	80.90
Château Mouton Rothschild '70 (Pauillac)	540.00
Château Lafite Rothschild '70 (Pauillac)	605.00
Château Beau-Site '73 (St. Estèphe)	54.00
Château Capbern Gasqueton '70 (St. Estèphe)	94.50
Château Calon Segur '70 (St. Estèphe)	134.50
Château Calon Segur '73 (St. Estèphe)	120.00

Red Rhone

Châteauneuf-du-Pape '74 Domaine Coron	80.50

Red Burgundy

Beaujolais Superieur '74 Domaine Comte de Chabanne	43.10
Moulin-a-Vent '73 Domaine Coron	71.00
Côte de Beaune Villages '69 Domaine Doreau	77.25
Nuits-Saint-Georges '71 Clos de l'Arlot, Domaine Jules Belin	119.00
Beaune les Cent Vignes '64 Domaine Coron	126.00

	Price per unit (case)
Beaune les Cent Vignes '69 Domaine Coron	129.00
Pommard '72 Domaine Carré	130.50
Musigny '71 Domaine Dufouleur	275.00
Corton '69 Domaine Voarick	137.00
Clos Vougeot '70 Domaine Dufouleur	259.25
Grands Echezeaux '71 Domaine Engel	204.50
Chambertin Clos de Beze '73 Domaine Damoy	269.00
Chambertin '70 Domaine Bart	300.00

White Bordeaux

Château Ferrande '74 Graves	40.50
Château Romer du Hayot '73 Barsac	64.75

White Burgundy

Chassagne Montrachet '71 Domaine Delagrange	150.00
Meursault Clos du Cromin '71 Domaine Poil	121.50
Pouilly Fuissé '74 Domaine Desrayaund	62.55
Chablis Grand Cru Valmur '70 Domaine J. Moreau et Fils	99.25
Puligny Montrachet, Perrières '73 Domaine Bellicard	121.50
Corton Charlemagne '73 Domaine Gordot	180.90

Loire Valley

Sancerre '72 Domaine Roblin	65.50
Pouilly Fumé '72 Domaine Pabiot	69.50

Alsace

Ingersheim Gewürztraminer '73	48.60

Red Italian—Tuscany

Contessa Albani Masetti Chianti Classico Uzzano '71	53.90

Red Italian—Verona

Fratelli Poggi Bardolino '71	35.10
Produttori Associati Soave Valpolicella '71	35.10

	Price per unit (case)
Red Italian—Lombardy	
Inferno '69 Valtellina,	
Produced by Enologica	48.60
Sasella '64 Valtellina,	
Produced by Enologica	75.00
Red Italian—Piedmont	
Alfredo Prunotto Grignolino '71	42.50
Pio Cesare Barbera '70	42.50
Pio Cesare Nebbiolo d'Alba '67	62.10
Pio Cesare Barbaresco '64 Riserva	121.50
Pio Cesare Barolo '64	121.50
White Italian—Verona	
Produttori Associati Soave Classico	
'74	35.10
White Italian—Latium	
Vigneti di Colle Portella: A. DeSanctis	
Frascati '73	35.10
White Italian—Umbria	
Barberani Orvieto Classico	35.10
Roberto Bianchi Verdicchio dei Castelli	
di Jesi Classico	35.10
White German	
Piesporter Goldtropfchen Kabinett '73	
Wilhelm Wasum	40.95
Bernkasteler Doktor, Spätlese '73	
Wwe. Dr. H. Thanisch	276.00

ALEXANDER C. MCNALLY, HEUBLEIN, INC., IMPORTERS

$500 Wine Cellar

	Price per unit (case)
Red California	
Beaulieu Vineyard Burgundy	$29.00
Inglenook Vineyards Zinfandel	35.00
White California	
BV Beauclair Johannisberg Riesling	45.00
Inglenook Vineyards Chenin Blanc	31.00

	Price per unit (case)
Red Bordeaux	
Château St. Georges (St. Emilion)	78.00
Red Burgundy	
Bouchard Père & Fils Beaujolais Superieur	43.00
White Burgundy	
Bouchard Père & Fils Chablis	57.00
Loire Valley	
de Marconnay Anjou Rosé	38.00
Red Italian	
Gancia Valpolicella	35.00
White German	
Rheinhof May Wine	31.00
Red Hungarian	
Bulls Blood Egri Bikaver	40.00
White Hungarian	
Greyfriar Badacsonyi Szurkebarat	38.00

$1,000 Wine Cellar
(2 cases each of above, total 24 cases)

$5,000 Wine Cellar

	Price per unit (case)
Red California	
Inglenook Vineyards Gamay	$35.00
Inglenook Vineyards Zinfandel	35.00
Inglenook Vineyards Charbono	50.00
Beaulieu Vineyard Cabernet Sauvignon	50.00
BV Beaumont Pinot Noir	50.00
White California	
Inglenook Vineyards Chenin Blanc	31.00
BV Château Beaulieu Sauvignon Blanc	40.00
Inglenook Vineyards Johannisberg Reisling	50.00
BV Beaufort Pinot Chardonnay	50.00

	Price per unit (case)
Red Bordeaux	
Château St. Georges (St. Emilion)	100.00
Château Mayney (St. Estèphe)	150.00
Clos des Jacobins (St. Emilion)	154.00
Château Talbot (St. Julien)	210.00
Château Gruaud Laro e (St. Julien)	220.00
Château Lafite Rothschild (Pauillac)	237.00
White Bordeaux	
Château Lafaurie Peyraguey Sauternes	118.00
Red Burgundy	
Bouchard Père & Fils Beaujolais Superieur	43.00
Bouchard Père & Fils Gevrey Chambertin	100.00
Beaune du Château Rouge	108.00
Clos de la Mousse Beaune	111.00
Beaune Greves Vigne de l'Enfant Jesus	215.00
White Burgundy	
Bouchard Père & Fils Chablis	57.00
Beaune du Château Blanc	108.00
Domaines du Château de Beaune Chevalier Montrachet	170.00
Loire Valley	
De Marconnay Vouvray Blanc	45.00
De Marconnay Anjou Rosé	38.00
Rhone Valley	
Paul Jaboulet Tavel Rosé	$ 75.00
Hermitage La Chapelle Rouge	137.00
Hermitage Sterimberg Blanc	137.00
Paul Jaboulet Châteauneuf-du-Pape	140.00
Provence	
Château des Vannières Rosé	38.00
Red Italian	
Gancia Valpolicella	35.00
Mirafiore Bardolino	35.00

	Price per unit (case)
Ganchia Chianti Classico	51.00

White Italian
Mirafiore Orvieto	35.00
Gancia Soave	35.00

White German
Lorelei Liebfraumilch	31.00
Scholl & Hillebrand Rudesheimer Bischofsberg	46.00
Piesporter Goldtropfchen Moselle	49.00
Erbacher Markobrunn Schloss Reinhartshausen	73.00

Red Hungarian
Szekszardi Voros	35.00
Nemes Kadar	39.00
Egri Bikaver	40.00
Hajosi Cabernet	40.00

White Hungarian
Hungarian Riesling	33.00
Debroi Harslevelu	35.00
Greyfriar Badacsonyi Szurkebarat	38.00
Tokay Aszu 3 Puttonos	49.00

Portugal
Quinta Lisbon Red	25.00
Lancers Vin Rosé	41.00
Lancers Vinho Branco	41.00

Sparkling Wines
Gancia Asti-Spumante	64.00
Mirafiore Lacrima Christi	68.00
Beaulieu Vineyard Brut Champagne	72.00
Inglenook Vineyards Champagne Brut	78.00

Dessert Wines
Inglenook Pale Dry Sherry	27.00
Harveys Gold Cap Port	54.00
Bristol Cream Sherry	84.00

Japan
Kiku Masamune Sake	33.00

$10,000 Wine Cellar
(2 cases each of above, total 120 cases)

$100,000 Wine Cellar
(12 cases each of above, total 720 cases [$5,000 cellar selection]. Plus $40,000 of assorted rare auction wines, additional vintages of above basic selection, etc. Following are some examples.)

	Price per unit (bottle)
Portugal	
2 bottles Cockburn's Vintage Port '08	$ 100.00
Red California	
1 bottle Inglenook Burgundy '03	200.00
12 bottles Beaumont Pinot Noir '46	52.00
Bordeaux	
1 bottle Château Lafite (Pauillac) 1869	1,400.00
1 imperiale (eq. 8 bottles) Château St. Georges '45 (St. Emilion)	700.00
12 bottles Château Haut-Brion '07 (Graves)	52.00
12 bottles Château Latour '53 (Pauillac)	50.00
12 bottles Château d'Yquem Sauternes '55	75.00
Burgundy	
2 bottles Bouchard Père Clos Vougeot 1865	225.00
12 bottles Beaune Greves Vigne de l'Enfant Jesus '45	30.00
Rhone Valley	
12 bottles Hermitage LaChapelle '45	35.00
Italian	
12 bottles Barolo Mirafiore '47	25.00
German	
1 bottle Rauenthaler Huenerberg Auslese '21	200.00
1 bottle Steinberger 1895	210.00
1 bottle Ruedesheimer Apostelwein 1727	800.00

Price per
unit (bottle)

Hungarian
1 bottle Tokay Essence 1889   300.00

MICHAEL COLLINS, MUNSON & SHAW, IMPORTERS

$500 Wine Cellar

Red Burgundy
Beaujolais Village (Marquisat), young vintage ready
for drinking (1 case)
Medium-priced Côtes du Beaune (Jouvet), about 5
years old for present drinking (1 case)
Mixed case of more expensive Burgundy: Pommard,
Clos Vougeot, Volnay, etc, 5-7 years old (1 case)

White Burgundy
Chablis or Pouilly Fuissé (Jouvet) young vintage
(1 case)
Beaujolais Blanc (Marquisat) (1 case)

Red Bordeaux
"Petite château" (Château Teyssier, Château d'Arche)
from a reliable Bordeaux shipper (Dourthe Freres),
about 5 years old (2 cases)
Classified growth from the Medoc: Château Lynch
Bages, Château Léoville Las Cases, about 5-7 years
old (1 case)

Miscellaneous
Corbieres, Côtes du Luberon, Muscadet, Sancerre
Adriatica Yugoslav wines—assorted and of young
vintages

$1,000 Wine Cellar & $2,000 Wine Cellar

Would include proportionately more of the same wines
plus one case of Champagne (Laurent Perrier), an
assortment of fortified wines (Duff Gordon Pinta
Sherry, Cockburn Special Reserve Port) and one case
Red Côtes du Rhone (Chapoutier "La Marcelle"
Châteauneuf-du-Pape).

$5,000 Wine Cellar, $10,000 Wine Cellar, Up

Call in an expert for consultation.

CHARLES S. MUELLER, KOBRAND CORPORATION, IMPORTERS

$500 Wine Cellar*

(6 bottles each—total 18 wines)

*This is a get-acquainted cellar for today's enjoyment and the near term. This could be combined with my $5,000 cellar for a complete working cellar.

	Price per unit (bottle)
Red Bordeaux	
Ginestet Fort Medoc '70	$ 4.49
Château des Arras '70	$ 4.39
White Bordeaux	
Ginestet Graves Extra '73	$ 3.19
Red Burgundy	
Beaujolais Villages Jadot '74	$ 3.98
Beaune Boucherottes '70 estate bottled by Louis Jadot	$ 8.49
White Burgundy	
Macon Blanc Villages Jadot '74	$ 3.98
Pic Chablis '74	$ 4.98
Rosé	
Moc-Baril Rosé d'Anjou '74	$ 2.98
Château d'Aqueria Tavel Rosé '73 estate bottled by J. Olivier	$ 4.39
Rhine	
Madrigal Johannisberger Riesling '75	$ 3.89
Moselle	
Piesporter Goldtropchen Spatlese '71 Orig. Abf. Lehnert Matheus	$ 5.00
Champagne and Other Sparkling Wines	
Taittinger Brut La Française Champagne	$12.98
Bouvet Brut (Saumur)	$ 5.98

	Price per unit (bottle)
Spanish	
Cabernet Sauvignon '70, 100% varietal, estate bottled by Jean Leon	$ 4.39
Loire Valley	
Barre Muscadet de Sevre et Maine '74	$ 3.29
Italian	
Nozzole Chianti Classico Riserva '69	$ 4.19
Dessert Wines (3 bottles)	
Dow's Boardroom Tawny Porto	$ 9.98
Red Rhone	
Gigondas "Cuvée du Président" '70	$ 3.98

$5,000 Wine Cellar*
(1 case each—total 26 wines)

*The following wines were selected from current availabilities for the person who wishes to have an outstanding cellar of imported wines suitable for appreciation and aging. It should be augmented by fine California wines to be selected on individual tasting from stocks available in the local market.

	Price per unit (bottle)
Champagne	
Taittinger Comtes de Champagne Blanc de Blancs, Brut '69	$25.98
Red Bordeaux	
Château Margaux Premier Grand Cru Classe '71 (Margaux)	$35.00
Château Margaux Premier Grand Cru Classe '67 (Margaux)	$40.00
Domaine de Chevalier '71 (Graves)	$19.00
Château Petit Village '70 (Pomerol)	$12.00
Château Larrivet Haut Brion Rouge '66 (Graves)	$ 8.00
Château de Segonzac '70 (Cotes de Blaye)	$ 4.50
White Bordeaux	
Château Climens Premier Cru '70 (Barsac)	$24.00

Price per
unit (bottle)

Red Burgundy
Beaune Clos des Ursules '71
    estate bottled by Louis Jadot $ 2.98
Corton Pougets '71
    estate bottled by Louis Jadot $16.00
Volnay Santenots '70 mise en bouteilles
    au domaine, Reserve Numerotee,
    Domaine des Comtes Lafon $ 8.80
Clos de Vougeot '71 estate bottled,
    Reserve Numerotee, L'Heritier-
    Guyot $10.75

White Burgundy
Corton Charlemagne '71
    estate bottled by Louis Jadot $17.00
Chevalier Montrachet "Les Demoiselles"
    '73 estate bottled by Louis Jadot $13.45
Chablis Grand Cru Vaudesir '71
    estate bottled by Albert Pic $ 7.70
Clos Blanc de Vougeot '73 Reserve
    Numerotee, L'Heritier-Guyot $11.00

Red Italian
Nozzole Chianti Classico Riserva '64
    estate bottled by L. Rimediotti-
    Mattioli $ 5.70

Red Spanish
Cabernet Sauvignon '70
    estate bottled by Jean Leon $ 4.40

Red Rhone
Gigondas "Cuvée du Président" '70 $ 6.00

German
Eltviller Sonnenberg Spatlese '71
    Orig. Abf. Langwerth Von Simmern $ 6.00
Hattenheimer Nussbrunnen Riesling
    Spatlese '71 Langwerth Von
    Simmern $ 8.00
Piesporter Goldtropfchen Auslese
    Silberne Kammerpreismunze '71 Orig.
    Abf. Lehnert Matheus $10.00

	Price per unit (bottle)
Urziger Wurzgarten Auslese '71 Erz Abf. Weingut Pfeiffer	$ 7.00
Scharzhofberger Spätlese '71 Orig. Abf. Egon Muller	$ 8.00
Graacher Himmelreich Beerenauslese '71 Orig. Abf. Joh. Jos. Prum	$50.00
Steinberger Riesling Trockenbeeren- auslese '71 Orig. Abf. Verwaltungder Staatsweinguter	$65.00

JULIUS WILE, JULIUS WILE SONS & CO., IMPORTERS

$500 Wine Cellar*

*This is a "taster's cellar," aimed at providing the newcomer with the widest possible selection for his money. As he gains experience with wine, he will expand the cellar to taste and pocketbook.

	Price per unit (bottle)
Bordeaux District Claret	
Prats Médoc (3 bottles)	$ 3.99
Prats St. Emilion (3 bottles)	4.29
Bordeaux Petit Château Claret	
Prats Château Malbec Bordeaux Superieur (2 bottles)	4.69
Prats Château Falfas Côtes de Bourg (2 bottles)	4.49
Prats Château Peymelon Bordeaux Superieur (2 bottles)	4.59
Bordeaux District White	
Prats Graves (2 bottles)	2.88
Prats Sauternes (2 bottles)	3.98
Bordeaux Petit Château White	
Prats Château Piron (Graves) (2 bottles)	3.95
Prats Château de Laulan (Sauternes) (2 bottles)	4.98

Bordeaux "Classified Growth" Claret

	Price per unit (bottle)
Prats Château Cos d'Estournel (6 bottles)	13.45

Beaujolais
Chanson Beaujolais (1 bottle)	3.29
Chanson Beaujolais Villages St. Vincent (1 bottle)	4.25
Chanson Brouilly St. Vincent (1 bottle)	4.98

Red Burgundy
Chanson Côtes de Beaune Villages St. Vincent (2 bottles)	6.75
Chanson Beaune St. Vincent (2 bottles)	7.95
Chanson Beaune Clos des Feves St. Vincent (2 bottles)	11.80

White Burgundy
Chanson Mâcon Blanc (2 bottles)	3.19
Chanson Chablis (2 bottles)	6.49
Chanson Pouilly-Fuissé (2 bottles)	7.49

Rosé
| Chanson Rosé des Anges (2 bottles) | 2.89 |
| Château Ste. Roseline (Provence Rosé) (2 bottles) | 3.98 |

Red Italian
| Villa Antinori Chianti Classico (3 bottles) | 3.98 |
| Villa Antinori Riserva Chianti Classico (1 bottle) | 5.99 |

Veronese
Antinori Bardolino (1 bottle)	2.98
Antinori Valpolicella (1 bottle)	2.98
Antinori Soave (1 bottle)	2.98

White Italian
Villa Antinori Bianco (1 bottle)	3.19
Antinori Est! Est!! Est!!! (1 bottle)	3.09
Antinori Orvieto Abbocata (1 bottle)	3.09

Red Spanish
| Paternina Banda Azul (1 bottle) | 2.98 |

	Price per unit (bottle)
Paternina Viva Vial (1 bottle)	3.98
Paternina Gran Reserva (1 bottle)	5.85

White Spanish
Paternina Rinsol (1 bottle)	2.98
Paternina Banda Dorada (1 bottle)	2.59
Paternina Reserva (1 bottle)	4.89

Alsatian
Willm Cordon d'Alsace (1 bottle)	2.69
Willm Riesling (2 bottles)	3.85
Willm Gewürztraminer (1 bottle)	4.85

Rhine
Deinhard Rheinritter (1 bottle)	2.98
Deinhard Hanns Christof Liebfraumilch (1 bottle)	3.98
Deinhard Liebfraumilch Lilac Seal (1 bottle)	5.79

Moselle
Deinhard Moselmaid (1 bottle)	2.98
Deinhard Green Label Bereich Bernkastel (1 bottle)	3.98
Deinhard Bernkasteler Lilac Seal (1 bottle)	5.79

Champagne
Bollinger Extra Dry (1 bottle)	9.95
Bollinger Special Cuvée (1 bottle)	11.45
Bollinger Vintage Brut (1 bottle)	13.75

Rhone
Chanson Côtes du Rhone (1 bottle)	2.69
Chanson Châteauneuf-du-Pape St. Vincent (1 bottle)	7.95

Loire Valley
Chanson Muscadet (1 bottle)	3.39
Chanson Pouilly-Fumé (1 bottle)	6.35

Spanish Sherry
Williams & Humbert Dry Sack Sherry (4 bottles)	5.59

	Price per unit (bottle)
Williams & Humbert Pando Dry Sherry (1 bottle)	5.25
Williams & Humbert Canasta Cream Sherry (1 bottle)	5.59

Dessert Wines

Robertson's Dry Humour Porto (1 bottle)	4.98
Leacock St. John Dry Madeira (1 bottle)	4.15
Cherry Elsinore Danish wine (1 bottle)	3.45

Aperitifs

Raphael Aperitif Wine (4 bottles)	3.69
Cazalis & Prats Dry Vermouth (1 bottle)	2.39
Cazalis & Prats Sweet Vermouth (1 bottle)	2.39

8

My Most Memorable Wine and One for a Desert Island

Now for the really tough questions. You are a wine professional. You've tasted literally thousands or even tens of thousands of wines and vintages. Of them all, which single glass of wine is your most memorable?

Another toughie: you're going to be stranded on a desert island, where you'll spend the rest of your life. You can take only one bottle of wine with you. Which would it be?

I posed these questions to some of my favorite wine professionals and, hardly to my surprise, got some very interesting answers. Match your own choices against them, or use them as guidelines to build a dream wine cellar (even if only in your dreams). In any case, here they are:

My Most Memorable Wine

HARRY G. SERLIS, retired president, The Wine Institute, San Francisco; consultant, Robert Mondavi Winery, Oakville, California: A 1928 Mouton Rothschild, which I drank in 1972 at the chateau with Baron Philippe. The wine was superb and had rested in the cellars at Mouton undisturbed for the forty years after bottling.

JOE MONOSTORI, winemaker, Parducci Wine Cellars, Ukiah, California: A 1951 Beaulieu G. DeLatour Private Reserve Cabernet Sauvignon from the Napa Valley. I still have one bottle. Its slightly musty taste has never been duplicated in this region. The public can't get these, sad to say!

DAVID S. MILLIGAN, wine consultant, Miami, Florida; former

president, Dennis & Huppert, Importers: Château Lafite 1949, one of the greatest postwar vintages—and I'm happy to say I was able to have more than one glass of it. Apart from the fine summer, one of the reasons why the wine was so good was that during and immediately after the war no replanting of the vineyards was possible, so the average age of the vines was higher than normal. Also, there was a great shortage of fertilizers, and yields generally were low. These factors, coupled with the use of the more old-fashioned methods of winemaking, produced really great wines in most of the postwar vintages. When I drank the 1949, some ten years ago, it was perfectly mature and the epitome of fine claret with a magnificent almost nutty aroma, and was smooth and delicate, with much complexity on the palate.

HANNS KORNELL, president and winemaker, Hanns Kornell Champagne Cellars, Napa, California: A 1900 Hungarian wine, Four Puten Tokaji Aszu. I was born in 1911. Because of my parents' delight in this event, my father bottled in 1911 the 1900 Tokaji. It was very sweet, with a dark gold color and an extremely fine bouquet. One of these bottles is still in my cellar, and before I go into the green pastures I would like to enjoy the taste with my family.

MADELINE GREENBERG, writer, *Playgirl,* New York *Sunday News Magazine,* and other publications: Chateau d'Yquem '47, tasted at a Heublein auction a couple of years ago. It was exquisitely full and complex.

EMANUEL GREENBERG, wine consultant and writer, *Playboy* and other publications: Gonzales Byass Amontillado Del Duque. It is not in regular distribution, but I'm told it may be special-ordered wherever Tio Pepe (Gonzales Byass' best-known Sherry) is sold. It is superb and bone-dry.

J. ALLAN MAYS, director of public relations, Taylor Wine Co., Hammondsport, New York: A sip of altar wine when I was an altar boy in the Episcopal Church many years ago. This was my introduction to the beverage and the start of a lifelong friendship with wine.

RICHARD H. ELWOOD, president, Llords & Elwood Winery, Beverly Hills, California: The first glass of Champagne shared with my bride immediately following the wedding ceremony.

GERARD YVERNAULT, director, wine division, Kobrand Corporation, Importers, New York City: Château Margaux 1900, which I enjoyed on my first visit at the chateau with

Bernard Ginestet, it *propriétaire;* I have always had a weakness for round numbers.

JOSEPH S. CONCANNON, JR., president and winemaker, Concannon Vineyard, Livermore, California: Beaulieu Vineyard Private Reserve Cabernet Sauvignon 1970.

ROBERT MONDAVI, president, Robert Mondavi Winery, Oakville, California: A bottle of 1893 Cabernet Sauvignon that John Daniels, when he was with Inglenook, gave me from his library. We had a special dinner to commemorate the opening of this wine. I pulled the cork three hours in advance of the dinner, and the aroma filled the entire room. It had been my pleasure to drink many old Bordeaux wines, but up to this time never had I experienced a bouquet which was more pronounced in distinctiveness and character.

MYRON NIGHTINGALE, winemaker, Beringer Vineyards, St. Helena, California: 1926 Mouton-Rothschild.

SHELDON WASSERMAN, writer, *Barron's, Les Amis de Vin:* A '29 Richebourg, Liger Bel Air.

KARL L. WENTE, president and winemaker, Wente Bros., Livermore, California: A glass of 1929 Trockenbeerenauslese Schloss Vollrads that I had at Vollrads in 1949. I remember it vividly. It was the finest Trockenbeerenauslese I have ever had.

RUSSELL T. WOODBURY, marketing manager, Cresta Blanca Winery, San Francisco, California: At the risk of sounding slightly parochial, I would say that my most memorable glass of wine contained Cresta Blanca Premier Sémillon. This was the first "boytrytized" wine ever successfully grown in the United States. Boytrytis cinerea was innoculated into the grapes in near-hothouse conditions. The resulting wine achieved a delicate sweetness and finesse akin to an exceptional year of Château d'Yquem. This wine was produced from 1959 to 1963 and, unhappily, is not in current production.

FERDINANDO D. GARBANI, hotel and restaurant manager, House of Banfi, importers, Farmingdale, New York: The wine that made my career in this industry possible, Merlot del Ticino, a visitor from France to my native Switzerland. It became one of the best locally raised and vinified grapes, producer of a simple, honest wine with brilliant ruby red color and the hidden softness of strong character.

JULIUS WILE, senior vice president, Julius Wile Sons & Co., Importers, New York City: An 1877 Chanson Clos des

Feves. When I was in Beaune visiting Chanson several years ago, they brought the wine out of their private family cellar to show me a wine made during the same year that Julius Wile Sons & Co. was founded. The wine had a fantastic bouquet, still had a great deal of body and so little sediment —quite typical of Beaune wines—that we drank every bit of it.

CHARLES S. MUELLER, executive vice president, Kobrand Corporation, importers, New York City: The 1934 Beaune Clos de Ursules of Louis Jadot which was served to me at Madame Jadot's home. The vintage chosen was in honor of my birth year.

LOUIS P. MARTINI, president, Louis M. Martini Winery, St. Helena, California: A glass of Louis Martini 1957 Pinot Noir. I drank it about three years ago. The wine had been bottled in magnums and had developed into a beautifully rounded, full-bodied Pinot Noir with a full bottle bouquet. It was allowed to breathe for about two hours and was obviously at its peak.

DANIEL MIRASSOU, president, Mirassou Vineyards, Soledad, California: Without question, Mirassou Cask '59 (1959) from our vineyard in Gilroy, California. It is an extremely rich and full-bodied yet balanced Zinfandel. The alcohol is 13.9, the total acid about .68. The last bottle I drank was two months ago. It indicated a certain amount of oxidation, which the cork promptly showed itself responsible for. It remains my favorite wine, and for those who have it properly stored with a good cork, it should live another ten years easily. I was offered a trade on my last four bottles, in exchange for anything I wanted in a certain gentleman's cellar . . . and I didn't take it.

AUGUSTIN HUNEEUS, president, Paul Masson Vineyards, Saratoga, California: The wine that influenced my decision to become associated with Paul Masson. At the time, I knew that some outstanding wines were produced in California, many of them comparable in quality to excellent vintage wines of Europe. But I was not prepared to find a truly great wine bearing a California label. However, through the settlement of an estate, I came into possession of two bottles of Paul Masson Santa Cruz Mountains Pinot Noir 1945. When I opened one of the bottles and sampled its contents, I experienced my most memorable moment in wine tasting. The wine was soft in texture, rich in body, with a subtle and evocative taste—it was superb.

Desert Island Wine

My "desert island" question really threw respondents. Most of them refused to believe I meant they could have only one bottle—a *single* bottle—for the rest of their lives. Instead, they understood me to ask (psychologists could have a field day with this one!) what *single wine* they could drink for the rest of their lives, bottle after bottle, never changing it but apparently having an unlimited quantity.

I'll save the psychological insights for another time. Suffice it to say here that both types of answers proved interesting enough to pass along. Here they are, starting with the respondents who took the desert island hypothesis seriously:

FERDINANDO D. GARBANI: This is not a choice, it is an ultimatum! A promise of a very short future, an imminent departure from this valley of tears! Faced with such a cruel fate, all dreams of future glories and all inhibitions, if any, would give way to more sober thoughts. Memories of infancy, family, friends would rush through my human attic. In order to clarify matters and put history in the right perspective, I would have to return to the wine that made it all possible, thanks to a simple and memorable initiation of many years ago—yes, Merlot del Ticino. In this crucial moment, I would reflect in its brilliant ruby red color and think of happy moments with friends, family, and wine.

RICHARD H. ELWOOD: Llords & Elwood Ancient Proverb Port. An occurrence which compelled such a decision would surely lead to reflecting on life's fondest experiences. For reminiscing, or after dinner, or in the late evening, there is no wine better suited than a fine Port.

HARRY G. SERLIS: Robert Mondavi Cabernet Sauvignon 1970. I choose this because it is fine now, holds every promise of greatness, and will unquestionably improve and outlive me. Who could ask for more?

ROBERT MONDAVI: My own 1974 Cabernet Sauvignon when it has aged fifteen years—I hope I live that long. I'm particularly partial to it, because '74 was the first year in which we kept all our wine in contact with the skins after the completion of fermentation, from eight days to two weeks. This wine has a richness and softness which I feel will have the longevity found in truly great wines, yet with a gentle authority necessary in an elegant wine.

HANNS KORNELL: I would enjoy with my family the last

bottle of that 1900 Four Puten Tokaji Aszu that my father bottled the year I was born.

SHELDON WASSERMAN: I've never had a Tokay Essence, so I would choose an Essence from that great year of the nineteenth century, 1811—the year of the comet. If I couldn't get one, I'd probably pick a great pre-phylloxera Latour, Mouton, Lafite, Margaux, or Haut Brion, because I prefer clarets to all other wines.

JOE MONOSTORI: The 1969 Parducci Private Bottling Cabernet Sauvignon. Only five hundred cases were made. It will mature perhaps in 1990. What a wine! Rich and powerful, made from one late picking at Ukiah, balling 24 degrees (a measure of the grape's sugar content).

MYRON NIGHTINGALE: My own 1970 (Beringer) Cabernet Sauvignon.

AUGSTIN HUNEEUS: Paul Masson Pinnacles Estate Selection Cabernet Sauvignon Cuvée No. 843, the first bottling from plantings that Paul Masson vineyards made in Monterey County in 1962 and 1963. The combination of soil and climate in the Pinnacles Vineyard produces an aristocratic varietal grape with a distinctive flavor.

And now for the disbelievers . . .

EMMANUEL GREENBERG: A crisp, light, fino Sherry, which is a most versatile sip, along with tapas, or any number of courses, and continually interesting. A drink you can stay with. My preference is for Tio Pepe.

MADELINE GREENBERG: A fine California Chardonnay— Chalone, Spring Mountain, Freemark Abbey, or Robert Mondavi. Heitz is good, too, but a little too much oak for my taste.

RUSSELL T. WOODBURY: Any of the top Pinot Chardonnays being produced in California today—Freemark Abbey, Stony Hill, Sterling, Spring Mountain.

LEO SHAW, metropolitan marketing manager, Frederick Wildman & Sons, Importers, New York City: Louis Latour, whom I consider the finest shipper in all of Burgundy, produces a Pinot Chardonnay, a white wine made from the Chardonnay grape, the classic grape of Montrachet and Meursault. It is light and fruity, dry without being austere, well-balanced, easy to drink. I have had it with red meat as well as white, and it holds up beautifully. While anything repetitive can be a bore, I feel I could live with this particular wine for the rest of my life. The bigger and more complex the wine, the richer is becomes—literally too rich for my blood for any sustained period of drinking and too difficult to consume daily.

JULIUS WILE: I am particularly partial to red Bordeaux, and therefore, hoping for longevity, I would pick a 1970 Chateau Cos d'Estournel. Though not quite ready for drinking now, it should last forever.

CHARLES S. MUELLER: Taittinger Comtes de Champagne, Blanc de Blancs, Brut 1969, the finest Champagne in the world, would certainly serve me well for my remaining days. While I have enjoyed a great number of extraordinary wines in my life, this particular one can be drunk any time of the day and would bring much joy.

AUGUST SEBASTIANI, president and winemaker, Sebastiani Vineyards, Sonoma, California: Zinfandel has always been my favorite for everyday drinking. It is a wine which mixes well with many meals and one you can consume frequently without getting tired of it. It is vivacious and young, and this combined with its fruitiness and bouquet make it my natural choice. I'd select Sebastiani 1972 Vintage Reserve Zinfandel.

KARL L. WENTE: I think if one has to select a single bottle of wine for the rest of his life, it should be something he is quite familiar with and has often had. I think I would settle on a Livermore Sauvignon Blanc. It would go well with most everything and also stand up with heavier dishes but is still delicate enough to go with light ones. It is a wine that I would not become tired of. (My friend Karl is too modest to say so, but his own Sauvignon Blanc, from California's Livermore Valley, is one of that state's most highly praised white wines.)

DAVID S. MILLIGAN: It would have to be one of my favorite Bordeaux chateaux, probably Latour, or possibly Lynch Bages, both typical of that great commune of Pauillac. I prefer the slightly richer style of that region, and the vintage I would pick at the moment would be 1959, which has a soft charm that makes it very appealing for immediate drinking.

LOUIS P. MARTINI: The 1968 Louis Martini Zinfandel. It is the best all-purpose wine I can think of, with the most unsatiating characteristics. I would be much less apt to tire of it day in and day out than more complex, richer wines.

DANIEL MIRASSOU: My preference changes each vintage and for each given environmental circumstance. If I'm going to marry a white wine, I suppose it would be a Chenin Blanc. Year in and out, I probably drink more of this than any other wine. My favorite vintages are 1970, 1973, and 1969, in that order. I'm biased, of course, but with the thousands of wines I've tasted in my life, most have been Mirassou, and I've grown accustomed to them.

GERARD YVERNAULT: Beaujolais-Village Jadot, current vintage. The criterion here must be versatility; I would want a wine I could drink on all occasions, whether at a formal dinner or a family picnic, and with all kinds of dishes. The most versatile wine I know is Beaujolais-Villages Jadot, current vintage. André Gagey, managing director of Maison Louis Jadot, year after year selects the most elegant and typical cuvée of Beaujolais to create a wine of distinction, in each vintage reflecting all the characteristics of that particular year.

9

Cooking with Wine

For many people, cooking with wine has taken on an aura it doesn't deserve. Brought to mind are images of an auditorium-sized kitchen, dozens of pots with creamy sauces bubbling out of them, dozens of emtpy ones hanging overhead, a staff of white-hatted sub-cooks huddling around white-hatted rank-and-file cooks, while a four-hundred-pound chef stands by gazing serenely at the tumult . . .

Well, that *is* part of the cooking-with-wine scene. But it isn't the only part. The fact is, wine cookery is no less appropriate in your average garden variety studio apartment mini-kitchen. And why should things be otherwise? Why should uncorking a bottle and pouring a liquid from it be regarded as a formidable and complicated culinary skill?

That's all there is to it. No chopping, peeling, grating—just pouring. And as a result, your food is perked up, tenderized, and flavored.

It need not be expensive, either. You needn't use your last seventy-five-dollar bottle of 1941 Beaulieu Cabernet Sauvignon. You needn't even use a three-dollar bottle. Any jug wine will do, and while sellers of expensive wines like to say that the better the wine you use, the better the dish will turn out, I happen to know that's not true. One of the most magnificent dishes of *boeuf bourgignon* I ever tasted was made not with Chambertin or Richebourg but with Taylor's Burgundy. Frankly, I wouldn't drink it except under duress (though I find some of Taylor's other wines delightful), but it worked splendidly as a cooking agent.

If you're hesitant to cook with wine because you fear adding all those calories, forget it—you won't add calories. While there are plenty of them in alcohol, the alcohol evaporates in the heat of cooking. No calories are added to the dish. Indeed, you could serve wine-cooked victuals to teetotalers (if

Wine and Food Combination Table

	Foods
Soups	Cream Soups
	Meat and Vegetable Soups
Sauces	Cream Sauce and Variations
	Brown Sauce and Variations
	Tomato Sauce
	Cheese Sauce
	Dessert Sauces
Meats	Pot Roast-Beef
	Pot Roast-Lamb and Veal
	Gravy for Roasts
	Stew-Beef
	Stew-Lamb and Veal
	Ham, Baked-Whole
	Liver, Braised
	Kidneys, Braised
	Tongue, Boiled
Fish	Broiled, Baked or Poached
Poultry & Game	Chicken, Broiled or Sautéed
	Gravy for Roast or Fried Chicken and Turkey
	Chicken Fricassee
	Duck, Roast-Wild or Tame
	Venison, Roast, Pot Roast or Stew
	Pheasant, Roasted or Sautéed
Fruit	Cups and Compotes

there are any left these days) and not violate their ethical precepts.

If the recipe you're following doesn't call for wine, don't be afraid to experiment. A dollop of wine will enhance almost any dish. Or use wine as a water substitute for stews. The table on page 131 is a good guide for wine types and volume with standard dishes.

While most dishes will benefit from wine, some absolutely demand it. Not all of these require elaborate preparation. Some, in fact, are quite simple. Herewith, some of my favorite convenience recipes.

Amount	Wine Type
1 tsp. per serving	Dry white or Sherry
1 tsp. per serving	Dry red or Sherry
1 tbsp. per cup	Dry white or Sherry
1 tbsp. per cup	Dry red or Sherry
1 tbsp. per cup	Dry red or Sherry
1 tbsp. per cup	Dry white or Sherry
1 tbsp. per cup	Port
¼ cup per lb.	Dry red
¼ cup per lb.	Dry white
2 tbsps. per cup	Dry red, white or Sherry
¼ cup per lb.	Dry red
¼ cup per lb.	Dry white
2 cups (for basting)	Port
¼ cup per lb.	Dry red or white
¼ cup per lb.	Dry red or Sherry
½ cup per lb.	Dry red
½ cup per lb.	Dry white
¼ cup per lb.	Dry white or red
2 tbsps. per cup	Dry white, red or Sherry
¼ cup per lb.	Dry white
¼ cup per lb.	Dry red
¼ cup per lb.	Dry red
¼ cup per lb.	Dry white, red or Sherry
1 tbsp. per serving	Dry white, red, rosé, Sherry or Port

Snacks to Serve at Wine Tastings

Party Steak Pot

2 pounds tender beef steak, cut about 1 inch thick
¼ cup butter
1½ teaspoons plain or seasoned salt
⅔ cup dry white or rosé wine
¼ cup catsup
2 teaspoons cornstarch
¼ teaspoon dried dill
Black pepper
Assorted crackers and other snack breads

Trim all excess fat from meat, then cut steak into bite-size cubes about ½ inch thick (2 pounds of beef should produce about 48 cubes). Brown steak quickly in heated butter, turning and sprinkling meat with salt during browning. Do not crowd the skillet with beef chunks; this will prevent even browning.

When browned, cubes should be transferred to chafing dish or other serving container. Blend wine, catsup, cornstarch, dill and pepper to taste; stir into pan drippings. Cook and stir until mixture boils and thickens. Then pour over steak cubes, stirring to combine meat and sauce. Serve with fondue forks or long cocktail picks for spearing meat. (Serves 8 to 10.)

Fondue

3 oz. Gruyère cheese per person
3 oz. Emmenthal cheese per person
1 clove garlic (optional)
4 oz. dry white wine per person

1 oz. Kirsch (a spirit distilled from cherries) for every 3 persons
2 teaspoons cornstarch
Dash each, nutmeg and white pepper
Cubes of bread

Shred cheese. If desired, cut garlic in half and rub into inside of fondue pot, chafing dish, or top of double boiler. Discard garlic, pour in wine, add cheese, and cook over low heat or boiling water, stirring constantly, until cheese melts and mixture is smooth. Blend cornstarch with kirsch (you may substitute brandy or Sherry) and stir into mixture. Add nutmeg and pepper. Stir 4 to 5 minutes longer, until smooth and slightly thickened.

Serve at once, keeping fondue hot over spirit lamp or candle warmer. Each guest in turn spears a cube of bread with a wood pick or fondue fork, dips it into the pot, and twirls it to keep the fondue on the bread.

Appetizers

Sherried Olives

1 8-oz. can pitted ripe olives
Dry Sherry

Drain liquid from olives and discard. Place olives in pint jar or other container with cover. Add enough Sherry to cover completely. Cover and let stand overnight. Drain olives and serve with salad or as an appetizer. (Remaining Sherry can be used to flavor meat or fish.)

VARIATIONS: If desired, add one of the following to the olives and Sherry: 1 clove garlic, sliced; a few fennel seeds; a little oregano and basil; ½ teaspoon hickory liquid smoke; dash of Tabasco sauce.

Stuffed Celery Rounds

1 celery heart
1 cup grated Cheddar cheese
Dry white wine

Separate celery stalks and trim to an even length. Dry thoroughly. Blend cheese with enough wine to make a stiff paste. Fill stalks with the cheese, generously. Reshape them, placing smaller stalks together first and arranging larger ones around them. Press together closely. Wrap and chill thoroughly. Cut into thick slices to serve. (About 16.)

Sherry Sesame Sticks

10 oz. pie crust mix
Dash salt
 1 cup grated sharp Cheddar
    cheese
¼ cup dry Sherry
 2 tablespoons sesame seeds

Combine pie crust mix, salt and cheese, mixing lightly with a fork. (If sticks of pastry mix are used, crumble them into a bowl.) Add Sherry and mix until other ingredients are evenly moistened; shape dough into a ball. Roll to a 12-inch square on lightly floured board. Sprinkle sesame seeds evenly over dough and roll lightly with rolling pin to press seeds into dough. Cut into strips 3″ × ¾″. Arrange on ungreased baking sheets. Bake at 450° for 8 to 10 minutes. Remove to wire rack to cool before storing in an airtight container. (About 4 dozen.)

Sherried Appetizer Roll

 5 eggs, separated   Ham filling
½ teaspoon cream of tartar   Olive nut filling

⅓ cup dry Sherry
¾ cup sifted all-purpose flour
1 teaspoon salt
1 teaspoon baking powder
2 tablespoons fine dry bread crumbs

Egg filling
2 3-oz. packages cream cheese
2 tablespoons light cream or milk

Beat egg whites with cream of tartar until very stiff. With same beater, beat yolks well. Add wine and beat again. Resift flour with salt and baking powder. Add to egg yolk-wine mixture, and beat until smooth. Pour over egg whites, and fold in carefully. Turn into jelly roll pan (10″ by 15″ by 1″) lined with greased waxed paper and sprinkled with crumbs. Bake at 350° for 15 minutes.

Invert pan onto damp towel, and strip off waxed paper. Fold towel over roll, and cool completely before filling. When roll is cold, spread ham filling over ⅓ the length, olive nut filling across second ⅓, egg filling over last ⅓. Roll up as for jelly roll. Soften cream cheese and mix with cream or milk. Spread over top and sides of roll. Chill well before slicing. (Serves 8.)

Ham Filling: Mix 1 cup finely chopped or ground cooked ham with ¼ cup mayonnaise, 2 teaspoons dry Sherry and 3 tablespoons minced green pepper.

Egg Filling: Chop 4 hard-cooked eggs. Add 1 teaspoon prepared mustard, ¼ cup mayonnaise, ½ teaspoon salt and 2 tablespoons each chopped parsley and pimiento.

Olive Nut Filling: Combine ½ cup chopped ripe olives, ¼ cup chopped walnuts, 1½ tablespoons chopped pimiento and ¼ cup mayonnaise, and mix well.

Tomato-wine Aperitif

4/5 qt. Riesling or other dry white wine
2¼ cups tomato juice
2 drops Tabasco sauce

½ teaspon Worcestershire sauce or 1 teaspoon soy sauce
½ teaspoon seasoned salt
Ice cubes, 1 tray

Combine all ingredients, mixing until blended, chill. Serve

in chilled glasses. Garnish with lemon wedges or pickled vegetables on skewers. (Makes 10 4-oz. servings.)

Soups

Savory Chicken Chowder

4 pounds frying chicken pieces	2 cups Pinot Blanc or other dry white wine
1 onion	2 cups diced pared potato
6 whole cloves	1 lb. cream-style corn
2 carrots	2 cups light cream or whole milk
2 stalks celery	2 tablespoons finely chopped parsley
4 teaspoons salt	
1 bay leaf	
3 cups water	

Place chicken in large kettle. Peel onion and stud with whole cloves. Add to chicken along with pared carrots, celery, 3 teaspoons salt, bay leaf, water and 1 cup wine. Bring to a boil, lower heat, cover, and simmer until chicken is tender, about 1 hour. Remove chicken and vegetables from stock. Add potatoes to liquid and simmer until tender. Meanwhile, remove skin and bones from chicken; cut meat into generous chunks. Discard bay leaf, whole cloves. Puree vegetables removed from stock by mashing or blending smooth in blender. Return chicken pieces and vegetable mixture to soup. Add remaining salt and wine, corn and light cream. Heat slowly until piping hot. Sprinkle with parsley just before serving. (Serves 6 to 8.)

Sherried Cheese Soup

½ cup finely chopped onion	1½ cups dry Sherry
½ cup butter or margarine	2 cups shredded sharp cheddar cheese
⅔ cup sifted flour	⅔ cup toasted almonds
2 teaspoons seasoned chicken stock base	⅔ cup crisp-cooked bacon
1 teaspoon dry mustard	⅓ cup each chopped green pepper and pimiento
1 teaspoon paprika	
1 teaspoon salt	
5 cups milk	

Cook onion in butter or margarine until soft but not

browned. Blend in flour, chicken stock base, mustard, paprika, and salt. Gradually stir in milk. Cook, stirring frequently, over moderate heat until mixture boils and thickens. Stir in Sherry and cheese. Continue to heat slowly until cheese melts. Serve hot with toasted almonds, crisp bacon, chopped pimiento and green pepper, and additional Sherry for final seasoning. (Makes about 1½ qts.)

Veal Vegetable Soup

3 lb. veal shanks	¾ cup chopped onion
2½ quarts water	1 cup sliced celery
1½ cups Sémillon or other semi-dry white wine	1 cup sliced carrot
	1½ cups sliced potato
1 bay leaf	1 lb. tomatoes
1 tablespoon salt	10 oz. corn
¼ teaspoon powdered thyme	2 tablespoons chopped parsley
1 clove garlic, minced	

Combine veal shanks, water, wine, bay leaf, salt, thyme and garlic, and simmer 1 to 1½ hours, until meat is very tender. Cool sufficiently to handle, and remove bones and gristle from meat. Dice veal and return to broth. Add onion, celery, carrot, potato and tomatoes, and simmer until vegetables are tender (about 20 minutes). Add corn and cook 5 minutes longer. Remove bay leaf, and sprinkle soup with parsley. (Makes 3 qts.)

Gazpacho

1 clove garlic	¼ cup chopped green pepper
1½ cups tomato juice	
½ cup dry red wine	1 tablespoon wine vinegar
1½ cups peeled and diced fresh tomatoes	1 teaspoon salt
	¼ teaspoon pepper
⅓ cup diced cucumber	Few drops liquid hot pepper seasoning
¼ cup minced green onion	

Rub bowl with cut clove garlic. Discard garlic. Combine all ingredients in seasoned bowl and mix well. Chill for 4 hours before serving. (Serves 4 to 6.)

Main Courses

Glazed Pork Loin

1 center-cut pork loin roast (about 4½ to 5 lbs.)	⅓ cup medium Sherry
1 teaspoon salt	3 tablespoons catsup
¼ teaspoon pepper	1½ tablespoons soy sauce
	1½ tablespoons honey

Rub pork with salt and pepper and place in shallow roasting pan. Roast at 325° for 3 hours. (If meat thermometer is used, internal temperature should be 180°.) Combine Sherry with all remaining ingredients. Spoon over roast, and bake 30 minutes longer, basting frequently with Sherry mixture, until roast is nicely glazed. Meat thermometer should register 185° when meat is done. (Serves 8.)

Filet of Sole Florentine

3 large bunches fresh spinach	2 tablespoons butter
½ teaspoon onion powder	2½ tablespoons flour
1 teaspoon salt	⅔ cup light cream or whole milk
Dash white pepper	⅓ cup Sémillon or other semi-dry white wine
Dash mace	
1¼ pounds filet of sole	¼ cup grated Swiss cheese
1¼ teaspoons seasoned salt	Paprika
1½ tablespoons chopped parsley	

Wash spinach well and remove coarse stems. Cook in only the water clinging to the leaves, and just until wilted. Drain well and chop. Drain again, squeezing out all excess moisture. Mix with onion powder, ½ teaspoon salt, pepper and mace. Turn into shallow 1¼-quart baking dish. Sprinkle sole with seasoned salt and parsley. Roll up filets and place on top of spinach. Melt butter and blend in flour. Stir in cream or milk, and cook, stirring, until sauce begins to thicken. Add wine and remaining ½ teaspoon salt. Cook until sauce boils. Remove from heat, and stir in 3 tablespoons cheese. Spoon over sole and spinach. Sprinkle with remaining tablespoon cheese and paprika. Bake at 350° until sole is cooked through (about 25 minutes). (Serves 4.)

Wine-Poached Prawns

1 pound shelled deveined prawns or large shrimp	1 cup sliced fresh brown mushrooms
½ cup Pinot Blanc or other dry white wine	1 cup chopped celery
1½ cups chicken broth	½ cup sliced green onion
¼ teaspoon basil, dill or fine herbs	2 tablespoons cornstarch
	1 tablespoon lemon juice
½ teaspoon celery salt	2 tablespoons dry Sherry
½ teaspoon paprika	1 tablespoon finely chopped parsley

Rinse and drain prawns or shrimp; turn into large skillet. Pour on wine and broth. Add herbs, salt and paprika. Cover and simmer until prawns turn pink and are tender (about 10 minutes). Add mushrooms; simmer 5 minutes. Add celery and onion; simmer 5 minutes. Blend cornstarch with lemon juice and Sherry. Stir into sauce. Cook and stir until smooth and thickened. Add parsley and salt to taste. (Serves 5 to 6.)

Beef Stew

3 pounds lean beef stew meat	1 beef bouillon cube
	¾ pound small boiling onions
1½ teaspoons salt	
½ teaspoon pepper	2 cups fresh mushrooms, halved
½ teaspoon paprika	
¼ teaspoon allspice	2 cups zucchini chunks
2 tablespoons oil	2 tablespoons cornstarch
2 cups plus 2 tablespoons full-bodied red dry wine	

Cut beef in 1½-inch cubes. Mix salt, pepper, paprika and allspice; sprinkle over meat. Heat oil, and brown meat slowly on all sides. Add 2 cups wine and bouillon cube, and heat to boiling. Cover, and place in oven. Bake at 300° for 1½ hours. Meanwhile, prepare vegetables. Peel onions, cover with water, and boil 10 minutes. Drain. After meat has cooked 1½ hours, add onions, mushrooms and zucchini. Cover, and return to oven until vegetables are tender (30 to 40 minutes). Blend cornstarch with remaining 2 tablespoons wine, and stir into stew. Heat to boiling, stirring gently, and cook until gravy is slightly thickened. (Serves 8.)

Chicken with Vegetables, Chinese style

3 large half-breasts of chicken, boned and skinned
1 teaspoon powdered ginger
¾ teaspoon salt
¼ teaspoon paprika
2 tablespoons oil
1½ cups diagonally sliced celery, ¼ inch thick

½ cup green pepper strips
½ cup coarsely chopped onion
1 lb. sliced baby tomatoes
½ cup rosé wine
2 tablespoons soy sauce
1 tablespoon cornstarch
1 tablespoon cold water

Remove bones and skin from chicken. Cut chicken into strips 2½″ × ½″. Mix ginger, salt, and paprika, and toss with chicken strips. Heat oil in skillet, add chicken pieces, and sauté 5 minutes over moderate heat, stirring frequently. Push chicken to one side, add fresh vegetables, and stir-fry for 5 minutes. Add tomatoes, wine, and soy sauce; heat to simmering. Turn heat low, cover, and cook 5 minutes. Blend cornstarch with cold water, stir into mixture. Cook, stirring constantly, until sauce boils and thickens slightly. (Serves 4.)

Vegetables

Fresh Vegetable Casserole

6 potatoes, pared and sliced
4 tomatoes, diced
3 carrots sliced
¾ cup diced celery
2 onions, chopped
2 cloves garlic, minced
3 tablespoons chopped parsley

1 green pepper, sliced
1½ teaspoons salt
1 cup water
¾ cup Sherry
¼ cup salad oil

Place potatoes in shallow baking dish. Mix remaining ingredients and place on top of potatoes. Bake at 375° until potatoes are tender (45 to 60 minutes). Serve hot or cold. (Serves 6 to 8.)

Marinated Mushrooms

1 pound fresh mushrooms   ½ cup salad oil
¼ cup dry red wine   1 tablespoon garlic salt

Rinse mushrooms well under running water; remove and discard stems; drain caps. Combine wine with oil and garlic salt; pour over mushroom caps and allow to marinate for several hours or overnight. Stir occasionally. Serve on cocktail picks. (Makes 20 to 25 mushrooms.)

Barbecue Potato Casserole

1 qt. small whole cooked   ¼ teaspoon dried dill
  potatoes   ½ teaspoon garlic salt
½ cup Sémillon or other   1 tablespoon wine vinegar
  semi-dry white wine   ¼ cup mayonnaise
¼ cup salad oil   ½ cup sour cream
4 or 5 finely chopped   Crisp cooked bacon, crum-
  green onions   bled

Gently combine hot potatoes, wine, oil, onions, dill, salt and vinegar; marinate for 1 hour. Add mayonnaise and sour cream, and turn into small casserole or baking pan. Heat at 350° or on barbecue grill until potatoes are hot (about 20 to 30 minutes). Top with crumbled bacon. (Serves 5 to 6.)

Tomatoes with Relish Rice

½ cup dry white wine   3 tablespoons chopped
1 cup water   pimiento
2 chicken bouillon cubes   1½ tablespoons finely
½ teaspoon salt   chopped green onion
¾ cup long grain rice   ⅓ cup mayonnaise
⅓ cup chopped green pep-   2 tablespoons wine vinegar
  per   6 large tomatoes
⅓ cup chopped celery

Combine wine, water, bouillon cubes, and salt, and heat to boiling. Stir in rice, cover and cook over low heat for 20 minutes. Cool. Combine green pepper, celery, pimiento, onion, mayonnaise and wine vinegar, and toss lightly with rice. Peel tomatoes, cut a slice from top of each, and scoop out insides. Drain tomatoes unside down, then heap with rice mixture. Serve will chilled. (Serves 6.)

10

The Wine Mixologist

"We Spaniards like wine," observes Juan de Ayala Cortes, Prince of Spain. "We Spaniards like fruit. So what could be more natural than to mix the two? We call the combination sangría, and I have never met a person who didn't like it."

Neither have I. Sangría caught the fancy of North Americans during the Spanish tourist boom of the mid-1960's and has become one of the most popular leisure-time drinks of the U.S. and Canada. Actually, it's only one of many wine combinations that can multiply your beverage serving options at a fraction of the price of other drinks.

Most wine lovers bristle at the thought of altering even slightly the taste of their favorite *vino*, let alone mixing it with anything so taste-dominant as fruit. The trick is, don't use your favorite. Use the least expensive wine of a given type that you can find. The other ingredients will mask the wine's defects, the result being a pleasant—though by no means sophisticated or complex—refreshment.

The practice of mixing probably developed in the Mediterranean countries during the summer. Wine was, and still is, the standard mealtime beverage, but it isn't a real thirst-quencher, so thirsty Mediterraneans took to stretching it with mineral water. Also, no doubt, people found that certain inexpensively made wines lost their character between harvests, a result of both oxidation and the summer heat. Adding fruit and/or fruit juices masked the unpleasant, stale taste.

Both approaches persist in Mediterranean countries today. It's very common to find patrons of a *trattoria* or *brasserie* on a hot day ordering a carafe of wine and a bottle of mineral water and mixing equal parts or two parts of water to one of wine. I stress, one does not (unless shamefully extravagant) use an expensive wine.

In Spanish *cafés* during the summer, sangría outsells wine

two- or three-to-one. Again, you do not make it with your 1938 Marquès de Riscal. Any jug wine will do. In fact, some people—I among them—whip up a batch of sangría every time they come upon an otherwise undrinkable bottle of wine. This might be the remaining half of a gallon jug that you left standing for a week; oxidation has rendered the wine unpalatable, but adding fruit, particularly citrus, neutralizes the off-taste: meanwhile, the alcohol remains, and the result is a totally acceptable—indeed, delightful— refreshment.

Other occasions for sangría-making might be when you buy a bottle that has maderized or has a faulty cork, or when you experiment with your favorite wine merchant's *el cheapo* special and find you can't stomach it straight, or when a bottle in your cellar falls victim to a bad cork, heat, or some other wine-destroyer. As long as the wine hasn't actually turned to vinegar, chances are you can save it.

Of course, you can make sangría from unspoiled wine, also. Or if you're really lazy and don't mind paying two or three dollars for something you yourself can prepare for 50 to 75 cents, you can buy ready-bottled sangría.

There are many other wine preparations currently being marketed, including one from Taiwan that I number among my favorites: New Dynasty Plum Wine. It's great on the rocks with a sprig of mint. In addition to the plum base, the blend includes tea. This provides a tannic quality which plums do not possess but which is imparted to grape-based wines by the skins, seeds, and stems.

In sum, wine mixtures are refreshing, only mildly alcoholic, a great way to use otherwise unusable wine, and—if you presently have no unusable wine—a good way to get maximum volume and satisfaction from inexpensive wines. On the budget side, consider this: two gallons of sangría, including the fruit, can be made for under five dollars. The punch can serve a party of twenty to thirty people without leaving anyone of normal appetite thirsty. To serve just one can of beer each to thirty people would cost about nine dollars.

Herewith some recipes for aspiring wine mixologists.

Cold Drinks

Sangría

1 grapefruit
½ gallon dry wine (white or red)
½ gallon apple juice
1 lemon
1 orange

2 pieces of noncitrus fruit seasonally available (my favorite choices are peaches, pears, apples and strawberries)

Cut the grapefruit into quarters or eighths, combine with wine and apple juice. Cover and let stand in refrigerator or cool room for 16 to 32 hours. (Standing time of less than 16 hours will produce a palatable drink but lacking some of the tartness that the liquid absorbs from the grapefruit skins.) Slice thin wheels of orange and lemon, add to mixture, let stand another 2 hours. Dice remaining noncitrus fruit, let stand another 15 minutes. Serve over ice or from punch bowl filled wih ice. (Makes about 1 gallon before ice is added; serves 20 to 30 light sippers or 8 to 10 thirsty guests.)

Tomato Cooler

1 fifth dry or semi-dry white wine
18 oz. tomato juice
Juice of ½ lemon
1 tablespoon Worcestershire sauce

1 small cucumber, thinly sliced
1 pimiento-stuffed green olive per person
Ice cubes

Chill all ingredients beforehand. Then combine wine, tomato juice, lemon juice and Worcestershire sauce in tall pitcher. For garnish, twist ends of cucumber slice around green olive, sliding onto a bamboo skewer. Serve over ice.

Optional additional garnish: lemon slices sprinkled lightly with dill weed. Another interesting option: instead of using ordinary ice cubes, freeze tomato juice in ice tray and put 2 or 3 cubes in each glass. This keeps drink from becoming diluted, as with ordinary ice. (Makes about 1 quart before poured over ice.)

Sherried Grapefruit Cocktail

6 oz. frozen grapefruit juice 1½ cups cold water
 concentrate ¾ cup dry Sherry, chilled

Shake all ingredients together and serve very cold, in prechilled glasses. (8 servings.)

Golden Frappe

⅓ cup sweet white wine 2 teaspoons lemon juice
⅓ cup orange juice Finely crushed ice
 2 teaspoons sugar

Stir sugar into wine-orange juice mixture until it dissolves. Stir in lemon juice. Pour over finely crushed ice in Tom Collins glass or large stemmed glass. Serve with a straw. (1 tall serving.)

Red Lemonade

Juice of 1 lemon 8 to 10 oz. cold dry red wine
1½ teaspoons superfine 2 slices lemon
 sugar
 6 oz. cracked ice

Combine wine and lemon juice. Add sugar and stir to dissolve. Pour over cracked ice in a tall glass and garnish with lemon slices. (1 tall serving.)

Spritzer

1 lemon 4 oz. cold club soda
6 oz. cold dry white wine Ice cubes

With a small, sharp knife, carefully peel the lemon in a spiral, as you would an apple. The peel should be in 1 piece, resembling a corkscrew. Drop the peel into the glass, add ice cubes and white wine, and fill the glass with cold club soda. (1 tall serving.)

Vermouth Cocktail

2 cups dry Vermouth 5 stuffed green olives or pearl
2 teaspoons fresh lime or onions
 lemon juice

5 twists lime or lemon peel   Ice cubes

Measure Vermouth and lime juice into cocktail shaker or pint jar. Add ice and stir vigorously until mix is well chilled. Pour into cocktail or all-purpose glasses, adding twist of lime peel and stuffed olive or onion to each glass. (20 servings.)

Orange Cooler

1 quart orange juice
2 cups semi-dry Sherry
 or white wine
Powdered sugar to taste

Sprigs of mint and orange
 slices for garnishing
Ice cubes

Mix 2 parts orange juice to 1 part wine, sweeten to taste, serve over ice cubes in tall glasses. Garnish each cooler with a sprig of mint and a half slice of orange.

Tomato Vermouth

2 cups chilled tomato juice
1 cup dry Vermouth

2 tablespoons fresh lemon
 juice

Shake well together and chill before serving. (8 servings.)

Red Fruit Freeze

1 fifth dry red wine
6 oz. frozen concentrate for
 raspberry-lemon punch

6 oz. water
Juice of 1 lemon
12 sprigs of fresh mint

Mix and freeze in ice cube trays until crystallized, like a frappé cocktail. Spoon into frosted wine glasses and drink with short straws. Garnish with mint. (12 servings.)

Golden Cocktail

1 pint chilled apple juice
1 cup dry Vermouth

Peel of 1 lemon

Stir apple juice and Vermouth together; chill thoroughly. Serve with twist of lemon peel in each glass. (8 servings.)

Frosty Pineapple Cream

1½ cups sweet white wine
1 pint vanilla ice cream
⅛ teaspoon salt
¼ teaspoon ginger

8½-oz. can crushed pineapple
Chilled sparkling water or ginger ale

Blend all but sparkling water or ginger ale in electric blender or with eggbeater. Pour ½ cup of mixture into tall glass. Fill with sparkling water or ginger ale; stir gently. (6 servings.)

Guava Cooler

1 fifth dry red wine
12 oz. guava nectar
1 tablespoon lemon juice
1 cup lemon-lime carbonated beverage

1 pint large stemmed strawberries
Ice cubes

Chill all ingredients thoroughly. Just before serving, combine wine, guava nectar, lemon juice and carbonated beverage in punch bowl. Garnish with strawberries and serve over ice. (9 servings.)

Garden Cooler

2 cups boiling water
2 tablespoons tea leaves
1 cup dry red wine
1 cup orange juice

¼ cup lemon juice
⅔ cup sugar to taste
Sprigs of fresh mint
Ice cubes

Pour boiling water over tea leaves; let stand 5 minutes. Stir, then strain. Combine strained tea with wine, orange juice, lemon juice, and sugar. Chill thoroughly. To serve, pour over ice in tall glasses. Garnish each serving with a sprig of mint. (4 servings.)

Fruited Wine Cooler

1 cup sliced hulled strawberries
¼ cup sugar
1 tablespoon lemon juice

1 fifth chilled dry red wine
1 banana, sliced
Cracked ice

Crush strawberries with sugar, lemon juice and 1 cup wine. Cover and chill. Strain and discard pulp. Combine strawberry essence with remaining chilled wine. Pour over cracked ice. Garnish with skewer of strawberries and banana slices. (4 servings.)

Champagne Cooler

1 bunch grapes	12 pineapple chunks
½ cantaloupe, scooped into balls	2 cups dry red wine
	1 fifth Champagne

Drop a grape, cantaloupe ball or pineapple chunk into each division of an ice cube tray, add red wine and freeze. Place 3 to 5 cubes in a tall glass and fill with chilled Champagne.

NOTE: Wine cubes do not freeze into solid blocks like ice made with water. They have an attractive crackled appearance and come out of the tray easily. They will thaw rapidly and should be used at once. (4 servings.)

Sherried Orange Nog

3 eggs	2 to 3 tablespoons sugar
1 cup dry or medium Sherry	⅛ teaspoon cinnamon
½ cup orange juice	¼ teaspoon nutmeg
½ cup milk	

Beat eggs until light and fluffy. Beat in all remaining ingredients until blended, adding sugar to taste. Serve well chilled. (4 servings.)

Spiced Wine Punch

24 whole cloves	6 oz. frozen lemonade concentrate
24 whole allspice	
1 tablespoon broken cinnamon sticks	48 oz. pineapple juice, chilled
1 medium-sized ginger root	2 fifths dry red wine, chilled
1 cup sugar	1 quart sparkling water, chilled
2 cups water	Block of ice

Combine spices, sugar and water; boil 15 minutes. Cool and strain. In a punch bowl mix spiced syrup and frozen lemonade concentrate. Stir in pineapple juice and wine. Add block of ice. Just before serving, add sparkling water. Garnish with clove-studded orange slices. (50 servings.)

Hacienda Wedding Punch

6 oranges	2 cups lemon juice
6 lemons	½ gallon dry white wine
4 cups sugar	2 fifths Champagne
2 cups water	2 fifths sparkling water
½ cup white corn syrup	Block of ice
¼ teaspoon salt	
2 quarts pineapple or orange juice	

Peel oranges and lemons. Cut peel in thin strips, place in saucepan. Add sugar, water, syrup and salt. Bring to boil, stirring to dissolve sugar. Lower heat; simmer 15 minutes. Cover and cool; remove peel. Add cold flavored syrup to fruit juices and white wine. Pour over block of ice in large punch bowl. Let stand about ½ hour, stirring once or twice. Add well-chilled Champagne and sparkling water immediately before serving. Orange and lemon peels may be used again as garnishes.

NOTE: Large blocks of ice in the punch bowl dilute the punch much less than ice cubes. To save time, make your own blocks by freezing in ice trays without cube dividers. Add color to ice blocks by using fruit juice instead of water, or by freezing fruit or flowers in the liquid. (80 servings.)

Hot Drinks

Some like 'em hot, especially for winter picnics and aprés-ski parties. Hot wine drinks that are spiced and sweetened are called "mulls" or "mulled wine." Originally, they were heated with a red-hot poker thrust into the crock of wine. Today, it's much easier to rely on a saucepan on top of your stove or in your fireplace.

Mulled Red Punch

¼ cup brown sugar	¼ teaspoon powdered cardamom
2 teaspoons dehydrated	

orange peel
2 teaspoons powdered
  cloves

1 teaspoon powdered cinnamon
2 gallons sweet red wine

Mix sugar, orange peel and spices thoroughly. Tie 1 teaspoon of mixture in small square of cheesecloth or stuff into emptied teabag. Simmer wine, but do not bring to boil (boiling makes alcohol evaporate).

In a mug, pour ½ of wine over bag of spices. Let steep for several seconds, then remove bag to serve. One bag should flavor 28 servings. Store unused spice mixture in airtight container. (28 servings.)

Skiers Punch

1 fifth dry red wine
1 quart Hawaiian punch
1 bay leaf

6-inch-strip lemon peel,
  ½ inch wide

Combine all ingredients and heat slowly for 10 minutes, but do not allow to boil. Serve hot. Lemon peel is kept in the punch bowl as a garnish. (Makes about ½ gallon.)

Hot Sherried Lemonade

1 teaspoon whole cloves
1 teaspoon whole allspice
1 stick cinnamon

1 quart lemonade
1 fifth dry Sherry
1 cup water

Combine spices in 1 cup water and boil 5 minutes. Add lemonade and wine, heat to simmer. Serve. (Makes about ½ gallon.)

Olympic Wine Torch

3 cups apple juice
20 whole cloves
4 cinnamon sticks
Peel of 1 lemon, cut into
  strips

Juice of 1 lemon
1 fifth dry red wine
1 fifth sweet red wine (Port
  is ideal)
½ cup brandy

Simmer apple juice, cloves, cinnamon and lemon peel 15 minutes. Strain, add lemon juice, wines, simmer again. Heat brandy, ignite it and ladle slowly into hot wine. Serve in pre-heated mugs, cups or glasses. (25 servings.)

Swedish Glog

¾ cup light or dark raisins
1 tablespoon whole cardamom
2 teaspoons whole cloves
3-inch cinnamon stick
1½ cups water
1 fifth dry red wine
½ cup sugar
¼ cup blanched almonds

Rinse and drain raisins; peel and crush cardamom, using mortar and pestle or sturdy knife. Combine cardamon, cinnamon stick, cloves, ½ cup of raisins and water; simmer ½ hour. Strain and add liquid to wine; stir in sugar and heat to simmering. Serve hot, with almonds and raisins in each cup. (12 servings.)

Merry Sherry

2 cups Sherry
6 cinnamon sticks
¼ cup sugar
¼ cup lemon juice
1 lemon, thinly sliced

Heat Sherry with 1 stick cinnamon and sugar, just to boiling. Add lemon juice and pour into pre-heated cups. Garnish each cup with thin slice of lemon and cinnamon stick for stirring. (5 servings.)

After-Ski Bowl

12 very small apples
3 or 4 tablespoons white corn syrup
¼ cup sugar
½ teaspoon cinnamon
3 cups dry white wine
1½ cups apple cider
¼ teaspoon nutmeg
Peel of 1 lemon

Roll apples in corn syrup to coat, then in mixed sugar and cinnamon; bake at 400° F. for 15 minutes. Meanwhile mix and heat other ingredients for 15 minutes over very low heat. Serve in wide mugs, pre-heated; float one of the apples in each mug. (12 servings.)

Cinnamon Sherry Toddy

1 quart eggnog (commercially prepared or home-made from any standard recipe)
1 cup Sherry
¼ teaspoon cinnamon
1 cup milk
¼ teaspoon salt
1 egg white
16 cinnamon sticks

Mix eggnog, Sherry and powdered cinnamon; beat well. Stir in milk and salt; heat gently to below boiling. Beat egg white to soft peaks; fold into hot nog. Serve with cinnamon sticks for stirring. (16 servings.)

Minted Spiced Red Punch

1 quart apple juice
2 sticks cinnamon
1 teaspoon spearmint leaves
¼ cup sugar
1 fifth dry red wine

Simmer apple juice, cinnamon and spearmint leaves together 5 minutes. Add sugar and wine. Reheat and strain into heat-proof glasses. (10 servings.)

Spiced Tea

1 quart boiling water
1½ tablespoons black tea (or 4 tea bags)
¼ teaspoon ground allspice
¼ teaspoon ground cloves
16 cinnamon sticks
½ to ⅔ cup sugar
1 cup orange juice
2 cups sweet red wine
1 fifth dry red wine

Combine boiling water with tea, allspice and cloves; add sugar to taste. Cover and let stand 10 minutes. Strain out tea, add orange juice and wine, reheat. Serve with cinnamon stick for stirring. (16 servings.)

Pomegranate Warmer

4 fresh pomegranates
½ cup sugar
1 fifth sweet white wine
(Optional: 1 cup sweet red wine)

Cut pomegranates in halves and squeeze, using an orange reamer. Pour juice through a fine sieve to strain out seeds.

Add sugar and stir until dissolved. Add wine, and heat just to simmering.

Optional: if deeper color is desired, add red wine. NOTE: punch can be made with grenadine syrup instead of fresh pomegranates; use ¾ to 1 cup. (7 servings.)

Honey-Buttered Sherry

1 fifth Sherry	2 sticks (3-inch) cinnamon
½ cup honey	1 strip (3-inch) orange peel
½ cup unflavored wine vine- gar	1 strip (3-inch) lemon peel
	6 teaspoons butter

Combine wine, honey, vinegar, cinnamon, and peels. Bring to boil, lower heat, and simmer 10 minutes. Remove cinnamon and peels. Drop 1 teaspoon butter into each serving cup. Pour hot wine and stir. Cinnamon stick and peels may be used again as garnishes. (Makes about 1 quart.)

Red Nectar

1 fifth dry red wine	3 cups papaya nectar
¼ cup sugar	

Combine all ingredients and heat to simmering. Serve hot in heat-proof glasses. (10 servings.)

Herbed Wine

1 fifth dry white wine	½ teaspoon dried basil
¼ teaspoon dill seeds	2 tablespoons sugar
½ teaspoon rosemary leaves	1 tablespoon lemon juice

Combine all ingredients and heat to simmering. Strain and serve hot in heat-proof glasses. (6 servings.)

Spiced Red Punch

1 cup granulated sugar	½ teaspoon whole cloves
½ cup brown sugar	½ teaspoon anise seeds
1¾ cups water	½ teaspoon powdered ginger
⅓ cup lemon juice	1 strip orange peel
2 sticks cinnamon	½ gallon dry red wine

Combine sugars, water, lemon juice, spices, and orange

peel. Bring to boil, lower heat, and simmer 10 minutes. Strain and discard whole spices and peel. Combine the spiced syrup and wine, and heat to simmering, either in electric coffee maker or large pan. Serve hot. (Makes about 10 cups.)

Classic Mulled Wine

½ cup sugar	⅛ teaspoon nutmeg
¼ teaspoon cinnamon	⅛ teaspoon cardamom
¼ teaspoon allspice	1 fifth dry red wine
¼ teaspoon cloves	

Thoroughly mix sugar with spices. Heat wine. Pour about ½ cup wine into each glass. Add about 1 tablespoon spice-sugar mix, and stir until dissolved. Serve in mugs or heat-proof glasses. (6 servings.)

Mulled Sherry

1 package sweetened lemonade mix	½ teaspoon cinnamon
	½ teaspoon cloves
1 cup orange-flavored instant breakfast drink	1 fifth Sherry
	Optional: 1 fifth apple cider

Combine lemonade mix, orange-flavored breakfast drink, cinnamon and cloves, and mix well. Store in airtight container. When ready to serve, spoon 1 tablespoon of the dry mixture into heat-proof mug or glass. Heat Sherry to simmering. Pour desired amount into each mug, stir to blend flavors.

Optional: Before heating Sherry, mix with equal volume cider. (12 servings.)

Wassail Bowle

6 apples	3 cloves
1 cup sugar	1 tablespoon grated lemon rind
2 fifths Sherry	
½ teaspoon nutmeg	4 eggs
½ teaspoon cinnamon	

Bake apples, cored and filled with sugar. Meanwhile, in double boiler, heat Sherry with spices, ½ cup sugar, and lemon rind. Beat 4 egg yolks and whites separately until whites are stiff; fold together. Add hot wine slowly to eggs; beat until frothy. Put baked apples in bowl and pour hot liquid over. Serve in heat-proof glasses.

NOTE: the name wassail comes from a cheery salute that went with the ancient drink in Northern Europe. (12 servings.)

Midnight Tea

1 tablespoon tea leaves	2 tablespoons lemon juice
3 cups boiling water	1 lemon, thinly sliced
½ cup orange marmalade	Sugar to taste
1 fifth dry white wine	

Cover tea leaves with boiling water. Steep 5 minutes; strain; add orange marmalade. Bring to boil; simmer 10 minutes; strain again. Add wine, lemon juice, and sugar to taste. Simmer again. Put thin lemon slice in each cup and pour liquid over. (16 servings.)

Hot Chocolate Supreme

1 package instant hot chocolate	1 cup water
	1 tablespoon Sherry

Blend instant hot chocolate and water, then add Sherry. (1 serving.)

California Glog

¾ cup sugar	2 cups Sherry
Dash of bitters	1 cup brandy
2 cups dry red wine	Raisins and unsalted almonds

Mix wines, brandy, bitters. Add sugar, stirring until it dissolves. Heat mixture until piping hot. Place 1 large raisin and 1 almond in each pre-heated mug or cup and pour in Glog. (13 servings.)

11

Some Thoughts on Wine, Notable and Quotable

Here's to good wine! Kings it makes gods, and meaner creatures kings.

—*William Shakespeare*

Wine moistens and tempers the spirits and lulls the cares of the mind to rest. . . . It revives our joys and is oil to the dying flame of life. . . . If we drink temperately, and small draughts at a time, the wine distills upon our lungs like sweetest morning dew. It is then the wine commits no rape upon our reason, but pleasantly invites us to agreeable mirth.

—*Socrates*

One cannot imagine the wine-drinker in solitude. The real *amateur* of wine can only enjoy it along with friends, sharing with them the art of conversation and the art of drinking.

—*Jean Drapeau*

Men who can have communion in nothing else can sympathetically eat together, can still rise into some glow of brotherhood, over food and wine.

—*Thomas Carlyle*

A table without wine
Is an organ without bellows,
A woman without hair,
A family without children.

—*Anonymous*, inscribed on a wall in an inn at Parenzo, Italy

Fill every beaker up, my men,

Pour forth the cheering wine;
There's life and strength in every drop—
Thanksgiving to the vine!
—Albert Corton Greene

Never think of leaving wine to your heirs. Drink it yourself
and let them have the money!
—Martial

I rather like bad wine. One gets so bored with good wine.
—Benjamin Disraeli

We preserved our constitution with Claret while the Tories
destroyed theirs with Port.
—Lord Byron

The bottle you drank before must not make you regret the
bottle to come.
—French proverb

The wine-grower is a warrior. He has to fight the vagaries of
the weather, storms, frosts, insects, disease, rot, hail, and
bad luck. This is why every bottle is worthy of respect and
every glass must be drunk with the honors it deserves. That
soil, that man, that fight are embodied in your glass of wine.
—Anonymous Italian poem

You Americans have the loveliest wines in the world, you
know, but you don't realize it. You call them "domestic"
and that's enough to start trouble anywhere.
—H. G. Wells

Nothing more excellent or valuable than wine was ever
granted by the gods to man.
—Plato

Give me a bowl of wine; in this I bury all unkindness.
—William Shakespeare

Let us drink the juice divine,
The gift of Dionysius, god of wine.
—Anacreon

A house with a great wine stored below lives in our imagination as a joyful house, fast and splendidly rooted in the soil.

—*George Meredith*

Come, fill the Cup, and in the Fire of Spring
Your Winter-garment of Repentance fling. . . .
A Book of Verses underneath the Bough,
A Jug of Wine, a Loaf of Bread—and Thou
Beside me singing in the Wilderness—
Oh, Wilderness were Paradise enow!

—*Omar Khayyám*

A good doctor is like wine:
He cures sometimes,
He relieves often,
He consoles always.

—*Anonymous*

I wonder often what the vintner buys, one half so precious as the stuff he sells.

—*Omar Khayyám*

Who prates of war or want after taking wine?
—*Horace*

In water one sees one's own face; but in wine one beholds the heart of another.

—*French proverb*

A man cannot make him laugh—but that's no marvel; he drinks no wine.

—*William Shakespeare*

Drink no longer water, but use a little wine for thy stomach's sake . . .

—*Saul of Tarsus (Paul)*
I Timothy 5:23

Wine can with good right be considered the most healthful, the most hygienic of beverages. Also, among those which

are known today, it is the one a person prefers to all the others, if only he is given the chance to accustom himself to it.
—*Louis Pasteur*

Now that the wine
Has set their heads whirling,
Go and prepare
A wonderful party
If on the way
You meet some young lady,
Try also to bring
Her along.
Let the dancing
Be spontaneous.
They can do the minuet,
The gavotte,
Or the waltz,
Just as you like;
And I in the meantime
Behind the scenes
Will be flirting
With this one and that one.
Ah, to my list
Tomorrow morning
You will have to add
At least ten names!
—*Lorenzo Da Ponte*, Librettist
Wolfgang Mozart's *Don Giovanni*

Fill the goblet to the brim with choicest wine.
Let pleasure be born, let sorrows die.
Have done with all hatred, do away with all scorn.
Let only love and jollity reign here.
Let us taste and enjoy the cure of all ills,
That brings renewed life to every heart.
Let us drive away the dull cares of the soul;
Let pleasure be born, let sorrows die.
—*Francesco Piave and Andrea Maffei*,
Librettists
Giuseppe Verdi's *Macbeth*

Here's to the sparkling wine that chases all our troubles,

That lightens our hearts in sweet intoxication.

—*Guido Menasci and Giuseppe*
Targioni-Tozzetti, Librettists
Pietro Mascagni's
Cavalleria Rusticana

Libiamo, libiamo ne' lieti calici,
Che la belleza infiora;
E la fuggevol, fuggevol ora
*   s' innebrii a voluttà.*
Libiam ne' dolci fremiti
Che suscita l'amore
Poichè quell' occhio al core
Onnipotente va.
Libiamo, amore, amor fra i calici
Più caldi baci avrà.
Libiamo; amor fra i calici
Più caldi baci avrà.

Let us drink, let us drink from festive cups
That with beauty are adorned;
And the fleeting, fleeting hour
With sensuous pleasure will be replete.
Let us drink with sweet excitement
Arising out of love
Because of a glance that reigns supreme
After having pierced the heart.
Let us drink, love, for the warmest kisses of love
Lie within the wine cup.
Ah, let us drink,
Love finds the warmest kisses within the cup.

—*Francesco Piave and Andrea Maffei,*
Librettists
Giuseppe Verdi's *La Traviata*

Questions and Answers About Wine

[Every segment of "Enjoying Wine with Paul Gillette" has produced questions from viewers, sometimes in the hundreds or even thousands. The following are a sampling of those I think most people would find interesting.

If you have a question about wine, I'll be happy to try answering it, either on the air or in future books. Mail it to: Question Department, "Enjoying Wine with Paul Gillette," 2362 Valejo St., San Francisco, CA 94123. If you'd like a personal reply, enclose a stamped self-addressed envelope.]

Q. SHOULD WATER BE SERVED AT A MEAL WITH WINE?

"Should" questions always make me nervous, because I'm concerned about falling into the old let-my-palate-be-your-measure trap. Let me stress that my answers to this and all other "should" questions represent personal opinion, not an objective standard or rule. If what I say doesn't make sense to you, disregard it.

That having been noted, I'll observe that most wine drinkers rarely if ever drink water at meals except during hot weather, when some mix water or mineral water with wine to help quench a thirst. Nonetheless, some people do like water on the table, even in cold weather. My personal rule is to serve water unless I know that my guests never use it.

Q. DOES THE SHAPE OF A WINE GLASS REALLY MATTER?

Shape is partly a matter of esthetics, partly tradition, and partly practicality. An inward curving rim enhances your perception of the wine's nose. A narrow bowl, as in the tulip or flute, preserves a sparkling wine's bubbles. A stem insures that you can lift the glass without fingerprinting the bowl (thus marring your enjoyment of looking at the wine) or warming the wine from the heat of your hand.

With few exceptions, the traditional glass shapes possess qualities that enhance the most distinctive features of the wine being served. Those traditional shapes are: for Pinot Noir-based wines, the spherical Burgundy bowl; for Cabernet Sauvignon-based wines, the U-shaped Claret glass; for light whites, the small spherical Moselle glass; for full-bodied whites, the pear-shaped tastevin (sometimes also used for reds, particularly younger ones); for sparkling wines, the flute or tulip (the latter sometimes is also used for nonsparkling whites or reds, particularly younger ones); for Sherry, Port and other fortified wines, the tulip, flute, or tube-like classic Sherry glass.

Of course, any glass is better than none. Ultimately, the only really undesirable glasses are those which detract from a wine's most distinctive qualities. That means colored glasses, or those without stems, or those with engraving or other distractions on the bowl. If your budget or living space permits only one set of glasses, a good multi-purpose choice would be the tulip, the tastevin, or the U-shaped Claret glass.

Q. SHOULD YOU SERVE THE WINE YOU'VE CHOSEN FOR YOUR MAIN COURSE ALSO WITH THE SOUP COURSE, OR IS THERE SOMETHING MORE APPROPRIATE TO DO?

There are three approaches to the problem. One is to serve wine only with the main course. Another is to serve the same wine with the entire meal. A third is to serve different wines with each course.

For me, the last is by far the most desirable. Not only does it permit my guests and me to enjoy a variety of wines, but also it allows for precision-matching of wines and foods so that each enhances the most distinctive properties of the other.

Of course, budget and number of guests are important considerations. Not too many people would serve five wines with a five-course dinner if only two guests are present. Conversely, if you have twelve guests, it's likely you'll need at least three bottles of wine. So why not take advantage of the possibilities and serve three different wines?

The traditional order of service is light to full-bodied, dry to sweet, white to red. Obviously there is some overlap in these categories, so it's silly to regard this as a hard and fast rule. But it applies much more often than not.

A popular wine to serve with soup is dry Sherry. Since an opened bottle of Sherry will last indefinitely without loss of character, you needn't worry about wasting what your guests don't consume.

Q. WHEN YOU SERVE ICE CREAM FOR DESSERT, SHOULD YOU SERVE WINE WITH IT? IF SO, WHICH WINE? SHERRY? PORT?

A sweet sparkling wine is a good choice for dessert. Most people I know would serve the wine not with the dessert itself, but between the previous course and dessert. Most guests I know would drink the wine before beginning dessert, whether dessert was ice cream, a pastry, or whatever. It's all a matter of taste, of course; but I think most people will find that no wine, sweet or dry, is really enjoyable drunk side-by-side, sip-to-bite, with ice cream, cake, or other sweet foods.

Sherry, particularly cream (sweet) Sherry, and Port are popular after-dinner wines. My preferred sequence is dessert, coffee, and *then* Sherry or Port.

Q. IS THERE AN EASY WAY TO GET A CORK OUT OF A BOTTLE? PERHAPS IT'S THE CORKSCREW I USE, BUT INVARIABLY HALF THE CORK GETS LEFT IN THE NECK OF THE BOTTLE AND ULTIMATELY WINDS UP IN THE WINE.

A good cork—one that is sufficiently thick and has been kept moist through continuous contact with the wine in the bottle—will not break in half when you try to remove it, unless you do something with the corkscrew that is so weird I can't presently conceive it.

Follow this uncorking procedure: (a) use a corkscrew whose screw is at least two inches long and hollow in the center (see Chapter Five); (b) twist the screw into the center of the cork, inserting it deeply enough to penetrate the bottom of the cork; (c) lift the cork straight up (this will happen automatically if you use any of the leverage-type corkscrews); (d) employ even pressure rather than jerking.

If you use these techniques and the cork breaks off, chances are 999 in 1,000 that it's a bad cork. If this happens to you consistently, consider switching wine merchants and/or brands.

Q. HOW DO YOU SUPPOSE PEOPLE BEGAN COOKING WITH WINE?

My guess is that the practice developed in regions where water was unhygienic and/or foul-tasting, and where wine was both abundant and inexpensive.

Bear in mind that national cuisines frequently feature the more available local beverages for stewing, sautéeing, steaming, etcetera. Thus, many German and Belgian dishes are made with beer, many Scandanavian and North American ones with milk.

A liquid used for cooking imparts taste to the food. However, the alcohol in wine or beer evaporates when it boils, so the resulting dish is not really alcoholic and could be served in good conscience to teetalers.

Q. IS COOKING WITH WINE EXPENSIVE?

It needn't be. The qualities that make a wine expensive are generally lost during cooking, so there is no point in using any wine that costs more than one or two dollars a bottle. Some chefs insist that they use only prime wines in their preparations, but I have a feeling that if they're telling the truth they're buying the wine with someone else's money. I've tried making two batches of the same recipe, side-by-side, using an expensive wine in one and an inexpensive in the other. Neither I nor the people I served could tell the two apart. Some of my guests were chefs.

In wine country, chefs frequently use not the wine itself but pomace, or the remains of pressed grapes. As Gerard Yvernault has pointed out, pomace of Pinot Noir appears in the original recipes for *Boeuf Bourguignonne*.

In any case, most recipes call for a relatively small quantity of wine—rarely more than half a cup per person—so even if you use a fairly expensive wine, the added cost of the dish will be rather small.

Q. HOW CAN ONE BOTTLE OF WINE BE A HUNDRED TIMES MORE EXPENSIVE THAN ANOTHER?

Many factors contribute to the price of wine: variety of grape, cost (including taxes) of the real estate on which it is grown, cost of various winemaking procedures (it is more expensive to age wine in small barrels than in large casks), costs of shipping and storing, profit, and demand.

With super-expensive wines—those costing, say, twenty dollars or more per bottle—demand generally is the main factor. A vineyard like Château Lafite-Rothschild, probably the best-known in Bordeaux, sells in certain prime vintages at over a hundred dollars per bottle. If people are willing to pay it, Baron Elie de Rothschild will happily accept their money. But it certainly does not cost the baron twenty times as much to make his wine as it costs Château Pedesclaux, a few kilometers down the road in the same township of Pauillac, to make the wine it sells for four or five dollars a bottle.

Age is another big factor. No wine that I know of, including Lafite-Rothschild, ever sold for as much as twenty dollars a bottle when it was first released by the winery. However, when a vintage is regarded as prime, shippers and retailers stock up on the biggest names and boost the price as the wine's reputation grows and demand increases.

If you take the trouble to scout vintages year by year, you generally can buy prime vintages immediately on their release from the winery, then cellar them and let their value grow as they age. It usually is difficult to buy prime vintages of the best-known French names, because shippers corner the market in anticipation of making a real killing. However, prime vintages in California, Germany, Italy and other countries usually are quite freely available. All you have to know is what to buy.

Q. WHEN EXACTLY DOES ONE DECANT A WINE?

Decanting serves two purposes: (a) it permits you to pour an older wine off its sediment, which would mar the taste, nose and clarity if it were remixed with the wine as you poured from the original bottle; (b) it aerates an underage red wine, thus enhancing nose and taste. There's no need to decant under other circumstances.

Q. WHY ARE NORTH AMERICAN WINES SWEETER THAN THOSE OF EUROPE AND SOUTH AMERICA?

They aren't always. In the lower price range (say, three dollars a bottle), North American wines probably are generally sweeter. Winemakers tell me they find these wines easier to sell. (North Americans, importer Julius Wile suggests, like to talk dry but drink sweet.) However, I haven't found North American wines priced over three dollars a bottle to be generally more or less sweet than those of other countries.

"Sweetness," incidentally, is used by wine professionals to describe sugar content. It's possible for a wine to seem sweet to the average palate even though it may contain no sugar whatever. The pseudosweet taste is provided by fruit acids, particularly those of the *vitis labrusca* species of grape, used predominantly in New York and Canadian wines.

Q. I'M SERVING A SHRIMP APPETIZER AND A PASTA WITH RED SAUCE FOR THE MAIN COURSE. MY GUESTS ARE NOT BIG DRINKERS, SO I'D PREFER TO SERVE ONLY ONE BOTTLE OF WINE. SHOULD IT BE RED OR WHITE?

My own choice would be a light-bodied red, perhaps a Zinfandel, Gamay, Beaujolais, Bardolino, Cirò, or inexpensive Chianti. However, I could also enjoy a bone-dry white—say a Frascati or an Orvietto Bianco Seco—with the meal.

It's a safe general rule to serve red wine with red sauce, but it isn't mandatory. Some Italians drink only white wine during hot weather, whatever the food.

By the way, if you believe your guests wouldn't consume two full bottles of wine, you might try serving two half bottles. That would be my preference for your meal. I'd serve a bone-dry white with the shrimp and a light red with the pasta.

Q. WHAT IS CONSIDERED THE PROPER GLASS FOR SHERRY? ALL I'VE EVER SEEN ARE THOSE THIMBLE-LIKE GLASSES THAT ARE DIFFICULT TO HOLD. THERE MUST BE A BETTER WAY.

There are several classic Sherry glasses from Jérez de la Frontera, the city in Spain where the wine called Sherry originally was produced. ("Sherry" is believed to be an English mispronunciation of "Jérez.")

Probably the most popular glass is stemmed with an almost cylindrical bowl—the top is just a few millimeters narrower than the bottom. The glass holds about four ounces. Another favorite among Spaniards is stemless and perfectly cylindrical; it holds about three ounces. Still another is stemmed with an almost spherical bowl and holds about four ounces.

I don't care for the latter two, "proper" though they are,

and I'm less than in love with the first, preferred though it generally is. My own preference is a tulip or flute-shaped glass, which I find easier to handle. The tulip and flute also permit me to enjoy the nose of the Sherry, a difficult feat with the classic glasses from Jérez.

Q. I UNDERSTAND THAT IN ITALY GRAPES ARE CRUSHED BY FOOT. I ASSUME THEY WASH THEIR FEET, BUT SOMEHOW IT SEEMS UNSANITARY. WHY DO THEY CONTINUE THIS ARCHAIC CUSTOM?

I know of nowhere in Italy where grapes are presently crushed by foot. It's much easier and quicker to use a mechanical crusher, even if only a small hand-operated one for home winemaking. All Italian commercial wineries that I have visited use up-to-date equipment.

The only place I know where grapes still are crushed by foot is Portugal, where the practice is employed ceremonially in a few small towns as part of a harvest celebration in which most townspeople take their turn in the crushing trough. Usually the crushers wear boots. In any case, the wine is purified during fermentation, no matter what germs may have been in it before.

Q. I USED TO BE ABLE TO GET ITALIAN WINES, ESPECIALLY CHIANTI, IN THOSE CHARMING BOTTLES WITH BASKETS ON THE BOTTOM. NOW THEY'RE VERY HARD TO FIND. IS THE REED BECOMING SCARCE?

No, but the cost of weaving it has become prohibitive. These days very few producers use basket-bottomed *fiaschi* and the number is ever-dwindling.

Q. I HAVE NEVER DRUNK WHAT I CONSIDER A GOOD ITALIAN WHITE WINE, BUT I LOVE THEIR REDS. IS THE EMPHASIS ON REDS RELATED TO THE LARGE AMOUNT OF TOMATO SAUCE ITALIANS EAT? IF THERE ARE DECENT ITALIAN WHITES, WOULD YOU RECOMMEND ONE?

Italy does produce more red than white wine, and I think you're right when you conjecture that this relates to the prevalence of tomato sauce in Italian cooking. However, there are many, many Italian white wines. When you say you've never drunk what you consider a good one, I suspect that one or both of the following factors is responsible:

(a) Most Italian whites are considerably more full-bodied than the typical white of Germany, France or the United States. Perhaps you don't like full-bodied whites.

(b) Most Italian whites are meant to be consumed when very young and do not travel well. Perhaps the ones you drank were over the hill or suffered from maderization or some other defect relating to handling or shipping.

I'd recommend that you try a very young (no older than two years, preferably younger than one) wine from a shipper whose Italian reds appeal to you. Among types of wine you might try are Soave, Frascati, and Verdicchio.

Q. I FIND IT NEXT TO IMPOSSIBLE TO OPEN A BOTTLE OF CHAMPAGNE WITHOUT EXPLODING THE CORK. IS THERE SOME WAY TO PREVENT THIS?

Use the step-by-step procedures I outlined in Chapter Five. Be certain that the wine is very cold, and don't shake the bottle before opening it. After you've removed the wire cage, be sure to turn the bottle while holding the cork firm, not vice versa.

Q. WHY DO MOST WOMEN PREFER WHITE WINE TO RED WINE? DO YOU THINK IT HAS TO DO WITH THEIR PHYSICAL MAKEUP?

I doubt that there is a general preference among women for white or red. However, I've found that newcomers to wine, particularly in North America, tend to favor lighter, fruitier, sweeter, and less complicated wines. Perhaps the women you've observed have not been drinking wine for very long.

As to why newcomers favor these wines, California wineman Jerry Vonne makes the point that most native-born North Americans grew up drinking soft drinks and perhaps find themselves most strongly attracted, at least initially, to wines that resemble these drinks.

This, in my opinion, is one reason for the great popularity in North America of the crackling rosés, like Lancers and Mateus of Portugal or Lambrusco from Italy, none of which enjoys nearly as much popularity in the country that produces it.

Q. I RECENTLY ATE AT A RESTAURANT WHERE A

BOTTLE OF MATEUS SOLD FOR $15. I'D LIKE TO KNOW HOW A RESTAURATEUR JUSTIFIES CHARGING FOUR TIMES AS MUCH AS THE WINE COSTS AT RETAIL.

In my view, there's no explanation other than greed. The restaurateur buys his wine at fifteen to fifty percent less than retail. His only costs are storage, refrigeration, and occasional breakage of glasses. I think it's outrageous to charge more than one or two dollars above retail for a bottle of wine, and I refuse to patronize restaurants that do.

Q. I THINK THE REASON THE FRENCH ARE SO COMPLICATED WITH THEIR LABELING SYSTEM IS THAT THEY'RE BASICALLY CROOKS. THEY WANT US TO BE CONFUSED SO WE'LL PAY HIGH PRICES FOR WHAT WE'RE MISLED TO BELIEVE IS A TOP-RATED WINE. DO YOU AGREE?

There is no question that French wine labels are difficult to understand, even for people who are fluent in French. Much of the confusion relates to official designations and classifications. Spokesmen for the French wine industry say these guarantee the authenticity—and, by extension, the quality—of the wine. I say they are designed to limit production in order to keep prices up. In any case, the labels *can* be read and understood if you are willing to take the trouble to learn what the various designations mean. The major ones are discussed in detail in *Playboy's Book of Wine*.

I don't think the French wine industry as a whole is aiming to rip off the consumer. The fact is, some extraordinary French wines are available at three to five dollars a bottle. The trick is discovering them. If you're really interested, read a good book that focuses specifically on French wines; there are several listed in the bibliography at the end of this book.

Where the ripoff factor enters the picture with the French is, in my opinion, when certain producers seek to exploit the semi-informed consumer's knowledge of wine classifications and designations. It's well-known, for example, that the most celebrated wines of Bordeaux are chateau-bottled (that is, bottled by the vineyard where the grapes were grown). Such wines are named after the chateau (e.g., Château Margaux, Château Lafite-Rothschild). It's also well-known that the most highly prized wines of Beaujolais carry the names of nine communities, one of which is Moulin-a-Vent.

There is presently being marketed in the United States a wine named "Château Moulin-a-Vent." It is not a chateau-bottled wine in the sense that the term is employed in Bordeaux, nor is it produced in the prestigious Beaujolais community of Moulin-a-Vent. The producer has chosen a trade name that he presumably hopes will be confused with the more prestigious wines on whose labels "Château" or "Moulin-a-Vent" appear.

Yes, it's a ripoff. But knowledge is power, and if you take the trouble to learn what the various official designations and classifications are, you won't fall victim to an aspiring ripoff artist's legerdemain.

Q. GERMANY SEEMS GENERALLY TO PRODUCE SWEETER WHITE WINES THAN ANY OTHER COUNTRY. IS IT DUE TO CLIMATIC CONDITIONS, OR DO THEY TAMPER WITH THE WINE?

The sweetness in the most highly prized German wines comes from picking the grapes very late, after they have been attacked by the botrytis cinerea fungus, which reduces the amount of juice per grape without reducing the natural sugar content. This is a deliberate—and costly—choice that German vintners make because there is strong domestic and foreign demand for this kind of wine, which winemakers in other countries have never quite managed to duplicate.

However, Germany also produces some bone-dry whites. They are less well known outside the country than in Germany itself. They generally are labeled *"Kabinett."*

In years when sunshine isn't adequate to provide the desired level of natural sugar in grapes, German law permits addition of small quantities of sugar before fermentation. However, wines made with added sugar generally are in the lower price range; it is illegal to add sugar to the *Auslesen, Spaetlesen, Beerenauslesen,* and *Trockenbeerenauslesen* that most lovers of German wines prize.

Q. WHY DOESN'T GERMANY PRODUCE ANY RED WINE?

Germany produces a small quantity of red wine but exports very, very little of it. The wine is very light, closer to a rosé than to the well-known full-bodied reds of California, Spain, Italy, and other countries.

The main reason production is so small is that the prime

red wine grapes don't grow well in Germany, which has the world's northernmost vineyards. The classic white grapes of Germany—Riesling, Mueller-Thurgau, Sylvaner—require less heat and sunshine.

Q. I UNDERSTAND THAT THE YIELD OF GRAPES THROUGHOUT THE WORLD THESE PAST FEW YEARS WAS QUITE HIGH. IN FACT, I'VE READ THAT THE SUPPLY FAR OUTDISTANCES THE DEMAND. DOES THIS MEAN THE PRICE OF WINE WILL GO DOWN?

Wine prices already have dropped considerably from their 1973-74 highs. I bought in 1976, at under three dollars, internationally celebrated wines that couldn't be touched in 1973 for less than fifteen dollars. I bought at under two dollars a gallon—that's right, under two a *gallon*—a wine that two years earlier would have fetched five dollars a gallon.

Another spinoff of the grape glut is that producers who haven't dropped their prices generally are using lower-yield grapes in their blends. For example, several California producers now use thirty percent or more Chardonnay in their generically labeled Chablis. Before the grape glut, they used no Chardonnay in the blend.

Unfortunately, there's no such thing as a free lunch. Plummeting grape prices have bankrupted some growers and have induced others to switch to different crops. When supply and demand return to equilibrium, you can expect wine prices to resume climbing.

Q. THE CLIMATE IN THE SOUTHERN UNITED STATES IS VERY HOT, EVEN COMPARED TO COUNTRIES LIKE ITALY, SPAIN AND MOROCCO. WHY IS NO WINE PRODUCED IN THESE STATES?

The ideal climate for wine growing, in the opinion of most professionals, is where summers are long and cool. Too much sunshine, heat, or rain can ruin the grapes. Another problem is parasite infestation: while parts of Virginia seem to be ideal climatically, that state's agriculture researchers have been unable to develop a strain of grapevine that can resist the inevitable attacks of local insects.

Small quantities of wine are produced commercially in most states, but the character of these wines apparently has not been sufficiently noteworthy to attract consumers away from wines of the two largest producers, California (with over ninety percent of the nation's production) and New York. Perhaps as local demand increases, producers in other states will develop the resources to expand their marketing reach.

Q. I'VE BEEN MAKING WINE AT HOME FOR YEARS. RECENTLY A FRIEND TOLD ME I'M REQUIRED BY LAW TO FILE A FORM WITH THE GOVERNMENT TELLING THEM I'M DOING SO. IS THIS TRUE? IF SO, WHAT BUSINESS IS IT OF THE GOVERNMENT WHETHER I MAKE WINE?

Yes, home winemakers are required by law to register with the federal government, which has decreed that you can make a maximum of two hundred gallons a year. I don't think it's any business of the government whether you make wine, but apparently the pirates you and I have elected to public office chose to make it their business. If you disapprove, you might write to your congressman and senators. That probably won't change the situation, since the bureaucracy has a vested interest in maintaining the status quo; but at least you'll get a chance to blow off some steam.

Wine Dictionary*

Compiled by Peter A. Gillette and Paul Gillette

*All terms are defined only with respect to their application to grape-based wine, unless otherwise indicated. In English and other languages, foreign words frequently are used in their original language rather than in translation to describe wine and wine characteristics.

abboccato, *adj.* (It., ahb-boc-COT-oh), retaining a portion of natural sugar; ergo, sweet. Fermentation stops when alcohol concentration reaches 14 to 16 percent. If the crushed grapes contain more sugar than was needed to produce that concentration, the surplus will remain in the wine, sweetening it.

abfullung, *adj.* (Ger., AHP-fuyl-loong), bottling; usually used on pre-1973 labels as part of the phrase, "original-*abfullung*," meaning bottled on the estate of the grape-grower; not a permissible designation under current German wine laws.

abstich, *n.* (Ger., ahb-SHTEEKH), process of drawing off the wine from its lees.

abzug, *adj.* (Ger., ahb-TSOOG), bottled on the estate of the grape grower.

acerbe, *adj.* (Fr., ah-SERB), tasting of acid.

acetic acid, *n.*, the chief ingredient of vinegar, a result of the oxidation of the alcohol in wine or cider by acetobacters. It frequently appears in wines that have been exposed to air or heat.

acid, *n.*, tart-tasting chemical compound that is natural to wines; if a wine is deemed lacking in acid, it is spoken of as "flat"; if the acid level is deemed too high, the wine is characterized as "sharp" or "overly tart"; if the level is deemed correct, the wine is described as "balanced," "tart," "crisp," or "lively."

adega, *n.* (Port., ah-DAY-ga), wine warehouse.

aération, *n.* (Fr., ah-ay-rah-see-AWN), addition of oxygen to must or wine, usually by mechanical means.

aging, *n.,* maturing of wine, first in barrels, casks or other large containers, then in the bottles in which the wine is sold; the latter phase is called "bottle-aging."

agrafe, *n.* (Fr., ah-GRAFF), in production of sparkling wines, a clamp or metal clip to hold down the cork of the bottle while secondary fermentation builds up pressure inside the bottle.

aigre, *adj.* (Fr., EGkr), characterized by an acid undertone.

albariza, *adj.* (Sp., ahl-bah-REE-thah), of soil, white and chalky; applied particularly to the soil in the Jérez district of Spain, where Sherry is produced.

almijar, *n.* (Sp., ahl-mee-KHAR), in Spain, courtyard of pressing house where grapes are spread out to dry in the sun before pressing.

alt., *adj.* (Ger., AHLT), old.

amelioration, *n.* (same spelling in French, ah-may-lee-oh-rah-see-AWN), addition of sweetening agents, water and/or acids to the must or wine to obtain desired balance of alcohol or taste characteristics, or any other treatment of the wine (e.g., pasteurization) or addition to it (e.g., sulfur dioxide as a stabilizing or cleansing agent).

amontillado, *n.* (Sp., ah-mon-teel-YAH-do), dry and relatively pale Sherry; after the town of Montilla, where such wines are believed to originate.

amoroso, *n.* (Sp., ah-mo-ROH-so), dark and medium-dry Sherry.

aperitif, *n.* (Fr., ah-pay-ree-TEEF), beverage consumed as an appetizer.

appellation contrôlée, *n.* (Fr., ah-pell-lah-see-AWN kohn-troh-LAY), controlled name; the term, on wine labels, warrants that the wine was made within a given geographic area (the area usually appears between the two words, e.g., *"appellation Margaux controlée"*) under conditions specified by French law.

appellation d'origine, *n.* (Fr., ah-pell-lah-see-AWN doh-ree-ZHEEN), "name of origin"; the term, on wine labels, identifies the place where the wine was produced but not necessarily the place where the grapes were grown; it is generally used only on wines which are *not* produced under *"appellation controlée"* regulations, and apparently is intended to deceive unknowledgeable consumers, since there is no other reason for the expression to appear.

appleness, *n.*, subtle apple-like taste in a white or rosé wine, generally regarded as desirable.

apre, *adj.* (Fr., AH-pruh), rough-tasting, harsh-tasting.

argol, *n.*, a composition of potassium bitartrate that collects inside storage vats; also called wine stone.

aroma, *n.*, fragrance of the grapes from which a wine is made, as opposed to "bouquet," the smell of acids and other properties developed by the wine after the grapes were crushed; a wine has both aroma and bouquet.

arroba, *n.* (Sp., ahr-ROH-bah), measure holding 16⅔ liters.

arrope, *n.* (Sp., ahr-ROH-pay), wine concentrate used to sweeten and give color to a sherry.

art, *n.* (Ger., AHRT), character.

artig, *adj.* (Ger., AHR-tigg), smooth, rounded.

asciuto, *n.* (It., ah-shee-AH-toh), any dry wine.

assemblage, *n.* (Fr., ah-sawm-BLAHZH), blending.

astringent, *adj.*, tart, causing the mouth to pucker; a characteristic caused mostly by the tannin derived from grape skins and seeds.

aum, *n.* (Ger., OHM), cask, usually 160 liters.

auslese, *adj.* (Ger., OWZH-lay-zeh), made from selected bunches of fully ripened grapes.

baby, *n.*, 6.4 ounce bottle, usually used for sparkling wine; sometimes called a "split."

balanced, *adj.*, having all elements in good harmony; thus, having a harmonious blend of sugar, acidity, etc.

Balling, *n.*, measure of soluble solids, mainly sugar, in grape juice or must; expressed as degrees of balling.

barrica, *n.* (Sp., bahr-REEK-ah), cask.

barrique, *n.* (Fr., bah-REEK-eh), barrel (usual size: 50 U.S. gallons), also a standard Bordeaux measure equaling 24 cases each of which contains a dozen 24-ounce bottles.

basto, *n.* (Sp., BAH-stow), a coarse wine.

Baumé, *n.* (Fr., boh-MAY), scale that measures the specific gravity of liquids, often used to determine degree of sweetness in wines.

beerenauslese, *n.* (Ger., BAY-ren-owzh-leh-zeh), wine made from individually selected grape berries from late-ripened bunches that have been attacked by the botrytis cinerea fungus.

besitz, *n.* (Ger., buh-SITZ), proprietor.

bestes, *adj.* (Ger., BEST-ez), best.

big, *adj.*, robust (as opposed to light-bodied); however, in translation, *grand* in French, *grande* in Italian, *gran* in Spanish and Portuguese, are used to characterize a wine regarded as distinguished; and in Chile, *gran* is an official designation that the wine is at least six years old.

binning, *n.*, storing wines in bins containing a number of bottles, usually of the same wine, as opposed to storing in individual holders on racks or other devices.

bitter, *adj.*, excessively tannic; the trait may simply indicate the wine's youth, or it may be the result of leaving stems, stalks and seeds in the must for too long during fermentation, or of overlong aging in wood.

blanc de blancs, *n.* (Fr., BLAWN-duh-BLAWN), white wine made exclusively from white grapes.

blanc de noir, *n.* (Fr., BLAWN-duh-NWAHR), white wine made at least partially from red (black) grapes.

blending, *n.*, mixing various wines, usually to achieve a specific character, balance and/or year-to-year uniformity, but sometimes also for economy.

blume, *n.* (Ger., BLOOM) fragrance.

blumig, *n.* (Ger., BLOOM-ig), pleasant frangrance.

bocksbeutel, *n.* (Ger., BOX-boy-tel), squat, bulbous bottle originating in Germany and used principally for *steinwein,* a predominantly sylvaner variety; the word, *bocksbeutel,* derives from the bottle's resemblance to a goat's scrotum, literal translation of *bocksbeutel*). The bottle presently is used also in Portugal and Chile.

bocoy, *n.* (Sp., boh-Koy), cask holding about 162 U.S. gallons; used mostly in northern Spain.

bodega, *n.* (Sp., bo-DAY-gah), originally, a wine storage room built above ground; currently used also as generic term for any retail wine shop.

body, *n.*, density or consistency of a wine; that is, the proportion of soluble solids in it. A full-bodied wine contains many soluble solids; a light-bodied wine, very few.

bon goût, *n.* (Fr., bun GOO), good taste.

bór, *n.* (Hun., BOHR), generic term for wine.

bota, *n.* (Sp., BO-tah), small leather bag for carrying wine; by squeezing it, the drinker squirts the wine into his mouth without touching the vessel with his lips; in

Jérez, *bota* also describes a cask containing 132 U.S. gallons.

botrytis cinerea, *n.* (Lat., boh-TREE-tees chee-nair-AY-uh), a mold which attacks certain grape berries, reducing their liquid content without reducing their sugar.

bottle-aging, *n.*, storing wine in individual bottles, as opposed to bulk-storage in other containers, usually wood.

bottle-ripe, *n.*, ready for bottling.

bottle sizes: the following are the most common:

Miniature: 2, 3 or 4 ounces

Split (also called baby, nip, or quarter): 6.4 ounces

Half-pint: 8 ounces

Tenth: 12.8 ounces

Pint: 16 ounces

Fifth: 25.6 ounces

Aperitif: 30 ounces

Quart: 32 ounces

Magnum: 51.2 ounces

Half gallon: 64 ounces

Jereboam: 102.4 ounces

Gallon: 128 ounces

Rehoboam: 156 ounces

Methuselah: 208 ounces

Salmanazar: 312 ounces

Balthazar: 416 ounces

Nebuchadnezzar: 520 ounces

Demijohn: 627.2 ounces

The wine industry in America is in the process of converting to the metric system, which is used by much of the rest of the world. By January 1, 1979, all wine bottled after that date and sold in this country must be in specified metric size containers. Sizes presently most generally used for wine are listed below, along with the number of ounces and number of servings in each, and closest metric equivalents:

Approximate servings per bottle

Bottle	Fluid ounces	Approximate measurement for recipes	(Dinner and sparkling wines, 4-oz. serving)	(Dessert wines, 3-oz. serving)	Nearest metric bottle size
Split	6.4	¾ cup	1½	2	187.5 milliliters
Tenth (⅘ pt., a half bottle)	12.8	1½ cups	3	4	375 milliliters (12.68 oz.)
Fifth (⅘ qt., the most common size)	25.6	3⅛ cups	6	8	750 milliliters (25.36 oz.) 1 liter (33.81 oz.)
Quart	32	4 cups	8	11	
Half-gallon (bottle or jug)	64	8 cups	16	21	1.5 liters (50.72 oz.)
Gallon (bottle or jug)	128	16 cups	32	42	3 liters (101.44 oz.)

bouchonné, *adj.* (Fr., boo-shuh-NAY), characterized by a corky taste; an indication that the wine is defective.

bouillage, *n.* (Fr., boo-YAHZH), initial fermentation.

bouquet, *n.* (Fr., boo-KAY), fragrance of acids and other properties developed in a wine during fermentation and aging; as opposed to "aroma," the fragrance of the grapes that makes up the wine.

bowle, *n.* (Ger., BOW-luh), punch made with wine, herbs, fresh fruit, and liqueurs or brandy.

breed, *n.,* character of a wine attributable to the grape variety or varieties which it comprises.

brilliant, *adj.,* of such clarity that it reflects light.

brix hydrometer, *n.,* instrument for measuring soluble solids.

brut, *adj.* (Fr., BRWEET), the second least sweet degree of sparkling wine; originally, containing no sweetening agents; today, containing .5 to 1.5 percent sweetening. (A totally unsweetened sparkling wine today is usually described as "natural" or *"naturelle."*)

bukettreich, *n.* (Ger., boo-kett-RYESCH), rich bouquet.

bulk wines, *n.,* those stored, shipped or packaged in containers no smaller than 1 U.S. gallon; with sparkling wines, those which underwent secondary fermentation in a tank, usually of 1,000 gallons, rather than an individual bottle.

butt, *n.*, English measure of 151.3 U.S. gallons; also, standard sherry cask, measuring 129.6 U.S. gallons.

butte, *n.* (Hun., BYOOT), measure of 13.6 liters.

B.W., *n.*, bonded winery (official designation in California).

B.W.C., *n.*, bonded wine cellar (official designation in California).

candling, *n.*, testing a wine for clarity by holding it before a candle or other source of light.

capsule, *n.*, protective covering shaped to fit cork and part of the neck of a bottle.

carbonated wine, *n.*, one charged with carbon dioxide gas to produce bubbles.

cask, *n.*, container for storing and/or aging wine, usually 1,000 gallons or larger.

cave, *n.* (Fr., KAHV), storage place for wine, usually subterranean; thus, wine "cellar."

cellar, *n.*, storage place for wine, usually subterranean; also used to designate place of wine production, especially in Europe. ("Bottled in our cellars," or *"mis en bouteilles dans nos caves,"* does not necesarily mean the bottling took place underground.)

chai, *n.* (Fr., SHAY), storage place for wine; a Bordeaux term, usually used synonymously with "cellar" or "cave," although the place need not be subterranean.

chambrer, *v.* (Fr., shawm-BRAY), to take the chill off wine by letting it stand in the room where it will be served.

chaptalization, *n.* (Fr., shop-tah-lee-zah-see-OHN), addition of sugar to grape juice before fermentation to compensate for deficiency of natural sugar.

charmat process, *n.* (Fr., SHAR-mah), also *methode charmat*, in making sparkling wines, technique of inducing second fermentation in large tank instead of individual bottles.

charnu, *adj.* (Fr., shar-NOO), full-bodied.

chateau, *n.* (Fr., shah-TOH), property on which grapes are grown; thus, vineyard (original meaning, "castle," has been lost).

chateau-bottled, *adj.*, bottled on the property of the grape-grower, usually by him or under his direct supervision.

chill-proofing, *n.*, cooling of a wine before bottling to prevent clouding after bottling.

citric acid, *n.*, main fixed acid of lemons, oranges and other citrus fruits; small quantities found—and considered desirable—in wines.

claret, *n.,* generic term for light-bodied red table wine; despite French appearance, and despite fact that the term originally was applied to wines of Bordeaux, France, the word is English and is pronounced CLAIR-ett.

clear, *adj.,* unclouded, usually but not necessarily transparent.

climat, *n.* (Fr., KLEE-mah), vineyard; the term is used principally in Burgundy.

clos, *n.* (Fr., KLOH), literally, an enclosure; original application with regard to wine, a vineyard enclosed by a fence; now, any vineyard. The term is used principally in Burgundy.

cloudy, *adj.,* containing sediment or other substances in suspension rather than solution.

coarse, *adj.,* lacking finesse, usually because of excessive acidity.

Cold Duck, *n.,* a light red sparkling wine, often the result of mixing a red sparkling wine with a white one.

collage, *n.* (Fr., koh-LAHZH), process of clarifying a wine, usually with egg whites or other additives that later are removed.

color de vino, *n.* (Sp., koh-LORE day VEE-noh), concentrated wine added to Sherry for color and sweetness.

colorimeter, *n.,* instrument to measure depth of color.

common, *adj.,* not distinguished; a favorite word of wine snobs when referring to inexpensive wines.

commune, *n.* (Fr., koh-MYOON), subdivision of a French province, roughly equivalent to U.S. township; French wines frequently are identified by the commune in which they were produced.

concentrate, *n.,* grape juice from which a substantial portion of the original liquid has been removed by evaporation.

conservato, *n.* (It., kon-ser-VAH-toh), wine to which a boiled or concentrated wine has been added.

consumo, *n.* (Port. and Sp., kon-SOO-moh), any inexpensive wine, usually sold in bulk.

controlled fermentation, *n.,* conversion of sugar content of crushed grapes to alcohol and other byproducts, but in a regulated atmosphere in which the temperature of the must—and, therefore, the rate of fermentation—is controlled by refrigerating the fermenting vat.

cooper, *n.,* maker of barrels, casks, and other wooden containers.

cooperative winery, *n.,* winemaking enterprise owned and operated by the grape-growers themselves (as opposed to an outside party who buys grapes from different growers).

corky, *adj.,* having an odor and/or off-taste caused by a diseased cork.

corps, *n.* (Fr., KOHR), density or consistency of a wine; literally, body.

corredor, *n.* (Sp., coh-ray-DOHR), wine-broker; usually, someone who buys a variety of bulk wines, blends them, then bottles and ships them under his own name.

corsé, *adj.* (Fr., kohr-SAY), full-bodied.

cotto, *adj.* (It. KOHT-toe), heated; literally, cooked; refers generally to a fortified wine that was heated to increase alcoholic strength, a common practice in Marsala, Sicily, one of the better-known producing regions of Italian fortified wines.

coulant, *adj.* (Fr., koo-LAWN), smooth, easy-to-drink.

coupage, *n.* (Fr., koo-PAHZH), blending; usually, a second blending before bottling, as opposed to an initial blending of newly fermented wine before storage in wood for aging.

coupé, *adj.* (Fr., koo-PAY), blended, diluted; though any blended wine may be described, strictly speaking, as *coupé,* the term usually refers to a wine diluted with water.

crackling, *adj.,* characterized by slight effervescence, as opposed to the genuine "sparkle" of full secondary fermentation; under U.S. law, the term may be applied only to wines that underwent a slight secondary fermentation after being bottled; however, some producers introduce small quantities of carbon dioxide gas to a completely still wine to approximate the "crackling" character.

cradle, *n.,* container, usually wicker, that holds bottle at an angle designed to restrict sediment to the bottommost corner.

crémant, n. (Fr., CRAY-mawn), "creaming"; equivalent to the English, "crackling" (see above).

creszenz, n. (Ger., KRESS-senz), "the growth of"; appearing before a producer's name on a pre-1973 label, it indicates an estate-bottled wine.

criadera, *n.* (Sp., kree-ah-DAY-ra), the "nursery" in a Sherry

winery, where the wines age in wood before being introduced into the *solera* (see **"solera"**).

cru, *n.* (Fr., CREW), literally, "growth"; it refers specifically
to the place of growth, i.e., the vineyard; at various
times, official and semi- or unofficial French organiza-
tions have classified wines qualitatively by vineyard,
describing each class with an adjective, followed by
"*cru*"; e.g., "*premier cru*" (first growth), "*deuxième cru*"
(second growth), "*grand cru*" (great growth), "*cru
exceptionnel*" (exceptional growth); these expressions
mean that the wine produced from grapes grown in that
vineyard are generally regarded as ———— (insert appropriate adjective); they do *not* refer to a specific year's
"growth" as that term is used in English.

cru classé, *n.* (Fr., CREW klah-SAY), in Bordeaux, classified
growth; i.e., rated qualitatively during the official classification of 1855.

crush, *v.,* to squeeze whole grapes to pulp and juice; as a
noun, the term applies to the whole process of harvesting
grapes and crushing them: wine people thus speak of
"the crush" or "this year's crush."

crusher, *n.,* apparatus for crushing grapes; most such apparati
also separate the grape berries from the stems and are
called stemmer-crushers.

crust, *n.,* deposit usually found on lower surface of bottle
stored for several years or longer, especially bottle of
Port, sometimes called Crusted Port.

cups, *n.* (singular), particularly in England, an iced wine
drink that has been flavored with herbs, fresh fruit,
brandy and/or liqueurs.

cutting, *n.,* a piece cut from a grapevine for replanting.

cuvaison, *n.* (Fr., coo-vay-ZAHN), first stage of fermentation.
during which grape skins are left in the must to give a
red wine its color.

cuvée, *n.* (Fr., koo-VAY), blend of still wines, usually of different vintages, used as a base for sparkling wines; also,
in Champagne, the wine from the free run or first pressing of the grapes. The term often appears on sparkling
wine labels as "*cuvée reserve*" or with some other adjec-
tival indication that the *cuvée* in question was high-
quality; but the word, "*cuvée*," alone on a wine label is
without qualitative significance, and, in any case, none
of the "*cuvée*" variants is an official designation.

decant, *v.,* to pour from original bottle to another container; done with old wines to insure sediment won't cloud the wine or get into glasses when the wine is served, and sometimes also done with younger wines for aeration.

decanter, *n.,* container into which decanted wine (see above) is poured and from which it is served.

degorgement, *n.* (Fr., day-gorzh-MAWN), removal of sediment and other solids from bottle of sparkling wine before final corking.

delicate, *adj.,* not coarse; thus, soft, subtle.

delimited area, *n.,* region of production subject to specific wine laws or to sanctions of a wine-producers' organization; normally the name of a delimited area cannot legally be applied to a wine not produced from grapes grown within that region and under specifications of the relevant legislation or producers' organization rules.

demijohn, *n.,* measure of 4.9 U.S. gallons; usually a wicker-encased container.

demiqueue, *n.* (Fr., deh-mee-QYUY), cask holding about 228 liters; generally found in Burgundy.

demisec, *adj.* (Fr., deh-mee-SEK), literally, "half-dry"; in practice, the term usually is applied to wines that are rather sweet (5 to 7 percent sweetening).

denominazione di origine controllata, *n.* (It., deh-no-mee-naht-see-OH-neh dee oh-REEJ-ee-neh kohn-trol-LAHT-a), literally, "name of controlled origin"; the phrase, on an Italian label, warrants that the wine was produced from grapes grown in the specified area under conditions prescribed by law; often abbreviated as D.O.C.

densimeter, *n.,* device to measure sugar concentration in a liquid.

deposit, *n.,* crust or sediment formed in the bottle of an aging wine.

dépot, *n.* (Fr., day-POH), crust or sediment formed in the bottle of an aging wine.

disgorge, *v.,* to remove sediment and other solids from bottle of sparkling wine before final corking.

distinguished, *adj.,* exceptional and sophisticated; normally applied only to wines considered to possess perfect harmony of qualities.

domaine, *n.* (Fr., doh-MEHNN), estate; in Burgundy, used to designate a vineyard or the section of a vineyard tended by a single proprietor; wines produced exclusively from grapes grown by a single proprietor are legally classified as *"mise au domaine,"* i.e., *domaine-* or estate-bottled.

dosage, *n.* (Fr., doh-SAHZH), syrup made up of wine, sweetening agents(s) and sometimes brandy, added to most sparkling wines immediately before cooking; used to sweeten the wine and to fill the space in the bottle previously occupied by degorged solids.

douil, *n.* (Fr., doo-WEE), open cask in which grapes are carted from vineyard to pressing house; prevalent especially in Bordeaux.

doux, *adj.* (Fr., DOO), sweet; generally used to describe the sweetest degree of sparkling wine.

duft, *n.* (Ger., DOOFT), scent, fragrance.

dulce, *adj.* (Sp., DOOL-thay), sweet.

dur, *adj.* (Fr., DYOOR), harsh, coarse, young.

dry, *adj.,* lacking sweetness.

earthy, *adj.,* having a taste associated with soil.

ebullioscope, *n.,* instrument for determining the degree of alcohol in must or wine.

echt, *adj.* (Ger., EKHT), real, genuine.

edel, *adj.* (Ger., EH-dl), noble, unusually fine.

edelfaüle, *n.* (Ger., EHD-l-foy-leh), "noble mold," a fungus which attacks certain overripe grapes, reducing their overall volume of juice without reducing sugar—thus, making them sweeter.

edelgewachs, *n.* (Ger., EHD-l-guh-VEKHS), finest growth.

egrappage, *n.* (Fr., eh-grah-PAHZH), destemming of grapes.

egrappoir, *n.* (Fr., eh-grah-PWAHR), machine to destem grapes.

ehrwein, *n.* (Ger., EHR-vine), elegant wine.

eiswein, *n.* (Ger., ICE-vine), wine made from ripened grapes left on the vine during a frost; the grape is picked when some of its water is frozen; the remaining liquid concentration is commensurately sweeter.

envelope, *n.,* paper or straw cover or container put over bottle before shipping so that it will not break.

enzyme, *n.,* chemical component in yeast which induces fermentation.

epluchage, *n.* (Fr., eh-ploo-SHAHZH), process of removing undesirable berries from bunch of grapes before crushing.

erben, *n.* (Ger., EHR-ben), "heirs of" or "estate of," term frequently used on labels of estate-bottled wine.

erdig, *adj.* (Ger., EHR-dik), earthy.

estate-bottled, *adj.*, bottled on the property of the grape-grower, usually by him or under his direct supervision.

ester, *n.*, volatile compound formed by combination of acids and alcohol in wine; responsible for its bouquet.

estufa, *n.* (Port., es-TOO-fah), hothouse or heated cellar for baking young fortified wines in Madeira.

estufado, *adj.* (Port., es-too-FAH-do), baked.

ethyl alcohol, *n.*, the main alcohol found in wine, a result of yeast activity on the sugar in the grape.

extra dry, extra sec, *adj.*, with respect to sparkling wines, moderately sweet. The term obviously is an incongruity, since dry means lacking in sugar. Its use probably dates to a time when only two degrees of sweetness existed in sparkling wines, "sweet" (very sweet) and "dry" (not very sweet). Introduction of subsequent varieties of still less sweetness called for additional characterizations.

fad, *adj.* (Ger., FAHT), lacking taste, flat.

faible, *adj.* (Fr., FAY-bluh), weak.

fass, *n.* (Ger., FAHSS), cask containing about 160 U.S. gallons; the buying increment in the Rhine region of Germany.

faul, *adj.* (Ger., FOWL), having a mold-producing fungus; therefore, unclean.

fein, *adj.* (Ger., FINE), fine.

ferme, *n.* (Fr., FAIRM), a full wine that when aged possesses a coarseness it should have lost.

fermentation, *n.*, chemical process that transforms sugar into alcohol, carbon dioxide gas and other byproducts.

fett, *adj.* (Ger., FETT), big, full-bodied.

fiasco, *n.* (It., fee-AHS-coh), wicker-covered bottle, usually 1 liter or larger, used principally for Chianti.

fifth, *n.*, bottle in U.S. containing one fifth of a gallon, or 25.6 fluid ounces.

filtration, *n.*, process of clarifying wines by passing them through porous material, usually after immersing quantities of diatumaceous earth or some similar neutral substance to attract various particles that have been separated from the solution.

fining, *n.*, process of clarifying wines by adding materials (albumen, isinglass, lactic acid, blood, etc.) that combine with floating particles of sediment, then drop to the bottom of the container; the clarified wine then is pumped out, leaving the remaining solids. Note that fining and filtration are different processes. Fining is done at various stages in winemaking, but usually not after aging has begun. Filtration usually is performed only immediately before bottling.

fino, *n.* (Sp., FEE-noh), any very pale, dry and delicate Sherry; the term also is employed adjectivally, as in "a fino Sherry."

firn, *adj.* (Ger., FEERN), tasting of wood.

flagon, *n.*, ancient short-necked wine flask.

flask, *n.*, flat-sided container.

flat, *adj.*, of a still wine, dull, inspid, lacking in character; of a sparkling wine, lacking effervescence.

flavored, *adj.*, characterized by addition of flavoring.

flinty, *adj.*, sharp, dry, clean.

flor, *n.* (Sp., FLOHR), yeast which forms a film on the surface of the fermenting must and imparts a unique flavor to the wine; generally used in fortified wines.

flüchtig, *adj.* (Ger., FLERKH-tick), empty, light, fruity.

foil, *n.*, tin, lead or aluminum cap over mouth and neck of bottle.

fort, *adj.* (Fr., FOHR), strong, full-bodied.

fortified, *adj.*, possessing more than 16 percent alcohol by volume, a result of evaporation of non-alcohol liquids or, more commonly, addition of distilled spirts.

foudre, *n.* (Fr., FOO-druh), large aging cask.

foulage, *n.* (Fr., foo-LAHZH), the pressing of grapes.

foxiness, *n.*, strong grapy taste characteristic of many wines made predominantly from varieties of the *vitis labrusca* species of grape, native to North America.

fragrant, *adj.*, pleasing to the nose.

fresh, *adj.*, young, sprightly, clean, and usually highly acid.

frisch, *adj.* (Ger., FRISH), young, sprightly, clean, and usually highly acid.

frizzante, *adj.* (It., free-DZAHN-teh), characterized by slight effervescence, as opposed to the genuine "sparkle" of full secondary fermentation.

fruité, *adj.* (Fr., froo-wee-TAY), fruity.

fruit wine, *n.*, one made from a fruit other than the grape.

fruity, *adj.*, possessing a lively, clean, grapy flavor.

fuder, *n.* (Ger., FOO-dehr), wine cask containing about 960 liters, found principally in Moselle region.

full, *adj.,* containing many soluble solids; usually used as "full-bodied," in contrast to "light-bodied," which describes a wine containing few soluble solids.

fumet, *n.* (Fr., foo-MAY), bouquet.

fumeux, *n.* (Fr., foo-MUR), spirited.

gefällig, *adj.* (Ger., geh-FEH-lick), delightful, harmonious.

gefüllt, *adj.* (Ger., geh-FILL-t), robust, full-bodied, possessing fine bouquet and flavor.

gelatin, *n.,* a protein frequently used as a clarifying agent in fining.

gemarkung, *n.* (Ger., gheh-MAHRK-oong), legally delimited wine-producing area.

genereux, *n.* (Fr., zhay-nay-REHR), full-bodied wine with high alcohol concentration.

generic, *adj.,* named after a geographic area (Bordeaux, Chablis, Tokay) or a color (white, rosé); the term also is used as a noun, and a wine so-named is referred to as "a generic"—as opposed to "a varietal," which is named after the dominant grape variety.

generoso, *n.* (Port., jeh-neh-ROH-soh), full-bodied wine with high alcohol concentration, usually sweet.

gering, *adj.* (Ger., GHEH-rink), inferior.

getaufer, *n.* (Ger., gheh-TOWF-er), watered wine.

gewächs, *n.* (Ger., gheh-VEKHS), "property of," followed on wine labels by name of owner.

gezuckert, *adj.* (Ger., gheh-TSOOK-ert), sugared.

glatt, *adj.* (Ger., GLAHTT), smooth.

goldbeerenauslese, *n.* (Ger., GOLT-beer-n-owzh-lay-zuh), wine made from selected late-ripened grapes; the term appeared on German wine labels before 1973, when it was outlawed.

goût, *n.* (Fr., GOO), taste.

goût americain, *n.* (Fr., GOO-tah-may-ree-CAN), sweet sparkling wine associated with South American consumers.

goût anglais, *n.* (Fr., GOO-dawn-GLAY), dry sparkling wine associated with English consumers.

goût du bois, *n.* (Fr., GOO-duh-BWAH), woody taste.

goût du bouchon, *n.* (Fr., GOO-duh-boo-SHOHN), corky taste—the result of a diseased cork.

goût de paille, *n.* (Fr., GOO-duh-PIY-yuh), musty taste.

goût de pierre a fusil, *n.* (GOO-duh-pee-YAIR ah foo-ZEE), hard, flinty taste, usually associated with wines from the French district of Chablis.

goût de pique, *n.* (Fr., GOO-duh-PEEK), taste of vinegar.

goût de terroir, *n.* (Fr., GOO-duh-tehr-WAHR), earthy taste.

goût d'event, *n.* (Fr., GOO-day-VAHN), flavorless taste.

grafting, *n.,* inserting shoot or scion of one vine into the stock of another, in which it will continue to grow.

green, *adj.,* immature and not ready for drinking.

grossier, *n.* (Fr., groh-see-YAY), coarse full-bodied wine.

growth, *n.,* literal translation of French *"cru,"* referring to a vineyard; thus, wine growers speak of a "classified growth" not as a particular crop but as a vineyard which has been classified.

grün, *adj.* (Ger., GREWYN), immature and not ready for drinking.

halb-fuder, *n.* (Ger., HAHLP-fyuh-der), wine cask holding 480 liters, usually found in Mosel region.

halb-stück, *n.* (Ger., HAHLP-schtook), wine cask holding 640 liters, usually found in Rhine region.

harmonisch, *adj.* (Ger., hahr-MOHN-ish), well-balanced.

hart, *adj.* (Ger., HAHRT), acetic.

haute sauternes, *n.* (Fr., OH-so-TAIRN), literally, "high Sauternes," a phrase intended to suggest greater quality than in other wines from the French region of Sauternes; fact is, the designation is pure puffery on the part of the labeler and the expression appears only on wines exported to North America. However, some California winemakers use "haute Sauterne" (note absence of final "s") to designate certain medium-sweet to sweet still wines.

heavy, *adj.,* robust and full-bodied but lacking finesse.

hecho, *adj.* (Sp., AY-choh), ready for bottling.

hectare, *n.* (Fr., ECK-tehr), land measurement equal to 2.47 acres.

hippocras, *n.,* ancient cordial made of wine mixed with spices, often used as a medicine; Petronius wrote of it in *Satyricon;* predecessor of today's Vermouth.

hochgewächs, *n.* (Ger., HOKH-ghe-veks), superior vineyard; the term, once common on German labels, has been rendered obsolete by the 1973 wine law.

hock, *n.,* any dry white still wine of the type traditionally associated with Germany's Rhine region; the term, used mainly in England, is a corruption of "hochgewächs," which frequently appeared on labels of Rhine-produced wines.

hogshead, *n.*, large cask; size may vary from 63 to 140 U.S. gallons, except in Jérez, Spain, where it is fixed at 66 U.S. gallons.

holzgeschmack, *n.* (Ger., HOLTS-she-SCHMAHKH), woody taste.

honigartig, *n.* (Ger., HA-nikh-HARR-tick), honey-like aroma and taste, common to certain wines made from late-picked grapes.

hübsch, *adj.* (Ger., HOOPSCH), gentle.

hybrid vine, *n.*, one produced by crossing two or more varieties.

hydrometer, *n.*, instrument for determining specific gravity of a liquid.

ice wine, *n.*, wine made from ripened grapes left on the vine during a frost; the grape is picked when some of its water is frozen; the remaining liquid concentration is commensurately sweeter.

imperiale, *n.* (Fr., im-peh-ree-YAHL), bottle containing about 6 liters.

incrustation, *n.*, formation of crust-like solids in long-stored red wine.

injerto, *n.* (Sp., een-HEHR-toh), grafting.

insipid, *adj.*, lacking acidity.

isinglass, *n.*, gelatin obtained from fish, used as clarifying agent during fining of wine.

jarra, *n.* (Sp., HAHR-rah), jar containing about 12 liters.

jeroboam, *n.*, bottle containing about 104 ounces, usually used for sparkling wine.

jung, *adj.* (Ger., YOONG), young.

kabinett, *n.* (Ger., KAB-in-ett), wine deemed meritorious of "special attribute" status under German law; normally drawn from selected casks.

keeping qualities, *n.*, factors responsible for longevity of a wine.

keller, *n.* (Ger., KEL-ler), cellar.

kellerabfullung, *adj.* (Ger., KEL-ler-AHP-fil-loong), bottled on the estate of the grape-grower (literally, in his cellar).

kellarabzug, *n.* (Ger., KEL-ler-ahp-TSOOG), bottled on the estate of the grape-grower (literally, in his cellar); term rendered obsolete by 1973 German wine law.

konsumwein, *n.* (Ger., kon-ZOOM-vine), wine intended for local consumption; thus, not distinguished.

korper, *n.* (Ger., KOR-purr), density or consistency of a wine; that is, the proportion of soluble solids in it.

kräftig, *adj.* (Ger., KRAHFF-tick), robust, full-bodied, usually with high alcohol concentration.

krescenz, *n.* (Ger., KRESS-sents), "property of," followed on labels by name of owner.

lagar, *n.* (Sp., lah-GAHR), wine-pressing trough.

labrusca, *adj.*, pertaining to *vitis labrusca,* the main species of native North American grape, varieties of which include Catawba, Concord, Delaware, Niagara, Iona, Ives and Dutchess.

lebendig, *adj.* (Ger., luh-BENN-tick), fresh, with spicy flavor.

lees, *n.* (pl.), deposits of sediment that accumulate in a container of new wine as solids separate from the solution.

leger, *adj.* (Fr., lay-ZHAY), light-bodied.

legs, *n.* (pl.), streaks that run down the inside of a glass after wine has been swirled in it; as a rule, the heavier they are, the heavier-bodied the wine.

levante, *n.* (Sp., lay-VAHN-tay), a hot east wind that frequently blows over the Sherry-producing region of Jérez, accelerating the growth of grapes; legend has it that the wind originates in the Sahara, though there doesn't seem to be much meteorological support for this.

levulose, *n.*, principal sugar in grapes; a form of fructose.

lias, *n.* (pl.) (Sp., LEE-ahs), deposits of sediment that accumulate in a container of new wine as solids separate from the solution.

licoroso, *adj.* (Sp., lee-koh-ROH-soh), sweet, rich, heavy-bodied—usually applied to sweet Sherries and other fortified wines.

lieblich, *adj.* (Ger., LEEP-lick), delicate, gentle, light-bodied.

Limousin, *n.* (Fr., lee-moo-ZAN), variety of oak used in barrels and casks; widely regarded as one of the most desirable aging woods for wine.

liqueur de tirage, *n.* (Fr., lee-KURR duh tee-RAHZH), sweet solution composed of wine, sugar and yeast, generally added to sparkling wines after first fermentation to stimulate second fermentation; frequently described simply as "tirage."

liqueur d'expédition, *n.* (Fr., lee-KURR dex-pay-dee-see-

OWN), solution of sugar and wine added to sparkling wine before final corking to control degree of sweetness.

liquoureux, *adj.* (Fr., lee-koo-RERR), sweet, rich, heavy-bodied—usually applied to fortified wines.

maderisé, *adj.* (Fr., mah-duh-ree-ZAY), pertaining to a white wine that has taken on a woody taste and a dark hue, usually from oxidation, overaging or overexposure to heat and/or light.

maderized, *adj.,* pertaining to a white wine that has taken on a woody taste and a dark hue, usually from oxidation, overaging or overexposure to heat and/or light.

mager, *adj.* (Ger., MAY-ghurr), lacking in body.

magnum, *n.,* bottle containing about 52 ounces, or double the usual table size; used chiefly for sparkling wines.

maître de chai, *n.* (Fr., MAY-truh duh SHAY), cellarmaster.

malic acid, *n.,* one of the acids in grapes; similar to that in green apples.

mandel bitter, *n.* (Ger., MAHN-del bit-tur), wine with a taste reminiscent of bitter almonds.

manzanilla, *n.* (Sp., mahn-thah-NEE-lyah), strictly speaking, the dry wine, still or fortified, of the Spanish region of Sanlúcar de Barrameda; more commonly, colloquially in Spain and parts of the Americas, any dry Sherry.

marc, *n.* (Fr., MAR), pomace; the remains of skins, stems and seeds after grapes have been pressed; also, the brandy distillate often made from these remains.

matt, *adj.* (Ger., MAHTT), lifeless, insipid.

mature grapes, *n.,* those which have ripened to a point where their sugar-alcohol balance is deemed suitable for winemaking.

mature wine, *n.,* that which has aged to a point where it is deemed incapable of improving.

May wine, *n.,* any light, slightly sweet white wine infused with the fragrant leaves of the Woodruff plant; originates in Germany, popular also in England.

mellow, *adj.,* deemed correctly aged, soft, and well-rounded.

methuselah, *n.,* bottle containing about 208 ounces, or eight times the usual table size; popular in France for sparkling wines.

mild, *adj.,* lacking in character.

milde, *adj.* (Ger., MILL-duh), lacking in character.

mildew, *n.,* fungoid disease that attacks vines, damaging leaves and berries.

millésime, *n.* (Fr., mee-lay-ZEEM), vintage date.

mistelle, *n.* (Fr., meez-TELL), grape must to which brandy has been added to halt fermentation; used principally in aromatized and flavored wines.

moelle, *n.,* **moelleux,** *adj.* (Fr., mwah-LUH, mwah-LURR), applied to a wine that is rich and silky but not sweet.

moldy, *adj.,* characterized by an offensive nose and taste, the result of a musty barrel or of grapes on which certain fungi have grown.

moot, *n.* (Ger., MOOT), the crushed grapes—skins, stems, seeds and juice—before and during fermentation.

mosto, *n.* (Sp., MOH-stoh), the crushed grapes—skins, stems, seeds and juice—before and during fermentation; also applied colloquially in many Spanish-speaking countries to a young wine.

mou, *adj.* (Fr., MOO), flat-tasting, flabby.

mouillé, *adj.* (Fr., MOO-yah), diluted (i.e., with water; thus, pertaining to a watered wine).

mousseux, *adj.* (Fr., moo-SUH), sparkling; *n.,* any French sparkling wine made outside the district of Champagne.

mousy, *adj.,* having a musty [sic] taste and nose.

moût, *n.* (Fr., MOO), the crushed grapes—skins, stems, seeds and juice—before and during fermentation.

mulled wine, *n.,* a wine that has been sweetened, spiced and heated; may be cooled before serving but usually is served hot.

must, *n.,* the crushed grapes—skins, stems, seeds and juice—before and during fermentation.

mustometer, *n.,* instrument to measure sugar content of grape must.

musty, *adj.,* characterized by a disagreeable smell and taste of mold. (Note that this usage is completely unrelated to grape must.)

muté, *adj.* (Fr., moo-TAY), pertaining to a wine whose fermentation has been halted by addition of brandy.

natur, *n.,* **naturelle,** *adj.* (Fr., nah-CHOOR, nah-choor-ELL), made without addition of sugar or spirits; usually applied to sparkling wines that have not had the usual sweetening dosage.

naturwein, *n.* (Ger., NAY-choor-vine), one made without addition of sugar or spirits.

nebuchadnezzar, *n.,* bottle containing about 640 ounces, used on rare occasions for sparkling wine.

négociant, *n.* (Fr., neh-goh-see-YAWN), shipper.

nerveux, *adj.* (Fr., nair-VURR), lusty, possessing great longevity.

nervig, *adj.* (Ger., NURR-fick), robust, full, rich.

Nicolauswein, *n.* (Ger., nee-kohl-OWS-vine), made from grapes gathered on St. Nicholas Day, December 6.

noble, *adj.,* well-made from "aristocratic" (i.e., highly prized) grape varieties.

noble mold, noble rot, *n.,* a mold (deemed highly beneficial) which attacks certain grape berries, reducing their liquid content without reducing their sugar.

nonvintage, *adj.,* pertaining to a blend of wines from different years, or, less frequently, to a given year's wine which for one reason or another the producer chooses not to identify by year; in sparkling wines, "vintage" years generally testify to the producer's belief that the vintaged wine is superior to his usual product, whereas in still wines, certain producers almost always vintage all their wines and certain others almost never vintage any of theirs, depending mainly on the producer's blending practices.

nose, *n.,* fragrance.

nube, *adj.* (Sp., NOO-bay), cloudy.

nutty, *adj.,* characterized by a nut-like taste, particularly a walnut-like taste; said of Sherries, especially dry ones.

ochsle, *n.* (Ger., ERKS-leh), measure of soluble solids, mainly sugar, in grape juice or must; expressed in degrees; equivalent to English "balling."

octavilla, *n.* (Sp., ohk-tah-VEEL-lyah), cask containing about 16 gallons, usually used for Sherry.

oeil de perdrix, *n.* (Fr., OO-yuh duh pehr-DREE), wine of pinkish gold, usually an aged rosé; the term translates literally as "partridge's eye," which the color of the wine is perceived as resembling; the term also describes nonsparkling white wine made from red/black grapes (e.g., white Zinfandel).

oelig, *adj.* (Ger., EHRR-lick), oily; applied to a wine of considerable density that therefore pours slowly; not pejorative.

oenology, *n.* (ee-NOL-a-jee), the science of winemaking; sometimes spelled "enology."

oidium, *n.,* fungus disease that attacks vines.

oloroso, *n.* (Sp., oh-loh-ROH-soh), a type of Sherry, dark, sweet and full-bodied; unlike the contrasting finos, not made with flor yeast.

ordinaire, *adj.* (Fr., or-din-NAIR), not distinguished; a favorite pejorative of wine snobs.

organoleptics, *n.,* the science of judging wine by the senses (as opposed to by chemical analysis); such judging frequently is described as an "organoleptic evaluation."

oval, *n.,* an elliptical barrel or cask.

oxidation, *n.,* chemical change in wine (infusion with oxygen) brought about by exposure to air.

parfum, *n.* (Fr., pahr-FAM), fragrance (one speaks of the *parfum* of the wine whether pleasant or unpleasant).

passe-tout-grain, *n.* (Fr., pahs-too-GRAN), a wine made exclusively from Pinot Noir and Gamay grapes, usually in about one-to-three proportion.

pauvre, *adj.* (Fr., POH-vruh), poor; more specifically, flat.

Pedro Ximenez, *n.* (Sp., Pay-droh khee-MAY-neth), strictly speaking, a grape variety or the wine therefrom, used mainly for sweetening Sherries; colloquially in Spain, any very sweet Sherry.

pelure d'oignon, *n.* (Fr., peh-LOOR dwan-NYAW), brownish tinge that appears in some old red wines; literally, onion skin.

perfume, *n.,* fragrance (one speaks of the *perfume* of the wine whether pleasant or unpleasant).

perlé, *adj.* (Fr., pair-LAY), mildly effervescent.

perlwein, *n.* (Ger., PAIRL-vine), one that is mildly effervescent.

pétillant, *n., adj.* (Fr., pay-tee-LAWN), a (or pertaining to a) mildly effervescent wine.

petit, *adj.* (Fr., puh-TEE), small; by extension, poor, not well-made; a wine snob's pejorative.

petit chateau, *n.* (puh-TEE shah-TOH), a less-than-celebrated vineyard; one not numbered among those officially classified; not a pejorative.

pH, *n.,* measure of total acidity in a solution.

phylloxera, *n.,* a grapevine louse that attacks roots and leaves; an epidemic of them in the nineteenth century destroyed many vineyards in Europe and California, all of which subsequently had to be replanted with *vitis vinifera* shoots grafted to North American root stocks.

pièce, *n.* (Fr., pee-ESS), cask holding about 60 U.S. gallons, common in Burgundy.

pipe, *n.*, wine cask holding about 126 U.S. gallons, common in Spain and Portugal (the word pipe is English and is used principally by English merchants in Sherries and Ports).

piquant, *adj.* (Fr., pee-KAWN), sharp, biting, tart, but agreeably so; usually applied to young wines with captivating bouquet and taste.

piqué, *adj.* (Fr., pee-KAY), oxidized and therefore in the process of turning to vinegar.

pisador, *n.* (Sp., pee-sah-DOHR), person who treads on grapes during harvest (most have been replaced by mechanical crushers, but grapes are still crushed by foot in parts of Spain and Portugal).

plastering, *n.*, practice of adding gypsum to low-acid wine to give it balance.

plat, *adj.* (Fr., PLAH), flat, tasteless, dull.

plein, *adj.* (Fr., PLEEN), full-bodied.

pomace, *n.*, the remains of skins, stems and seeds after grapes have been pressed.

pop wine, *n.*, flavored wine, usually nongrape, usually also carbonated, with alcohol concentration of 7 to 12%.

pourriture noble, *n.* (Fr., poo-ree-TOOR NOH-bl), a mold (deemed highly beneficial) which attacks certain grape berries, reducing their liquid content without reducing their sugar.

powerful, *adj.*, having full bouquet (not a reference to a wine's alcoholic strength, as whiskey drinkers might imagine).

précoce, *adj.* (Fr., preh-KOHSS), fast-maturing; usually, mature before an analysis of grape-growing and winemaking practices would suggest it should be.

prensa, *n.* (Sp., PREHN-sah), apparatus that applies pressure to crushed grapes to force out remaining juice.

press, *n.*, apparatus that applies pressure to crushed grapes to force out remaining juice.

pressoir, *n.* (Fr., press-WAHR), apparatus that applies pressure to crushed grapes to force out remaining juice.

propriétaire, *n.* (Fr., pro-pree-eh-TAYR), owner of a vineyard; in Burgundy, vineyards are sectionally owned, and the propriétaire of each section may make and bottle his own wine under the vineyard name.

pulp, *n.,* fleshy inside of the grape.

puncheon, *n.,* cask of 80 to 165 U.S. gallons' capacity.

puttonyo, *n.* (Hun., poo-TAWN-yo), basket for gathering grapes during harvest; also an indication of the degree of sweetness in Tokaji (Tokay) wine, derived from the number of puttonyos (baskets) of overripe grapes added to a normal batch being crushed.

queue, *n.* (Fr., KER), cask holding about 120 U.S. gallons; common in Burgundy.

quinta, *n.* (Port., KEEN-tah), vineyard.

racking, *n.,* process of clarifying a new wine by pouring or pumping the liquid off its lees and into a new container.

rancio, *adj.* (Sp., RAHN-thee-oh), possessing great bouquet resulting from long storage; applied to Sherry.

rassig, *adj.* (Ger., RAHS-sick), possessing great character.

rauh, *adj.* (Ger., RHAW), harsh, coarse, immature.

raya, *n.* (Sp. RAH-yah), chalk mark on Sherry cask indicating the degree of sweetness of the contents.

redondo, *adj.* (Sp., ray-DOHN-doh), round, well-balanced.

refreshing, *n.,* process of adding a younger wine to an older blend to give it zestiness.

regional wine, *n.,* one named after the region in which it was produced (Chianti, St. Emilion, Rhine); however, when these same geographic names are applied to wines of the same type produced *outside* the region, the wines are called "generic" rather than "regional" wines.

reif, *adj.* (Ger., RIFE), mature, at its peak.

rein, *adj.* (Ger., RINE), pure, vinous.

reintönig, *adj.* (Ger., rine-TIRN-igh), round, well-balanced.

remuage, *n.* (Fr., rum-oo-AHZH), in production of sparkling wines, process of placing bottles neck downward on inclined racks so that sediment may separate from the solution and settle in the neck of the bottle, from which it is easily expellable; while in the racks, the bottles are jarred or shaken at intervals to enhance separation of sediment.

rich, *adj.,* possessing excellent bouquet, flavor and body.

riddling, *n.,* in production of sparkling wines, process of placing bottles neck downward on inclined racks so that sediment may separate from the solution and settle in the neck of the bottle, from which it is easily expellable; while in the racks, the bottles are jarred or shaken at intervals to enhance separation of sediment.

ripe, *adj.*, mature, at its peak.

robe, *n.*, the visual aspects of a wine—i.e., its color, clarity, and, in the case of sparkling wines, its sparkle.

robust, *adj.*, full-bodied; sometimes also connotes that the wine is slightly harsh or coarse.

rociar, *v.* (Sp., roh-thee-AHR), to refresh an older blend of wine by adding a younger wine.

rough, *adj.*, immature, harsh, coarse, not quite palatable; normally applied not to "bad" wines but to "good" ones that are deemed not ready for drinking.

rounded, *adj.*, well-balanced.

ruby Port, *n.*, a young Port wine with very deep red color.

rund, *adj.* (Ger., ROONT), well-balanced.

saccarometer, *n.*, instrument to measure sugar content of grapes or must.

sack, *n.*, English term originally applied to all Spanish fortified wines, now generally limited to those outside the Jérez de la Frontera district (those inside the district are called Sherry). The term frequently is taken as a corruption of *seco*, meaning "dry," but since all fortified wines at the time of its coinage were sweet, we prefer to regard it as a corruption of *secar*, "to export."

saftig, *adj.* (Ger., ZAHFT-tick), full-bodied, rich.

sancocho, *n.* (Sp., sahn-COH-choh), syrup used in Sherry blending to sweeten and color the wine; it is made by cooking the must.

sangria, *n.* (Sp., sahn-GREE-ah), a punch of wine and fresh fruit, sometimes fortified with brandy or other spirits.

sauber, *adj.* (Ger., DZOW-behr), clean; i.e., not "dirtied" by olfactory or taste sensations that distract from the original varietal ones.

schal, *adj.* (Ger., SCHAHLL), characterized by a moldy, tired taste.

schloss, *n.* (Ger., SCHLAWSS), vineyard (literally, "castle").

schlossabzug, *adj.* (Ger., SCHLAWSS-ahb-TSOOG), bottled on the estate of the grape-grower.

schneewein, *n.* (Ger., SCHNEE-vine), wine produced from grapes gathered when the vineyard is covered with snow.

schön, *adj.* (Ger., SHURN), rich, full.

schwefel, *n.* (Ger., SCHWEF-fel), sulphurous smell.

sec, *adj.* (Fr., SECK), lacking sweetness.

secco, *adj.* (It., SECK-coh), lacking sweetness.

seco, *adj.* (Sp. and Port., SECK-coh), lacking sweetness.

sediment, *n.*, crust or deposit found in casks, barrels, bottles or other containers, a result of solids in the wine separating from the solution.

sekt, *n.* (Ger., SEKT), sparkling wine.

silky, *adj.*, possessing admirable texture.

small, *adj.*, poor, not well-made; a favorite pejorative of wine snobs.

smooth, *adj.*, devoid of coarseness or harshness.

soft, *adj.*, low in acid (not a pejorative).

solear, *v.* (Sp., soh-lay-AHR), to dry in the sun—a practice employed in Jérez de la Frontera and other Spanish regions that produce fortified wines, to increase the sugar concentration of grapes before they are crushed.

solera, *n.* (Sp., soh-LAY-rah), a system of continuously blending wines by arranging casks in three or more tiers; the bottom tier contains the oldest wine, the next tier the next oldest, and so on; as wine is drawn from the oldest cask, it is replaced with wine from the next-oldest cask, and so on up the line; Spanish lore has it that the older wines give "guidance" to the young ones, helping them mature gracefully.

sommelier, *n.* (Fr., sum-mel-YAY), wine steward.

sophistiquer, *v.* (Fr., soh-fees-tee-KAY), to improve a wine by blending.

sound, *adj.*, well-balanced, possessing the desired vinous characteristics.

soutirage, *n.* (Fr., soo-tee-RAHZH), process of clarifying a new wine by pouring or pumping the liquid off its lees and into a new container.

soyeux, *adj.* (Fr., swah-YURR), possessing admirable texture.

sparkling, *adj.*, pertaining to wine which has undergone a second fermentation in a closed container; this creates a profusion of carbon dioxide bubbles, which make the wine "sparkle."

spätlese, *adj.* (Ger., SCHPAYT-lay-zuh), made from late-picked grapes.

spicy, *adj.*, lively, aromatic, fragrant, pungent.

spritzig, *n.* (Ger., SCHPRITS-ig), mildly effervescent.

spumante, *adj.* (It., spoo-MAHN-tay), sparkling.

starter, *n.*, a pure yeast used to induce fermentation (as opposed to the natural yeasts which develop on grape skins).

stemmer, *n.*, apparatus that separates grapes from their stems.

stemmy, *adj.*, having a taste characteristic of grape stems.

sturdy, *adj.*, full-bodied, robust; also applied on occasions to wines regarded as needing more aging.

süss, *adj.* (Ger., SERSS), sweet.

tannin, *n.*, acid derived from the skins, stems and seeds of grapes.

tart, *adj.*, high in acidity.

tartrates, *n.*, salts of tartaric acid, found in the lees or residues of wine after fermentation.

tastevin, *n.* (Fr., tast-VANN), implement for tasting wine; the classic tastevin is a flat silver cup with elevated sections along the sides to permit inspection of the wine's color: sommeliers frequently wear these around their neck; currently certain glasses of approximate pear-like contours also are described as "tastevins."

tawny, *adj.*, of a Port, characterized by a brownish or rusty tinge, a result of long aging and repeated fining (considered a highly desirable property).

tendre, *adj.* (Fr., TAND-ruh), delicate; usually, also fresh and young.

thief, *n.*, implement for drawing a sample of wine from a barrel; one common variety is a glass tube, dipped into the barrel, then covered so that suction will hold the wine inside as the tube is lifted from the barrel; another variety involves a cylindrical metal container that holds about an ounce, attached to a fine rod which is dipped into the barrel.

thin, *adj.*, deficient in body and/or alcohol concentration.

tierce, *n.*, cask holding about 42 U.S. gallons.

tirage, *n.* (Fr., tee-RAHZH), process of drawing wine from barrels (by whatever means).

tischwein, *n.* (Ger., TISH-vine), table wine; usually a reference not only to still wine but also specifically to tafelwein, that category of everyday blended still wines made from low-yield grapes, as opposed to *qualitätswein*, made from costlier grapes and regarded as special-occasion wines (though, of course, frequently drunk at table).

tonelero, *n.* (Sp., toh-nay-LAY-roh), person who makes or repairs barrels, casks and other wooden containers.

tonneaux, *n.* (Fr., tawn-OH), measure of about 900 liters, or 238 U.S. gallons, used in Bordeaux; usually the wines in this measure weigh about 2,000 pounds, or one ton; the English word, "ton," derives from *tonneaux*.

tourné, *n.* (Fr., toor-NAY), wine spoilage caused by lactic bacteria.

Traubenkelter, *n.* (Ger., TROW-ben-kell-ter), hydraulic grape press.

trocken, *adj.* (Ger., TROCK-en), dry. (And *sehr trocken* is "very dry." The terms are used on sparkling wine labels.)

Trockenbeerenauslese, *n.* (Ger., TROCK-en-bay-ren-OWZH-lays-eh), wine made from individually selected raisin-size grape berries that have been attacked by the botrytis cinerea fungus.

tun, *n.*, cask holding about 252 U.S. gallons.

ullage, *n.*, empty space in a barrel, resulting from loss of wine through evaporation or leakage; the barrel must promptly be refilled, or the air in it will oxidize the wine. One speaks of "topping up (i.e., eliminating) the ullage."

ungezuckert, *adj.* (Ger., OON-ga-tsook-ert), unsugared.

usé, *adj.* (Fr., oo-ZAY), past its prime.

uva, *n.* (It., OO-vah), grape.

varietal, *adj.*, named after the predominant grape variety. In the U.S., wines may be varietally named if at least 51 percent of the wine in the blend was made from grapes of the variety in question and the wine is deemed "characteristic" of the variety.

vat, *n.*, container of wood, concrete, glass or metal used for fermentation, storage, blending and/or aging.

vatting, *n.*, practice of blending or mixing wines (inevitably done in a vat).

vault, *n.*, underground storage place for wine.

V.D.Q.S., Vins Délimités de Qualité Superieure (Fr., VAN duh-lee-mee-TAY duh qual-ee-TAY soo-pehr-ee-URR), official French classification authenticating certain wines which fail to meet stricter standards for an *appellation controlée.*

velvety, *adj.*, possessing admirable texture.

vendange, *n.* (Fr., vahn-DAHNZH), harvest.

vendangeur, *n.* (Fr., vahn-dahn-ZHER), vineyard worker (grape-picker, general harvest laborer, etc.).

venencia, *n.* (Sp., vay-NEHN-see-ah), cylindrical container at the end of a long, fine strip of whalebone or a fine metal rod; dipped into barrel through bunghole to draw a sample.

verbesserte, *adj.* (Ger., fair-bess-EHR-tuh), pertaining to a wine in which fermentation has been enhanced by addition of sugar before or during fermentation; literally, "improved"; the process is called *verbesserung,* "improving."

vermouth, *n.,* a wine aromatized and flavored with herbs, roots, barks, bitters and other substances.

vert, *adj.* (Fr., VAIR), a wine too young to be drunk; literally, "green."

vid, *n.* (Sp., VEED), grapevine.

viejo, *adj.* (Sp., vee-AY-khoh), old, aged.

vif, *adj.* (Fr., VEEF), spicy, brisk, lively.

vigne, *n.* (Fr., VEEN-yuh), grapevine.

vigneron, *n.* (Fr., veen-yair-AWN), vineyard worker (more often, the owner of the vineyard and/or only those workers who actually tend the vines).

vignoble, *n.* (Fr., VEEN-yobl), vineyard.

vin, *n.* (Fr., VAN), wine.

viña, *n.* (Sp., VEEN-ya), vineyard.

viñadero, *n.* (Sp., veen-ya-DAY-roh), vineyard worker; usually, specifically those workers who actually tend the vines.

viñador, *n.* (Sp., veen-ya-DOHR), grape-grower; i.e., owner of the vineyard.

vin blanc, *n.* (Fr., VAN BLAWN), white wine.

vin cuit, *n.* (Fr., VAN KWEE), cooked or baked wine; a concentrate added to thin wines to give them liveliness and body.

vin de messe, *n.* (Fr., VAN duh MESS), sacramental or altar wines (literally, "mass wines").

vin doux, *n.* (Fr., VAN DOO), sweet wine.

viñedo, *n.* (Sp., veen-YAY-doh), a vineyard or a region in which there are vineyards.

vinée, *n.* (Fr., VEE-nay), vintage.

vinello, *adj.* (It., vee-NEL-lo), poor, thin, unpalatable.

viñero, *n.* (Sp., veen-YAY-roh), grape-grower, owner of vineyard.

vinetto, vinettino, *adj.* (It., vee-NEHT-to, vee-neht-TEE-noh), poor, thin, unpalatable.

vineux, *n.* (Fr., vee-NURR), vinosity, the collective characteristics of a wine.

vineyard, *n.,* plantation of grapevines.

vin, fin de marque, *n.* (Fr., VAN, FAN duh MAHRK), vintage wine.

vin gris, *n.* (Fr., VAN GREE), "grey" wine, usually a white wine made from a mixture of red and white grapes.

vinho, *n.* (Port., VEEN-oh), wine.

vinho claro, *n.* (Port., VEEN-oh CLAH-roh), unadulterated wine.

vinho generoso, *n.* (Port., VEEN-oh zheh-neh-ROH-zu), full-bodied wine with high alcohol concentration, usually sweet.

vinho surdo, *n.* (Port., VEEN-oh SOOR-doh), fortified wine.

vinho verde, *n.* (Port., VEEN-oh VEHR-day), generally, any white wine (literally, "green" wine); however, in some regions, especially northern Portugal, reds and rosés as well as whites will be called "verde" if deemed of such a character that they should be consumed young.

viniculture, *n.*, science of winemaking.

vinificator, *n.*, instrument that condenses alcohol vapors that rise from wine fermentation.

vini tipici, *n.* (It., VEE-nee TEE-pee-chee), characteristic wines; i.e., wines characteristic of given places; the term, *vino tipico,* frequently appears on wine labels, indicating that the wine is deemed characteristic of the area in which it was produced; sometimes this will appear as "*vino tipico di* (Chianti)," i.e., "characteristic wine of (Chianti, or wherever)."

vin mousseux, *n.* (Fr., VAN moo-SURR), sparkling wine.

vin nature, *n.* (Fr., VAN nah-TYOOR), unadulterated wine.

vino, *n.* (It. and Sp., VEE-noh), wine.

vino bianco, *n.* (It., VEE-noh bee-AHN-koh), white wine.

vino blanco, *n.* (Sp., VEE-noh BLAHN-koh), white wine.

vino corriente, *n.* (Sp., VEE-noh koh-ree-EHN-tay), wine intended to be drunk young; ordinarily deemed undistinguished.

vino da bottiglia, *n.* (It., VEE-noh dah boh-TEEL-yah), choice wine; literally, bottled-wine (as opposed to *vino da pasto,* wine served in flasks or carafes drawn from the barrel and intended for immediate consumption rather than for aging).

vino da pasto, *n.* (It., VEE-noh dah PAH-stoh), wine served in flasks or carafes drawn from the barrel and intended for immediate consumption rather than for aging; as opposed to *vino da bottiglia,* bottled-wine, choice wine.

vino de añada, *n.* (Sp., VEE-noh day ahn-YAH-dah), in

Sherry making, young, just-pressed wine, ready for first aging procedures.

vino de color, *n.* (Sp., VEE-noh day koh-LOHR), in Sherry production, a dark, fortified wine, usually baked, used for sweetness and color in final blending.

vino de cuerpo, *n.* (Sp., VEE-noh day KWEHR-poh), strong-bodied wine.

vino de Jérez, *n.* (Sp., VEE-noh day khay-RETH), Sherry; i.e., literally, wine from Jérez (de la Frontera).

vino de pasto, *n.* (Sp., VEE-noh day PAH-stoh), wine served in flasks or carafes drawn from the barrel and intended for immediate consumption rather than for aging.

vino maestro, *n.* (It., VEE-noh mah-EHS-troh), the "master wine"; i.e., a full-bodied wine blended with thinner, weaker ones to give them life and character.

vinometer, *n.*, instrument for measuring percentage of alcohol in wine.

vino nostrano, *n.* (It., VEE-noh noh-STRAH-noh), local wine.

vin ordinaire, *n.* (Fr., VAN or-din-NEHR), wine intended to be drunk young; normally deemed undistinguished.

vino rosso, *n.* (It., VEE-noh ROHS-soh), red wine.

vinosity, *n.*, the combined characteristics of a wine; its balance of body, bouquet and flavor.

vino tinto, *n.* (Sp., VEE-noh TEEN-toh), red wine.

vin rosé, *n.* (Fr., VAN roh-ZAY), pink wine.

vin rouge, *n.* (Fr., VAN ROOZH), red wine.

vin sec, *n.* (Fr., VAN SECK), dry wine.

vins, les grands, *n.* (Fr., VANS, lay GRAWN), "the great wines"; i.e., celebrated wines, usually famous vintages thereof.

vintage, *n.*, the annual gathering of ripe grapes; by extension, the wine produced from a given year's grapes.

vintager, *n.*, vineyard worker; usually, specifically those workers who gather the grapes at harvest time.

vintage wine, *n.*, any wine carrying a vintage date (thus, made exclusively or predominantly from grapes grown in that year); occasionally, however, the term is used colloquially to describe a wine considered unusually good (see "vintage year").

vintage year, *n.*, the year in which a vintage-dated wine was produced; in another context, more narrowly, a year deemed excellent for wine: in certain areas, it is customary to date wines only when the grape crop is deemed superior, and to market all others as blends without vintage dates; thus, a dated wine comes from a "vintage year" and in theory is superior to an undated wine; however, some producers have traded on the public's awareness of this practice, and thus many vintage-dated wines today are no better than wines not carrying a vintage date.

vintner, *n.,* person who makes wine.

viticulture, *n.,* science of grape-growing.

vitis labrusca, *n.* (Lat., VEET-ees lah-BROO-skah), main species of native North American grape, varieties of which include Catawba, Concord, Delaware, Niagara, Iona, Ives and Dutchess.

vitis vinifera, *n.* (Lat., VEET-ees vee-NEE-fer-rah), main species of native European grape, varieties of which include Chardonnay, Pinot Noir, Cabernet Sauvignon, Zinfandel, Nebbiolo, Sangioveto, Gewürztraminer, Riesling.

vornehm, *adj.* (Ger., FOR-nehm), aristocratic, elegant, refined.

weeper, *n.,* bottle with a leaking cork.

wein, *n.* (Ger., VINE), wine.

weinbau, *n.* (Ger., VINE-bow), science of grape-growing.

weinbauer, *n.* (Ger., VINE-bow-er), grape-grower; thus, in most cases, owner of the vineyard.

weinberg, *n.* (Ger., VINE-behrg), vineyard.

weingarten, *n.* (Ger., vine-GAHR-ten), vineyard.

weingut, *n.* (Ger., VINE-goot), vineyard.

weinlese, *n.* (Ger., vine-LAYZ-uh), vintage.

weinrebe, *n.* (Ger., vine-REH-buh), grapevine.

weinstock, *n.* (Ger., VINE-stock), grapevine.

weintraube, *n.* (Ger., vine-TROW-buh), grape.

wernig, *n.* (Ger., VEHR-nick), vinosity; the combined characteristics of a wine.

wine broker, *n.,* intermediary in the wine industry who arranges transactions between grape-growers and producers or shippers.

wine cellar, *n.,* storage place for wines; need not be subterranean.

wine cooler, *n.,* drink made of wine diluted with fruit juices, soft drinks, or other beverages, generally served over ice; also, a container in which wine is cooled.

wine grower, *n.,* person who cultivates a vineyard (more accurately, grape-grower) and/or makes wine.

winemaker, *n.,* person who makes wine; in commercial production, the title generally attaches to the person responsible for every step in winemaking, from grape-growing through aging and bottling; also called "oenologist," although these terms frequently are applied to assistants who do not have the winemaker's responsibility.

winery, *n.,* place where wine is made.

woody, *adj.,* characterized by the taste of wood, usually the result of aging overlong in wooden containers.

würzig, *adj.* (Ger., VUR-tsick), aromatic, fragrant, pungent.

xampan, *n.* (Sp., KHSAM-pahn), sparkling wine; a corruption of "Champagne."

Xeres, *n.* (Sp., khay-REHTH), original name of the town of Jérez de la Frontera, center of Spain's Sherry-producing region; also French name for Sherry.

yeasty, *adj.,* characterized by the taste or fragrance of yeast.

yema, *n.* (Sp., YAY-mah), the crushed grapes—skins, stems, seeds and juice—before and during fermentation.

yeso, *n.* (Sp., YAY-zoh), calcium sulphate; in Sherry making, the chemical often is added to the must during fermentation to enhance the wine's acid properties.

zapatos de pisar, *n.* (Sp., thah-PAH-toss day pee-SAHR), nail-studded shoes worn by grape-stompers in Spain.

zymase, *n.,* enzyme in yeast that causes vinous fermentation and converts sugar into alcohol and carbon dioxide.

Bibliography

AARON, SAM, AND FADIMAN, CLIFTON, *The Joys of Wine.* New York: Harry Abrams, 1975.
The color photography and its reproduction are superb, but the text is second-rate and the price borders on the scandalous. Aaron is a New York retailer who caters to the carriage trade, principally with the higher-priced wines of France and Germany, and this book reflects his biases without acknowledging them.

ADAMS, LEON D., *The Wines of America.* Boston: Houghton Mifflin, 1973.
The definitive work on wines produced in the U.S. and Canada. Significantly, wine experts in California, New York, and Ontario hail it as the best in the field, so who says you can't please all the people all the time? Be forewarned, however: the prose is sometimes as thick as the trunk of an eighty-year-old vine.

BESPALOFF, ALEXIS, *Guide to Inexpensive Wines.* New York: Simon and Schuster, 1973.
BESPALOFF, ALEXIS, *The Signet Book of Wine.* New York: New American Library, 1971.
Bespaloff is a former Bordeaux wineman who apparently can't resist plugging the product he used to sell. By inexpensive wines, he means those selling under $5 a bottle—which many people would consider far from inexpensive. Among those he really likes is Gallo's Hearty Burgundy—sorry, I'll pass on that one. I opened his *Guide* hoping he'd tout me on to some real steals about which he was uniquely knowledgeable, but no luck. *The Signet Book of Wine* purports to be a general introduction to wine. It isn't really that, but it does provide a concise guide to the more prestigious vineyards of Bordeaux and Burgundy.

BRAVERY, H. E., *The Complete Book of Home Winemaking.* New York: Collier, 1970.
The definitive how-to-do-it: everything you ever wanted to know but didn't know whom to ask.

CHROMAN, NATHAN, *The Treasury of American Wines.* New York: Rutledge Books, 1973.
A vineyard-by-vineyard discussion of the major California wineries, with a little additional material about a few New York

vintners. Chroman, a Los Angeles lawyer, doesn't hesitate to pass off his own opinions as facts or his personal tastes as standards for "good" wine. I wonder which wineries are his clients. The only partially redeeming feature is the four-color photography, which ranges from fair to excellent. Readers interested in individual California and New York vineyards will be better served by Adams' *Wines of America.*

CHURCHILL, CREIGHTON, *The Great Wine Rivers.* New York: Macmillan, 1971.
A celebration of the wines of France and Germany, most of whose vineyards are along riverbanks. Literate and entertaining.

EHLE, JOHN, *The Cheeses and Wines of England and France.* New York: Harper & Row, 1972.
Some people—I among them—favor the geographical approach to wine-food pairings. The theory is that wines and foods of the same region have developed in tandem and thus are usually most enjoyable when consumed together. If you share this view, plus have an appreciation of French or English wines or cheeses, this book is indispensable.

GILLETTE, PETER A., AND GILLETTE, PAUL, *Playboy's Book of Wine.* New York: Playboy Press, 1974.
No comment.

GINESTET, BERNARD, *La Bouillie Bordelaise.* Paris: Flammarion, 1975.
This may be the most candid, forthright, irreverent wine book ever written—by an insider, yet! Ginestet is a Bordeaux shipper. He also owns Château Margaux and is mayor of the township of Margaux, all of which makes him just about the last man you'd expect to assault the Bordeaux wine establishment. *Aux barricades!* Newcomers to wine may deem the whole thing a tempest in a, well, teapot, but seasoned wine-bibbers will find things to underline on every page. Hopefully an English translation will soon be available and will capture the stylistic elegance of a phrasemaker whose best can stand up alongside some of Voltaire.

GROSSMAN, HAROLD J., *Grossman's Guide to Wines, Spirits, and Beers.* New York: Charles Scribner's Sons, 1964.
Written for restaurateurs, bar owners, and wine retailers, this oft-reprinted volume is probably the best general guide to the more popular wines of France and Germany. However, it is weak on wines of other nations, notably Italy and the United States. There is much valuable information on cellaring, serving, et cetera.

HARDWICK, HOMER, *Winemaking at Home*. New York: Cornerstone Library, 1972.
A concise and useful guide for the home winemaker.

HOGG, ANTHONY, *Off the Shelf*. Essex: Gilbey House, 1972.
Written for retailers in England, this book contains valuable buying information for consumers also. Unfortunately, as with so many wine books, the author focuses chiefly on France and Germany.

THE ITALIAN NATIONAL WINE COMMITTEE, *Discovering Italian Wines*. New York: Ward Ritchie Press, 1970.
A promotional volume that doesn't pretend to be anything else, this book is well worth reading. It offers superb menus and recipes as well as a region-by-region discussion of Italian wines.

JOHNSON, HUGH, *The World Atlas of Wine*. New York: Simon & Schuster, 1971.
Around the world, vineyard by vineyard, with a writer who obviously loves his subject. The text sometimes sparkles, sometimes falls flat, but the photography is consistently first-rate, and Johnson has made a commendable effort to give wines of all nations equal attention.

LAMB, RICHARD, AND MITTELBERGER, ERNEST G., *In Celebration of Wine and Life*. New York: Drake, 1974.
The focus is historical, and the book abounds with previously unpublished photos and drawings from the Christian Brothers' Wine Museum, of which Mittelberger is director. Highly recommended for enthusiasts of wine lore.

LICHINE, ALEXIS, *Encyclopedia of Wines & Spirits*. New York: Alfred A. Knopf, 1968.
Lichine is a Bordeaux importer who has been all but beatified by certain groups of North American wine snobs, particularly in New York. His encyclopedia contains much valuable information, particularly about the wines of France, but his biases—personal and commercial—frequently obtrude, and he never acknowledges them.

MELVILLE, JOHN, *Guide to California Wines*. San Carlos, California: Nourse, 1972.
The vineyard-by-vineyard approach, with many superb photos. The book will be particularly useful to tourists who want to visit wineries.

MILLIGAN, DAVID, *All Color Book of Wine*. London: Octopus Books, 1974.
Probably the best all-around book of its kind. Milligan, former

president of the importing firm Dennis & Huppert, now a free-lance wine consultant, unabashedly acknowledges his present and past affiliations, then proceeds to write a book remarkably free of bias. The photography is superb.

NORMAN, WINSTON, *Fun with Wine*. New York: Pocket Books, 1972.

NORMAN, WINSTON, *More Fun with Wine*. New York: Pocket Books, 1973.

A delightfully light-hearted approach to wine with much information of value to the newcomer. Unfortunately, Mr. Norman, who was subsidized by the California wine industry, propagandizes unabashedly. This mars what could be two truly superb books.

RAINBIRD, GEORGE, *Sherry and the Wines of Spain*. London: Michael Joseph, 1966.

The prose is nigh impenetrable and the detail excruciating, but this is the definitive catalogue of Spanish wines.

RAY, CYRIL, *Bollinger*. New York: Pyramid Books, 1971.

A detailed history of the well-known House of Bollinger, Champagne producer. It is valuable for its multi-century perspective on Champagne production, but not the sort of tome that will keep you at the edge of your chair.

ROBOTTI, PETER J. AND FRANCES D., *Key to Gracious Living: Wine and Spirits*. Englewood Cliffs, New Jersey: Prentice-Hall, 1972.

Mr. and Mrs. Robotti own a New York restaurant that marks up wines as high as four hundred percent, and their book is an even bigger ripoff. I've never seen so much misinformation about wine presented with such apparent authority in such a small space.

ROWE, PERCY, *The Wines of Canada*. Toronto: McGraw-Hill, 1970.

The definitive catalogue of the impressive and still-growing wine industry of a nation that many people do not even realize produces wine.

SICHEL, ALLAN, *The Penguin Book of Wines*, Middlesex, England: Penguin Books, 1971.

An easy-to-read survey of European wines, principally those of France and Germany. Sichel is one of several very literate members of his family, long-time shippers with principal holdings in —guess where!—France and Germany.

SICHEL, PETER M. F., AND LEY, JUDY, *Which Wine?* New York: Harper & Row, 1975.

This purports to be a consumer's guide to wines of the world.

Peter M. F. Sichel does not conceal his commercial interest in wine—he is of the same family as the preceding Allan—and this is commendable. No less commendable, he discusses in detail and enthusiastically recommends some wines that he does not sell. Now if only he had made a clean breast and identified those of his recommendations which he does sell—such as Château Palmer, whose praises he sings fortissimo! But it's still a useful book for newcomers to wine-buying.

SIMON, ANDRÉ L., *The Commonsense of Wine*. New York: Bonanza Book, 1966.
In question-and-answer format, a nonstop, 280-page commercial for the wines the late Mr. Simon used to sell.

THOMPSON, BOB, ED., *California Wine*. Menlo Park, California: Sunset Books, 1973.
Vineyard-by-vineyard through the Golden State, with superb photos. An ideal guide for tourists who want to visit wine country.

VERONELLI, LUIGI, *The Wines of Italy*. Rome: Canesi Editore, undated.
The definitive reference work on Italian wines. Veronelli is witty and charming, particularly in his chapter introductions, but much of the vineyard-by-vineyard material will be far too detailed for the casual reader.

WAUGH, ALEC, *Wines and Spirits*. New York: Time-Life Books, 1968.
Here is another from the let-my-palate-be-your-measure school. Waugh states unabashedly, "Knowledge, along with constant tasting, can bring an appreciation of why and where and how we should enjoy our wines and spirits." *Should!?* Sorry, Alec, I hear a different drummer. But the photos by Arie deZanger are excellent.

About the Author

Paul Gillette, widely acclaimed novelist and television personality, is also a gourmet and a wine expert. He is co-author of THE PLAYBOY BOOK OF WINES. Dr. Gillette lives in San Francisco.

SIGNET Books of Interest

☐ **THE SIGNET BOOK OF CHEESE by Peter Quimme.** The complete guide to identifying, buying, storing, serving, and enjoying every variety of cheese from around the world. (#E7180—$1.75)

☐ **THE SIGNET BOOK OF COFFEE AND TEA by Peter Quimme.** The complete guide to evaluating, buying, preparing, and enjoying every variety of coffee and tea. This unique book is designed to tell you everything you need to know to experience the full range of dining delight that coffees and teas offer. (#W7149—$1.50)

☐ **THE SIGNET BOOK OF SAUSAGE (formerly titled: The Sausage Book) by Richard Gehman.** This unique book contains a wealth of information that includes all the secrets of sausage making and 103 mouth-watering recipes with step-by-step instructions that will introduce you to a whole new world of great eating!
(#W7066—$1.50)

☐ **THE LOS ANGELES TIMES NATURAL FOODS COOK-BOOK by Jeanne Voltz, Food Editor, Woman's Day Magazine.** Discover the joys of cooking and eating naturally with this book of over 600 savory, simple-to-follow recipes. Whether you are concerned with taste or nutrition, these delicious and healthy recipes—high in fiber content—will delight everyone from the gourmet chef to the dedicated dieter. (#E6815—$2.25)

☐ **THE SOUP-TO-DESSERT HIGH-FIBER COOKBOOK by Betty Wason.** The important new high-fiber, low-calorie diet that adds flavor and good health to every meal you eat! Low-calorie menus, hundreds of delicious recipes, food composition charts and a fiber diet dictionary make this book an absolutely essential kitchen companion for every cook who cares about good health and good eating. (#J7208—$1.95)

☐ **GOOD ... AP FOOD** by ... g ... .o- kitchen equipment and practical buying t... follow recipes from all over America, Europe, and the Caribbean, here's a feast of advice that will make your money go further and your meals more delicious.
(#W5919—$1.50)

☐ **THE WONDERFUL WORLD OF FREEZER COOKING** by Helen Quat. For the harried hostess and housewife comes a mouthwatering collection of recipes that can be prepared ahead of time and frozen. Also included is a section on international foods and party menus.
(#W6788—$1.50)

☐ **THE NO TIME TO COOK BOOK** by Roslyn Beilly. Dozens of fast and fabulous recipes for the gourmet on-the-go.
(#Y6188—$1.25)

☐ **GOURMET COOKING BY THE CLOCK** by William and Chesbrough Rayner. Here at last are full instructions to one of the fine points of cooking . . . the art of perfect timing. There are easy-to-follow recipes for everything from appetizers to desserts with each step of preparation and cooking timed by the clock. (#Q5436—95¢)

☐ **SIMPLY STEWS** by Shirley Sarvis. 42 ways to cook easy, exotic, elegant, economical, one-dish feasts. Why worry about late guests or a heavy schedule when you can serve gourmet main courses prepared ahead that improve with waiting and taste even better the next day!
(#T5405—75¢)

THE NEW AMERICAN LIBRARY, INC.,
P.O. Box 999, Bergenfield, New Jersey 07621

Please send me the SIGNET BOOKS I have checked above. I am enclosing $_____(check or money order—no currency or C.O.D.'s). Please include the list price plus 35¢ a copy to cover handling and mailing costs. (Prices and numbers are subject to change without notice.)

Name_____

Address_____

City_____State_____Zip Code_____
Allow at least 4 weeks for delivery